The Role of Culture
in Developmental Disorder

The Role of Culture in Developmental Disorder

Edited by

Charles M. Super
Judge Baker Children's Center
and Harvard University
Boston, Massachusetts

ACADEMIC PRESS, INC.
Harcourt Brace Jovanovich, Publishers
San Diego New York Berkeley Boston
London Sydney Tokyo Toronto

CR

ACADEMIC PRESS, INC.
1250 Sixth Avenue, San Diego, California 92101

United Kingdom Edition published by
ACADEMIC PRESS INC. (LONDON) LTD.
24–28 Oval Road, London NW1 7DX

Library of Congress Cataloging in Publication Data

The Role of culture in developmental disorder.

Includes index.
1. Developmental disabilities—Social aspects.
2. Cultural psychiatry.   3. Developmental disabilities—
Cross-cultural studies.   I. Super, Charles M. [DNLM:
1. Child Development Disorders—etiology.   2. Cross-
Cultural Comparison.   3. Culture.   WS 350.6 R7448]
RJ131.R63   1987   305.9'0816   87-1124
ISBN 0—12—676840—4 (alk. paper)

Contents

4   Sudden Infant Death Syndrome: An Anthropological Hypothesis

Melvin J. Konner and Charles M. Super

5   Alternatives to Mother – Infant Attachment in the Neonatal Period

Marten W. deVries

6   "Basic Strangeness": Maternal Estrangement and Infant Death — A Critique of Bonding Theory

Nancy Scheper-Hughes

7   Poor Readers in Three Cultures

Harold W. Stevenson, G. William Lucker, Shin-ying Lee,
and James W. Stigler
In cooperation with
Seiro Kitamura and C. C. Hsu

8   Self-Expression, Interpersonal Relations, and Juvenile Delinquency in Japan

Kosuke Yamazaki, Johji Inomata, and John Alex MacKenzie

9   The Straight Path: A Fijian Perspective on a Transformational Model of Development

Richard Katz and Linda A. Kilner

10   Child Psychiatry in an International Context:
        With Remarks on the Current Status of
        Child Psychiatry in China
        Felton Earls

Contributors

Numbers in parentheses indicate the pages on which the authors' contributions begin.

MOLLIE BLOOMSTRAND (9), School of Psychology, Georgia Institute of Technology, Atlanta, Georgia 30332

JAMES S. CHISHOLM (41), Department of Anthropology, University of New Mexico, Albuquerque, New Mexico 87131

MARTEN W. DEVRIES (109), Department of Social Psychiatry, University of Limburg, 6200 MD Maastricht, The Netherlands

FELTON EARLS (235), Department of Psychiatry, Washington University School of Medicine, St. Louis, Missouri 63110

GAEL D. HEATH[1] (41), Department of Anthropology, University of New Mexico, Albuquerque, New Mexico 87131

C. C. HSU (153), Children's Mental Health Center, Department of Psychiatry, National Taiwan University Hospital, Taipei 100, Taiwan, Republic of China

JOHJI INOMATA (179), Department of Psychiatry and Behavioral Science, Tokai University School of Medicine, Bohseidai, Isehara 259-11, Japan

RICHARD KATZ[2] (205), Harvard Graduate School of Education, Cambridge, Massachusetts 02138

LINDA A. KILNER (205), Harvard Graduate School of Education, Cambridge, Massachusetts 02138

SEIRO KITAMURA (153), Tohoku Fukushi Daigaku, 980 Sendai, Japan

MELVIN J. KONNER (95), Departments of Anthropology and Psychiatry and Yerkes Regional Primate Research Center, Emory University, Atlanta, Georgia 30322

[1]Present address: 2135 Monte Vista, Pasadena, California 91107.
[2]Present address: Department of Behavioral Sciences, College of Human and Rural Development, University of Alaska, Fairbanks, Alaska 99775-1380.

SHIN-YING LEE (153), Center for Human Growth and Development, University of Michigan, Ann Arbor, Michigan 48109

G. WILLIAM LUCKER[3] (153), Center for Human Growth and Development, University of Michigan, Ann Arbor, Michigan 48109

JOHN ALEX MACKENZIE (179), Department of English and American Literatures and Language, The National University System of Japan, Tokyo Suisan Daigaku, Minato-ku, Tokyo 108, Japan

G. MITCHELL (9), Department of Psychology, University of California at Davis, Davis, California 95616

NANCY SCHEPER-HUGHES (131), Department of Anthropology, University of California at Berkeley, Berkeley, California 94720

HAROLD W. STEVENSON (153), Center for Human Growth and Development, University of Michigan, Ann Arbor, Michigan 48109

JAMES W. STIGLER[4] (153), Center for Human Growth and Development, University of Michigan, Ann Arbor, Michigan 48109

CHARLES M. SUPER (1, 95), Judge Baker Children's Center, and Harvard University, Boston, Massachusetts 02115

KOSUKE YAMAZAKI (179), Department of Psychiatry and Behavioral Science, Tokai University School of Medicine, Bohseidai, Isehara 259-11, Japan

---

[3]Present address: Department of Psychology, University of Texas at El Paso, El Paso, Texas 79968.

[4]Present address: Committee on Human Development, University of Chicago, Chicago, Illinois 60637.

Preface

This volume concerns the ways in which culture conditions the problems of human development. Although developmental problems are experienced by individuals, their qualities and frequencies are strongly shaped by the human environment, shaped in ways that will not be obvious from examination of individuals alone. The chapters in this volume discuss how we structure our children's risks in general, and for some specific disorders. Taken as a whole, they present a sympathetic picture of the human species doing the best it can for itself as it learns the subtlety of its place in the world and the complexity of its own functioning. The panorama should be of interest to cross-cultural, developmental, life-span, and clinical psychologists; to medical, psychological, and psychiatric anthropologists; and to scholars in public health and medicine who are concerned with analyzing the patterns of mental and physical health of children and devising strategies for intervention. The volume is not a catalog of risks or a catalog of solutions. It presents a kind of questioning about developmental problems that I believe will prove both illuminating and fruitful.

One origin of the volume lies in conversations with colleagues from several disciplines about "comparative human development" as a field of scientific inquiry. Many of these conversations started at a faculty seminar organized by Sara Harkness, Richard Katz, Alan Harwood, Marten deVries, and myself; the seminar was sponsored by the Judge Baker Children's Center and generously funded by the John D. and Catherine T. MacArthur Foundation, to whom we are especially grateful. It was quickly evident in these conversations that for many of us "comparative" means comparison across cultures, because the monocultural limitations of present knowledge are severe, though not incurable. For others, comparison across time, historical and evolutionary, is critical, and for still others a comparison of species is necessarily implied. These diverse perspectives converge in the observation that the most appropriate model for human development is that of a biological organism participating in cultural reality.

A principal use of the comparative cultural approach is to explode false universals with the realization that people are very different in another time or place; diversity and behavioral adaptation are certainly hallmarks of our species. However there is usually an aftershock as well, rumbling up from the perception of often uncanny similarities. The Baoulé infant in the Ivory Coast investigates Piaget's matchbox and chain in exactly the same way as does an infant in Geneva. Traditional men of the New Guinea Highlands smile and frown and wrinkle up their noses in much the same expressions of emotion as do American social scientists. The investigation of culture necessarily leads to questions about specieswide characteristics and their biological foundations.

It follows that disciplinary perspectives must also be included among the comparisons. Formal collective knowledge — science — shares with individual cognition some features of development, as Piaget, Werner, Kuhn, and others have observed; of particular relevance here is the complementary interplay of differentiation and integration. The unprecedented growth of the social and behavioral sciences in the last half-century has been institutionalized primarily in the service of differentiation, that is, specialization of topic and methodology. Funding networks, scientific societies and journals, and other structures have become built around the academic disciplines, a progressive segregation or schizmogenesis that system theorists would recognize. Nevertheless, in the past decade there has been a renewed interest in intellectual synthesis across traditional divisions. In human development, the press for broader understanding is not only the direct result of an integrative cycle in public knowledge, but also a consequence of new applied concerns, from childhood psychopathology to public policy for children, where it is easily appreciated that the reality of human development is a seamless web, without dotted lines to demarcate academic territory. *The Role of Culture in Developmental Disorder* reflects this growth of transdisciplinary interests, and I hope it will contribute to its maturity.

The collection is intended to be provocative and stimulating, and I am grateful to a large number of colleagues who have afforded the stimulation — and on occasion, provocation — to conceive it. In particular, I acknowledge with pleasure the advice of a distinguished group of scholars who helped define possible topics and refine the one presented here: S. Anandalakshmy, Ph.D. (Lady Irwin College, India); B. G. Blount, Ph.D. (University of Georgia, U.S.A.); N. Blurton Jones, Ph.D. (University of California at Los Angeles, U.S.A.); T. B. Brazelton, M.D. (Harvard University, U.S.A.); J. S. Chisholm Ph.D. (University of New Mexico, U.S.A.); M. Cole, Ph.D. (University of California at San Diego, U.S.A.); P. R. Dasen, Ph.D. (University of Geneva, Switzerland); J. B. Deregowski, Ph.D. (University of Aberdeen, Scotland); M. W. deVries, M.D. (Rijksuniversiteit Limburg, The Netherlands); F. W. Earls, M.D. (Washington University, U.S.A.); T. M. Field, Ph.D. (University of Miami, U.S.A.); W. S. Hall, Ph.D. (University of Maryland, U.S.A.); S. Harkness, Ph.D., M.P.H. (Harvard University, U.S.A.); J. Kagan, Ph.D. (Harvard University, U.S.A.); R. Katz, Ph.D. (University of Alaska, U.S.A.); M. J. Konner, Ph.D., M.D. (Emory University, U.S.A.); A. Kleinman, M.D., M.A. (Harvard University, U.S.A.); J. B. Lancaster, Ph.D. (University of New Mexico, U.S.A.); R. M. Lerner, Ph.D. (Pennsylvania State University, U.S.A.); P. H. Leiderman, M.D. (Stanford University, U.S.A.); R. A. LeVine, Ph.D. (Harvard University, U.S.A.); E. A. Maritim, Ed.D. (Kenyatta University College, Kenya); H. Miyake, Ph.D. (University of Hokkaido, Japan); A. C. Mundy-Castle, Ph.D. (University of Zimbabwe); R. H. Munroe, Ed.D. (Pitzer College, U.S.A.); R. L. Munroe, Ph.D. (Pitzer College, U.S.A.); E. T. Prothro, Ph.D. (American University of Beirut, Lebanon); N. Scheper-Hughes, Ph.D. (University of California at Berkeley, U.S.A.); R. Serpell, Ph.D. (University of Zambia); R. A. Shweder, Ph.D. (University of Chicago, U.S.A.); H. W. Stevenson, Ph.D. (University of Michigan, U.S.A.); D. I. Slobin, Ph.D. (University of California at Berkeley, U.S.A.); S. J. Suomi, Ph.D. (National Institute of Child Health and Human Development, U.S.A.); D. A. Wagner, Ph.D. (University of Pennsylvania, U.S.A.); T. S. Weisner, Ph.D. (University of California at Los Angeles, U.S.A.); B. B. Whiting, Ph.D. (Harvard University, U.S.A.); J. W. M. Whiting, Ph.D. (Harvard University, U.S.A.); R. Yando, Ph.D. (Judge Baker Children's Center, U.S.A.).

CHARLES M. SUPER

The Role of Culture
in Developmental Disorder

1

The Role of Culture in Developmental Disorder

CHARLES M. SUPER

It would be traditional to open with a definition of culture. There is no shortage of inspirations, to be sure, for anthropologists have spent as much time in trying to delineate the core concept of their discipline as psychologists have in defining personality or, indeed, as developmentalists have in trying definitively to state the nature of development. For culture, definitions offered in the past range, in paraphrase, from "all the humanly constructed environment, physical, and social," to a narrower "system of shared meanings." It will be evident that I have in mind a very broad concept, but rather than draw sharp lines around it from the start, it may be useful to let "culture" remain a fuzzy concept as the chapters of this book are introduced. Similarly, for "developmental disorder" is intended a wide range of failures to continue healthy, happy, adaptive, skillful growth of mind and body, but to draw careful lines is unnecessary at this point.

More than unnecessary, a definitional approach would risk plunging us into the disciplinary insularity I wish to avoid. It would be possible, though artificial, to define rigorously "culture" or "development" if they are to be the isolated object of one's analysis. The goal of this chapter and volume, however, is to consider the relationship of culture and development or, more exactly, the relationship of humanly structured environments to dysfunctions in human growth, and the focus is on that domain of connection. A complete account of cultural influences on any particular problem in development is not attempted; that is beyond the present scope, and it is probably beyond the current state of knowledge. The chapters included here, however, offer the opportunity to consider disorders of development as a class of phenomena that reveal something of the nature of our children and also of the nature of the worlds we make for them.

Perspectives

Bloomstrand and Mitchell (Chapter 2, this volume) discuss the experimental literature on "normal reactions to abnormal events" among primates. Such reactions can include both adaptive and maladaptive features, and it is the maladaptive ones, necessarily maladaptive in a particular context, that constitute the disorders of major interest here. We are reminded in their review that the particular reactions that are "normal" are as much a characteristic of the species as the events that cannot be tolerated. By extension, the study of disorder must ultimately rest on a species-specific model of events the organism is prepared to cope with and its vulnerability to other, "abnormal" ones.

Chisholm and Heath's chapter (Chapter 3, this volume) is concerned with socially regulated prenatal influences, and in their evolutionary approach they tie a number of observed phenomena to a theory of adaptation and dysfunction. Variable characteristics of the infant, such as irritability, are viewed in light of their possible contribution to the inclusive fitness of the mother and infant (through facultative adaptation) and to the possible conflicts between the interests of the two. The early developmental plasticity of our species is seen as one route by which developmental dysfunction — of both parent and offspring — may be avoided. Greater knowledge of the mechanisms involved, the authors argue, can substantially alter our understanding of the positive and negative effects of early environment.

There are, of course, limits to our species' early plasticity, but the shape of those limits is not well sketched. Konner and Super (Chapter 4, this volume) hypothesize that some of the limits are challenged by the sleeping and feeding arrangements typical of families in the industrial West. They argue that this pattern of care may contribute to the vulnerability of some infants, already at biological risk, to the "sudden infant death syndrome." The authors point out that infant care in the industrial West has substantially contributed to lower risk for many disorders, such as infectious disease, and their speculation on increased risk for other problems is controversial. Whether or not they are correct in this one instance, however, the idea of a cultural pattern of elevated and decreased risk for various kinds of disorder at various ages lies behind most of the chapters of this volume.

deVries and Scheper-Hughes, in their separate chapters (Chapters 5 and 6, respectively, this volume), consider at different levels an issue foreshadowed by the first two chapters, namely, the nature of the earliest relations between mother and infant. Is it, as some theories hold, a win-or-lose task of mutual attachment and bonding or, as suggested here, a more active process on the mother's part of evaluating (at various levels of biological and psychological functioning) the viability of the emerging being? Drawing on a wide range of evolutionary, cross-specific, and cross-cultural material, deVries presents a model of maternal "choice" in rearing her infant that changes the picture of infanticide from that of a failed process to one extreme of a range of outcomes from a fully functioning system. Scheper-Hughes provides a detailed example of her presentation of early neglect and mortality in a Brazilian shanty town. Emphasizing social regulation of life and death, she explicitly postulates that bonding and attachment are "mediated by the mother's evaluations of her social and economic circumstances and, more important, by culturally derived meanings of maternity, fertility, nurturance, love, care, loss, and infant death" (p. 132, this volume). Her data bear eloquent testimony to the interconnections of women's lives and their children's survival.

Although infancy is a period of especially high risk, a "funnel" in natural selection that is shaped in part by culture, it is by no means the only time when functioning can go awry. Stevenson and his associates (Chapter 7, this volume) examine a problem central to modern middle childhood, poor reading. There has long been concern with the possible relationship of reading problems to the kind of orthography used to write, that is, the Roman alphabet, Japanese *kanji,* Hebrew characters, Arabic script, and so forth. After testing nearly 5000 children in 120 classrooms in 3 countries, the research team concluded that although the children's abilities to decode and interpret the written symbols of their culture were very similar, the cognitive characteristics of poor readers in English differ from those of children who are poor readers of Chinese and Japanese. In the latter two samples, unlike the first, the poor readers had substantially lower scores on verbal compared to performance tasks; in addition, more of the poor readers in those samples were also poor in mathematics, compared to the American sample, where there was greater independence of deficiencies in reading and mathematics. Beyond this general contrast, the authors conclude, if specific cognitive deficits are eventually found to underlie reading difficulty, such deficits are likely to differ according to culture. Important variation was also found among the three groups of parents in their awareness of and attitude toward the child's "problem." The pursuit of contributors at the cultural level to typical patterns of academic difficulty is a neglected but promising direction of research.

Yamazaki, Inomata, and MacKenzie (Chapter 8, this volume) delve deeply into Japanese culture and the history of family relations to present the roots of the "culture of youth" and juvenile delinquency in modern Japan.

Their twin theses, involving decreased parental authority and muted communications of attachment between mother and infant, will sound familiar to the Western reader but striking for their new meaning in the Japanese context. Indeed, the subtle but pervasive differences in meaning of the basic terms "self-expression" and "interpersonal relations" give pause in the task of transplanting theories of development. Does the decline of parental authority in one historical context mean the same thing in another? Do different expectations of family relations make the same level of objective conflict function differently in two cultures? These are but two of the fundamental problems raised by the authors' finely woven commentary on the quality of developmental disorder in young adults in Japan.

Culturally shaped ideals of what a life should be figure centrally in Katz and Kilner's presentation of the Fijian "straight path" (Chapter 9, this volume). In the island village they write about, there is a special role for the local "healer," who both facilitates individual functioning by enhancing its relationship to the spirit of the community and also leads the community under stress toward setting an adaptive path for individuals. This balancing act, both defining and invoking meanings at the center of psychological life, concentrates in one person dynamics of individual and community change and so represents an array of adaptive acts carried out, in one way or another, by peoples around the world. Choices involve risk, and the pattern of choices demanded by a culture, as well as the guidelines for making the choices, influences the risks of development throughout the lifespan. And the choices are passed on, for as children and young adults see their elders trying to find and follow the straight path, they learn the socially constructed dilemmas and the socially devised solutions.

The final chapter by Earls (Chapter 10, this volume) brings these abstract concerns to the reality of professional help for children and families around the world. Child psychiatrists, he points out, like psychologists, social workers, and others engaged in the task — indeed like the Fijian healers — derive their roles, their understanding, and their tools from a particular time and place in human history. Earls urges an international perspective for those who wish to promote children's mental health, and his specific priorities reflect the central theme of this volume. A basic organization of child mental health services, he advises, will require a knowledge of the local pattern of disorders and an understanding of how families cope with their vulnerabilities. As Western knowledge and Western professional structures are integrated into other settings, writes Earls, they will undergo changes not now predictable, but his five principles can be accommodated in a variety of structures. The same is true, of course, in Western societies, where professional structures are also responding to social change and new knowledge, and Earls emphasizes that the benefits of an international perspective are conferred on all sides.

Culture and Problems of Development

There are two related themes underlying the studies summarized above. The first picks up the question of what is meant by "culture," carefully avoided in the opening of this chapter. The second concerns the functional properties of culture as it regulates problems of development.

The idea that development is influenced by the environment is about as old as the idea of development. Although different schools of theory allot varying degrees of power to the environment, they share almost universally an interest in single dimensions of the environment, features that are isolated and measured. Sometimes these are "process variables," links in a causal chain such as maternal use of distal (e.g., talking) rather than proximal (e.g., touching) interactions with infants; sometimes they are larger conceptual chunks of reality such as socioeconomic status. Rarely in the developmental sciences, however, does theory acknowledge that environments have their own structure and internal rules of operation, and, thus, that what the environment contributes to development is not only isolated, unidimensional pushes and pulls but also structure.

The structure and function of human environments, especially their social aspects, has of course been the primary topic of study by anthropologists, sociologists, and more recently human ecologists. There is a long tradition in anthropology, especially, of examining the interrelations of physical ecology, social structure, and the culture of beliefs, values, and ritual. Child development became part of this academic tradition in the culture and personality school, now more generally referred to as psychological anthropology, and the psychocultural model proposed by the Whitings presents an ambitious integration. In brief, the model holds:

> 1. Features in the history of any society and in the natural environment in which it is situated influence
> 2. the customary methods by which infants (and children) are cared for in that society, which have
> 3. enduring psychological and physiological effects on the members of that society, which are manifested in
> 4. the cultural projective-expressive systems of the society and the physiques of its members" (J. W. M. Whiting, 1980, p. 155).

A large number of studies in this tradition have examined the effects on development of such varied cultural features as modes of infant carrying, adolescent initiation, maternal work load, parental ideology, sibling and peer relations, modernization, birth spacing, schooling, and daily chores (see, for example, Munroe, Munroe, & Whiting, 1980; also Harkness & Super, 1987, for an historical perspective). It is easy to recognize all these and many other aspects of life as strongly influenced by, indeed *to be,* the culture a child grows up in. In contrast, person-oriented research often treats "culture" as an independent variable at the same level as SES or language type, for example, and attempts to examine its effect free from "confounding" factors such as the social setting. One view in anthropology holds that there is no such essential nugget of culture, rather, that it is the complex coordination of these factors that is the culture (Harkness, 1983).

The connection of culture and developmental disorder that this volume draws attention to, then, extends previous work on culture and normal development to culture and normal reactions to abnormal events, where "abnormal" refers not to statistical frequency but rather to exclusion from the range of events the normal human organism can manage. There are, to be sure, individual vulnerabilities and strengths as well, but they too operate against a background of available experience. Culture includes the abnormal events our children face. All children are threatened by the immediate presence, if it occurs, of tetanus bacilli, open staircases, venomous snakes, sharp knives, unguarded fires, large metal-and-glass objects moving at high speed, malarial-infested mosquitoes, toxic chemicals, hostile enemies, and extremes of weather. Exposure to and protection from these are part of culture; they reflect modes of production, social structure, beliefs and values, knowledge, and technology. More difficult to specify, perhaps, are the psychological events that produce disorder, and a continuing thread in public attempts to improve children's lives is our shifting understanding of children's needs in the opening years. The complexity of the connections between development and the larger culture is part of what makes relevant policy so difficult to specify.

The multitude of connections also makes it easy to lose one's way in specifying the role of culture in developmental disorder. We have elsewhere tried to formulate the functional domains at the interface of culture and development, the "developmental niche" (Harkness & Super, 1983, 1985; Super & Harkness, 1981, 1982, 1986), and the results also serve as guideposts here. The immediate niche of development can be divided into three aspects. The first is the physical and social setting in which children spend their time. Who is with them, friends to play with or teachers to listen to, parents with psychic energy to invest or depressed adults who despair of their own future? Is the child exposed to pathogens and parasites or, prenatally, to stressed maternal physiology? Does the temperature require heavy clothing, thus limiting the practical methods of toilet training and affecting bodily cleanliness? As B. B. Whiting (1980) has observed, one of culture's most powerful influences is its role as a provider of settings.

A second feature of the niche is formed by the customs of child rearing proscribed and permitted by the culture. Are there rituals such as infant circumcision or cosmetic scarification? Does the community customarily lend support to the new mother? Do children sleep in their own beds or with their parents? Is there routine vaccination, dietary restraint, frequent washing, or common use of seat belts in high-speed travel that might decrease or alter the pattern of risk?

Finally, the psychology of caretakers is an important element in the niche, not only for its relationship to the settings and customs but also for the way it structures the myriad interactions of daily life. Are infants seen as hearty or fragile, isolated, and in need of attentive care or exploitive and in need of control? Does being a twin signal deformity or sacred status? Is it appropriate for fathers to be close to their children? What is the straight path for which children must be prepared?

Although each element of the niche can be related to features of the society (as anthropologists might want to do) and to variations in development (as the psychologist might), one is moved to consider the niche as a topic of analysis in its own right, because the features are interrelated with their own systematic properties. Customs are not sustained if they run counter to the beliefs and values of caretakers; children are not placed in settings thought to be harmful; and adult beliefs evolve in part on the basis of observing the effects of settings and customs. In addition, beliefs about the nature of children at different ages or stages or about the uniqueness of different children may dictate new settings or customs.

The settings, customs, and psychology of caretakers not only regulate the healthy emergence of human potential, they also shape the possibilities of disorder. At every stage of the etiology, expression, course, intervention, and final outcome of developmental problems, human culture structures the experience and adjusts the odds. Seeing the existence of and finding the nature of that role, as the present essays indicate, are not only intellectual tasks for the theoretician, they also form a basis for societally organized actions to improve children's lives.

References

Harkness, S. (1983). Culture and the interpretation of social behavior [Review of *Culture and early interactions*]. *Contemporary Psychology, 28,* 444–445.

Harkness, S., & Super, C. M. (1983). The cultural construction of child development: A framework for the socialization of affect. *Ethos, 11,* 221–231.

Harkness, S., & Super, C. M. (1985). The cultural context of gender segregation in children's peer groups. *Child Development, 56,* 219–224.

Harkness, S., & Super, C. M. (1987). The uses of cross-cultural research in child development. In G. J. Whitehurst & R. Vasta (eds.), *Annals of Child Development* (Vol. 4, pp. 209–244.) Greenwich, CT: JAI Press.

Munroe, R. H., Munroe, R. L., & Whiting, B. B. (Eds.). (1980). *Handbook of cross-cultural human development.* New York: Garland Press.

Super, C., & Harkness, S. (1981). Figure, ground, and gestalt: The cultural context of the active individual. In R. M. Lerner & N. A. Busch-Rossnagel (Eds.), *Individuals as producers of their development: A life-span perspective* (pp. 69–86). New York: Academic Press.

Super, C. M., & Harkness, S. (1982). The infant's niche in rural Kenya and metropolitan America. In L. L. Adler (Ed.), *Cross-cultural research at issue* (pp. 47–56). New York: Academic Press.

Super, C. M., & Harkness, S. (1986). The developmental niche: A conceptualization at the interface of child and culture. *International Journal of Behavior Development, 9,* 1–25.

Whiting, B. B. (1980). Culture and social behavior: A model for the development of social behavior. *Ethos, 8,* 95–116.

Whiting, J. W. M. (1980). Environmental constraints on infant care practices. In R. H. Monroe, R. L. Munroe, & B. B. Whiting (Eds.), *Handbook of cross-cultural human development* (pp. 155–179). New York: Garland Press.

2

Abnormal Behavioral Development in Primates

MOLLIE BLOOMSTRAND AND G. MITCHELL

Introduction

This chapter concerns abnormal behaviors displayed by nonhuman primates and the relevance of these to the field of human behavior. The chapter will first include an attempt to define the concept of abnormality, then will introduce the primates and examine the importance of animal models to human abnormal behavior. The remainder of the chapter will summarize the findings of many years of study of abnormal behavior in nonhuman primates. A brief look at the existence of abnormal behavior in natural settings will be followed by a more detailed analysis of abnormalities studied in the laboratory. Here an emphasis will be placed on areas of study that are most thoroughly addressed in the nonhuman primate literature: studies of social isolation, social separation, and child abuse. Finally, a concluding discussion on what the nonhuman primate findings have to offer investigators of human behavior will be presented.

Defining the concept of abnormality is not an easy task. Just as is true in the field of human behavior, no universally accepted definition of abnormal behavior has yet been generated in the field of behavioral primatology. Suomi (1982b) has most thoroughly described the concept of abnormal behavior, and his analysis will be outlined here. It has traditionally proven most useful to define the concept of abnormality in relative rather than in absolute terms.

Suomi has identified three approaches to defining abnormality. The first

The Role of Culture
in Development Disorder

approach is a *statistical* one which identifies rare behaviors as abnormal. If the great majority of the population does not display a particular behavior, then that behavior is deemed abnormal. Researchers using a second approach define abnormality in terms of pathology in a *medical* sense. This approach is typical of the psychiatric literature, and psychiatrists often assume underlying physiological malfunctions as the causes of abnormal behavior. These medical researchers call for the identification and treatment of such internal dysfunctions. The third approach is taken by most biologists, who define abnormal behaviors as *maladaptive* ones which reduce the likelihood of the passing of an organism's genes on to future generations. Abnormal behaviors can be defined in qualitative or quantitative terms. Stereotyped movements, bizarre postures, and various self-directed activities are examples of qualitatively described abnormalities. Other abnormalities such as hyperagressiveness or inadequate maternal behavior may be considered quantitatively distinct from normal behaviors (Capitanio, 1982). Obviously, employing different definitions of abnormality may lead to different decisions when classifying a certain behavior as normal or abnormal.

There are many *situational* factors that must be considered when defining abnormality. The context is important, because a behavior may be appropriate in one context and inappropriate in another. For example, the excessive rocking behavior observed in socially isolated rhesus monkeys *could* be considered "normal" because it is expected and widely exhibited under these specific environmental circumstances. If this same behavior was exhibited by a rhesus monkey in its natural environment, however, it would definitely be considered abnormal. Sackett (1968) claims that many "abnormalities" are probably of this type — they are actually dependent on processes in the environment rather than on permanent features of the animal itself.

The *age* of the animal studied is also an important consideration. A behavior that is part of the normal repertoire of an infant monkey, such as clinging to its mother, would be judged as quite abnormal if displayed by an adult animal. Both human and nonhuman primates who persistently display behavior patterns that their peers have outgrown or who engage in adult-like behaviors when they are still young are considered to be unusual and, hence, abnormal (Suomi, 1982b).

In the same fashion, the *sex* of an animal and the relation of any treatment experience to its *genetic* background must be evaluated when studying behavioral abnormalities (Mitchell, 1970).

Traditionally, two basic causes of abnormalities have been hypothesized: "bad genes" and "bad environments" (Suomi, 1982b). Abnormalities believed to be genetically caused have often been considered unpreventable and difficult or impossible to cure. Abnormalities believed to be environmentally caused have been considered avoidable (through the control of environmental influences on the organism), more easily reversed and more completely cured than genetically based abnormalities.

Most modern researchers now believe that abnormal behaviors are due to interactions of genetic and environmental factors. The expression of genes is greatly influenced by the physical and social environment in which the behavior occurs (Suomi, 1982a). There are significant individual differences in response to the same environmental stimuli. Some of these individual differences are undoubtedly genetically determined. In any case, certain environmental factors may be *necessary* for the expression of some abnormal behaviors, but they are not seen to be *sufficient* causes of those abnormalities.

The Primate Order

The nonhuman primates include around 200 different species of prosimians, monkeys, and apes, which we will categorize into seven major groups for our nonprimatologist readers (cf. Fobes & King, 1982):

1. Prosimians. This is a suborder of primates generally regarded as being more primitive than monkeys and apes. Structurally and behaviorally they are remarkably diverse but, in general, can be characterized as being more dependent on smell, as being less likely to have full binocular vision, and as having smaller brains than monkeys or apes. The prosimians include lemurs of Madagascar, lorises of Africa and Asia and the tarsiers of Asia among others. Some are nocturnal; some are not. Their social organizations include nearly solitary, monogamous, and multi-male, multi-female varieties. Little research has been done on abnormal behavioral development in prosimians.

2. Callitrichids. This is a family of New World monkeys which, in many ways, appear to be more prosimian in appearance than do other monkeys. Structurally they are small and behaviorally all of them are monogamous. Like prosimians they frequently use scent marking and smell, but they all have binocular vision. They are small brained as compared to other monkeys. The Callitrichids include marmosets and tamarins. All are diurnal. There has been some research done on abnormal behavioral development in callitrichids but not anywhere near as much as has been done on some of the other monkeys.

3. Cebids. This is a family of New World monkeys most of which look more monkey-like than do prosimians or callitrichids. Like prosimians, they are quite variable in size and diverse in their social organizations. They have excellent vision and therefore depend less on smell. The New World cebids include squirrel monkeys, spider monkeys, howler monkeys, titi monkeys, and night monkeys, among many others. The last two genera, titi and night

monkeys, are monogamous. Most of the rest show various forms of polygyny. There has been somewhat more research done on abnormal behavioral development in this group of nonhuman primates than on the two preceding taxonomic groups. The squirrel monkey, in particular, has been researched fairly extensively.

4. Colobines. This is an Old World subfamily of primates which includes primarily arboreal, leaf-eating monkeys of Africa, Asia, and the islands of the South Pacific. They are of varied and beautiful colors and sizes. Most of them live in large polygynous groups containing one or more males and many females, but two species are monogamous. They have excellent vision and have brains at least as large as those of the largest cebids. The colobines include colobus monkeys of Africa, langurs of Asia, the strange proboscis monkey of Borneo, and many others. All are diurnal. Little research has been done on abnormal behavioral development in these species.

5. Cercopithecines. This is an Old World subfamily of monkeys which includes both terrestrial and arboreal varieties of varied size, coloration, and social organization. All of them are polygynous, but the forms the polygyny takes are remarkably diverse. They too have excellent vision and large brains. This group of primates is the second most successful group on earth (next to humans). The cercopithecines include macaques (e.g., rhesus), baboons, vervets, mangabeys, geladas, and many other varieties. All are diurnal. Most of the research that has been done on abnormal nonhuman primate behavioral development has been done on this group of monkeys.

6. Hylobatids. This is the Old World group which includes arboreal, territorial, brachiating, and tailless lesser apes. They are intelligent, diurnal, and exclusively monogamous primates. There has been some (but not much) research done on abnormal behavioral development in this group, which encompasses the Asian gibbons and siamangs.

7. Pongids. This group includes only the great apes, the most intelligent and behaviorally complex of all nonhuman primates. All of them are diurnal, and, to varying degrees, they are both arboreal and terrestrial. Their social structures could hardly vary more from species to species. The pongids include the Asian orangutans and the African gorillas and chimpanzees. There are two different species of the latter, pygmy and common. Quite a lot of research on abnormal behavioral development has been published on this group of nonhuman primates, particularly on the common chimpanzee.

Relevance of Animal Models to the Study of Human Behavior

Historically, animal models of abnormal human behavior have not always been well received. More recently it has been reported that animal models of human psychopathology have become more respected in more clinical fields (Suomi, 1982c). This change in attitude has been attributed to changes in ideas about the biological basis of various psychopathologies and to an increasing sophistication in the animal models being used. Animal models must be carefully developed, interpreted, and evaluated, but they do afford a unique source of information for the study of human behavior.

Animal models represent a simplified version of the human phenomena in question, as these phenomena are expressed in a nonhuman organism (Suomi, 1982c). While the animal model of human behavior is not purported to be the perfect method of scientific study of human behavior, it certainly has many advantages over studies of human subjects. As Suomi (1982c) explains, animal models are not generally chosen because of their obvious strengths but because of problems inherent in attempting to conduct certain types of research with humans.

Ethical constraints eliminate the possibility of performing many studies of abnormal behavior on humans. For instance, it would never be acceptable to attempt to induce abnormalities in humans. Indeed, there is growing repugnance on the part of many toward those who would use animal models excessively. But, abnormalities that do exist in humans often cannot be documented as thoroughly as they may be with nonhuman subjects. Animals can (and, some would say, *must*) be more *intensively* observed and manipulated than humans. Therapeutic necessities often overrule strictly scientific goals when researchers work with humans. For example, it would certainly be unethical to withhold treatment from a human in the name of research.

Animal subjects offer some additional real advantages over human subjects. Laboratory animals usually have shorter lifespans than do humans and so allow the assessment of long-term consequences more efficiently than would be possible in humans. Animal studies are therefore generally more complete, because they allow a more thorough examination of subjects belonging to various age, sex, and individual history classifications than would be possible with humans. This greater breadth of information is helpful when attempting to generalize conclusions of a study. Thus, animals can be researched more *extensively,* as well as more intensively.

Problems with the use of animal models stem from the problem of generalizing between animal data and the human condition (Suomi, 1982a). Obviously, the degree of generality between an animal model and its intended human counterpart represents an important limiting factor when evaluating how useful the animal model will be. Many characteristics of nonhuman primates make them excellent choices for animal models of human behavior. Data on nonhuman primates are assumed to be particularly relevant to the study of human behavior because of the close evolutionary relationship among all primates including ourselves. The similar biochemical properties of the genes of humans and other primates have been used as an indication of shared evolutionary history. Lovejoy (1981) has estimated that 98% of the genes of any human are shared by a normal chimpanzee. This biological similarity is certainly a tremendous plus for nonhuman primate models when compared to other animal models of human behavior.

It is now generally recognized that advanced nonhuman primates also possess cognitive abilities that more closely resemble human mental capacities than ever would have been dreamed of 25 years ago (Suomi, 1982a). Combining this information with shared physiological properties (common to all primates) increases the value of nonhuman primate models for human behavior still further. Nonhuman primate models have enormous value for the study of human behavioral disorders. They can help in the understanding of the cause, symptoms, treatment, and prevention of many human behavioral abnormalities.

Abnormal Behavior in the Wild

A surprising number of primate field researchers have reported examples of spontaneously occurring behavioral abnormalities in wild animals. Indeed, it appears that very few feral populations are completely devoid of members exhibiting abnormalities (Suomi, 1982a). This may be somewhat unexpected since the "survival of the fittest" doctrine would seem to preclude the possibility of obviously "unfit" animals surviving for long in the wild. However, evolution does its work best when there is variety.

Fedigan and Fedigan (1977) have thoroughly described the development of an infant male Japanese macaque (*Macaca fuscata,* a cercopithecine) that appeared to have a severe case of cerebral palsy. Investigators inferred that this was the correct diagnosis after observing severe physical and motor problems soon after the animal's birth. The free-ranging troop the infant was born into was relocated in Laredo, Texas. The infant (called Wania 6672) had lower limbs that were deformed, and he could not cling to his mother as did the normal macaque infants in his group. As he grew older, more abnormalities were observed. The animal had difficulty with eye–hand coordination and seemed to lack binocular vision. He exhibited evidence of mental retardation; and, emotional instability was manifested in frequent "temper tantrums." His limb deformity made it impossible for him to locomote as did the normal monkeys, and, instead, he developed a method of hopping. This method was clumsy and slow, and he was not able to keep up with his peers.

Although one would expect this infant's probability of surviving in the wild to be quite low, he lived for over 13 months. His survival was attributed to the compensatory actions of the members of his troop, particularly of his mother. The infant's mother held him up while he was nursing, manually carried and retrieved him when he slipped off her. Throughout his life the infant's relationship with his mother was unusual. For example, weaning normally occurs when an infant is between 4 and 6 months of age. Independence from the mother is usually achieved well before she is again pregnant (at an infant age of 1 year). Wania 6672 was very abnormal in these respects. Most of his time was spent in contact or in close proximity to his mother. If separated from her, Wania 6672 emitted "lost" alarm calls almost incessantly. He did not forage for food as did the normal young macaques but was nursed by his mother throughout his 13 months of life. He spent very little time playing with his peers.

Other members of the troop interacted with Wania 6672 only infrequently. These interactions were accidental, and Wania 6672 displayed inappropriate behaviors during them. For instance, he was aggressive in response to play invitations by peers. The troop members were very tolerant of Wania 6672's abnormal behavior. They tended to ignore rather than to attack him when he threw temper tantrums. Adult males were once seen to protect Wania 6672 from the threat of a potential predator.

This example of an abnormal individual surviving as a direct result of the compensatory and tolerant behaviors of the members of its troop is not a unique example. Another well-documented case of "abnormal" behavior occurring in the wild is the reaction of an infant to the loss of its mother (see the section on Social Separation for a further discussion of this topic). This would be, of course, a very significant event in the life of any infant primate, as it is extremely dependent on its mother. The most common response to such a separation is psychopathological behavior followed by death (Suomi, 1982a). Goodall (cited in Suomi, 1982a) has reported such a response by a young male chimpanzee ("Flint") at the Gombe Stream Reserve in Africa.

Flint was 8 years old when his mother died. Flint had been unusually dependent on his mother and so was perhaps more vulnerable to severe effects of her loss than were other chimpanzees of his age. Flint died 25 days after his mother's death. During those 25 days he exhibited characteristics of severe depression. He became increasingly tense and apathetic and lost over one-third of his body weight. He spent most of his time alone and sat in a hunched-over posture. Four other young chimpanzees at Gombe have shown a response consisting of similar abnormal behaviors, two of whom died. While these reactions include the expression of psychopathological behaviors, they are expected, and so may be considered "normal" reactions to very traumatic events (Kaufman & Rosenblum, 1967; Plimpton & Rosenblum, 1983). These and many other examples of "abnormal" behaviors in the wild provide important evidence that not all primate societies attempt to eliminate behaviorally abnormal members, although some human cultures have certainly been known to do so (Suomi, 1982a).

Social Isolation in the Laboratory

The great majority of studies of abnormal behavior in nonhuman primates have been carried out in laboratories. A huge volume of literature dealing with the effects of social isolation on behavior has been generated, most of it on *M. mulatta,* the rhesus monkey (a cercopithecine).

Degree of Isolation

All types of isolation involve subjects raised under some condition of social deprivation. The most extreme form of deprivation studied in the laboratory has been termed total social isolation. This generally consisted of placing subjects in individual cages that had been completely enclosed by opaque walls. The subjects, most typically rhesus monkeys *(M. mulatta),* were thus isolated from both tactile and visual contact with other animals. Some isolation facilities also separated the animals from auditory contact with other monkeys through the use of various sound-shielding systems.

A second form of isolation was partial isolation. In this case the subjects were housed in individual cages which prohibited tactile contact but which allowed visual and auditory contact with other monkeys. This form of housing generally produced behavioral abnormalities which were similar to, although less severe than, those produced by total isolation procedures. Monkeys reared in any form of social isolation display a wide array of behavioral abnormalities. Mason (1968) has described the "primate deprivation syndrome" which includes: (1) abnormal postures and movements, (2) motivational disturbances (e.g., excessive fearfulness), (3) poor integration of motor patterns (e.g., inadequate sexual behavior), and (4) deficiencies in social communication. Isolate-reared animals fail to display certain normal developmental trends and engage in many distinctly abnormal behaviors.

Developmental Abnormalities in Isolates

A developmental trend normally observed in rhesus monkeys is the tendency for infants (particularly those under 2 months of age) to cling to almost any available social object (Harlow, 1958; Mason & Kenney, 1974). In contrast, isolates avoid social objects when they are available and instead cling to themselves. This posture generally involves self-clutching of the head and body by the arms and legs while remaining in a prone or sitting position. This posture is typically assumed by isolate-reared monkeys when they are in a stressful situation such as being placed in a novel environment. Infant and juvenile isolates tend to withdraw from novel stimuli whenever possible. In an unfamiliar setting they usually crouch, suck their thumbs or toes, clasp themselves, and engage in rocking or other stereotyped behaviors. This is in direct contrast to the extreme curiosity displayed by normally reared infant and juvenile rhesus monkeys, which tend to explore novel stimuli.

The comparative development of social play provides evidence for another distinction between isolate- and normally reared monkeys. Normal rhesus monkeys spend a great deal of their time involved in social play from the age of 3 or 4 months to puberty. Isolate-reared monkeys, on the other hand, rarely exhibit normal play behavior when given the opportunity. They do not engage in spontaneous outbursts of play and do not respond to playful invitations made by peers (Mears & Harlow, 1975). When partial isolates were allowed to contact each other in brief test sessions beginning at 25 days of age, clasping each other was the dominant social activity. Between 25 and 85 days of age, the amount of clasping decreased and social play increased. The same behavior pattern was observed when the isolates were separated after 85 days of age and were reunited at 150 days of age. Physical contact facilitated the development of the social interaction from clasping to play.

As stated earlier, isolate-reared monkeys display a number of behavior patterns that are seldom displayed by normal monkeys. Subjects raised in isolation spend a great deal of time engaged in self-orality; they suck their fingers and toes. Monkeys raised in normal environments rarely display comparable behaviors. Isolates often develop patterns of repetitive or stereotypic movements that are not recorded by observers of normal animals. These movements include stereotyped pacing, flipping, jumping, rocking, and crouching, and they increase in frequency and duration as the animal's level of fear increases.

Another type of movement pattern labeled "bizarre movements" or "nonrepetitive stereotyped movements" has also been observed in isolates. These movements *decrease* as the fear level increases (Mitchell, 1968). Berkson (1967) noted the similarity between the stereotyped movements of isolate nonhuman primates and the stereotyped acts of human beings with certain abnormal behaviors. He also noted that the number of different stereotyped behaviors that have been observed increases as one moves from monkeys (primarily cercopithecines) to apes (pongids) to humans. Perhaps even more bizarre than repetitive movement patterns are the self-aggressive behaviors displayed by many older juvenile and adolescent isolates. These may include self-biting, head banging, eye poking, and gouging (Berkson, 1967). It has been hypothesized that these unusual behavior patterns serve as a source of self-stimulation for isolates, whose environments certainly do not afford normal amounts of physical stimulation (Berkson, 1967; Goosen, 1981). But they also appear to be symptoms of an inability to handle excessive arousal.

There are substantial amounts of data which attribute many abnormalities of isolates to the lack of tactile contact with other monkeys. Harlow's (1958) early studies concerned the development of attachment of orphaned infant monkeys to inanimate surrogate mothers. The physical contact involving factors such as movement, clinging, sucking, and warmth influenced the formation of this attachment (Harlow & Zimmerman, 1959). An inanimate object in the cage with an infant monkey can decrease the types or frequencies of various abnormal self-directed behaviors (see Capitanio, 1982). If an introduced surrogate is soft and easily clasped, self-clasping by the infant is reduced. If the surrogate is moveable, the infant's rocking behavior is reduced. The more subtle *social* behaviors of infants raised on inanimate surrogates are not substantially improved; however, the monkeys do appear to be less fearful (Mason & Berkson, 1975).

Individually housed infants that are allowed tactile contact with another animal through the wire mesh of their cages do not develop many of the abnormalities that are typical of both total and partial social isolates (Missakian, 1969; Suomi, Collins, Harlow, & Ruppenthal, 1976). Essentially normal development seems possible when isolates are allowed brief, periodic physical contact with agemates. As little as 20 min of time together several times per week for the first 6 months of life have been shown to allow seemingly normal development (Rosenblum, 1961).

The "abnormal" behaviors attributed to social isolation have been interpreted as being the *normal* responses of animals in exceedingly abnormal environments (Berkson, 1967; Mason, 1978; Suomi & Harlow, 1978; Goosen, 1981). For example, the excessive sucking displayed by infant isolates may be a manifestation of the innate sucking response redirected from the mother's nipple (which is now unavailable) to what is available in the isolates' environment — namely, their own digits. In a similar fashion, self-clasping can be interpreted as the normal manifestation of the grasping reflex that would also typically be displayed to the mother. Repetitive stereotyped movements by isolates may be a result of the infants' need for movement. These stereotyped patterns are essentially eliminated when isolates have access to a moving cloth-covered dummy (Mason, 1968). In addition the infants with moveable dummies, as noted above, are less fearful and more active than their counterparts raised on stationary surrogates.

Time as a Factor in Isolation Effects

Both the duration of the isolation period and the age of the animal at the time of isolation affect the behavioral consequences of isolation. In general, greater durations of isolation lead to more severe and more persistent behavioral effects. When rhesus monkeys are totally isolated for the first 3 months of their lives, they display the typical disturbed behavior patterns when first removed from isolation. However, these disturbed behaviors are no longer noticeable after 8 weeks of living in normal housing conditions (Griffin and Harlow, 1966). In contrast, monkeys isolated for the first 6 months of their lives do not recover from their deprivation. Instead, they continue to develop abnormal social behaviors, communication abilities, and stereotyped movements (Harlow & Harlow, 1962; Mason, 1960; Sackett, 1965).

These abnormalities persist through adulthood unless some remedial treatment is given. Subjects isolated for more than 6 months from birth show increasing amounts of the same abnormal behaviors. These changes then are quantitative, not qualitative in character (Sackett, 1968; Harlow & Harlow, 1969; Mitchell, 1970). These abnormalities are also more resistant to change by treatment programs.

The subject's age at the time of isolation is an important factor in predicting the effects of deprivation. Monkeys isolated for the second 6 months of their lives do not exhibit behavioral effects as extreme as those of rhesus isolated for their first 6 months (Rowland, 1964). The animals isolated for the second 6 months are somewhat more normal, except that they show relatively high levels of aggressive behavior. Clark (1968) found that severe behavioral abnormalities develop only in monkeys isolated from birth. Periods of isolation beginning in adulthood produce few abnormalities other than increased aggressiveness (Suomi, 1982a). The general conclusion from these types of study is that as few as 6 months, but no less than 3 months of isolation, can produce the typical primate deprivation syndrome in rhesus monkeys, if that isolation begins at birth (Suomi, 1982a). It seems that even 3 months of life in a normal social environment somehow insulates monkeys from the most severe effects of isolation.

Some researchers have interpreted these findings as evidence for the existence of a critical period for the development of appropriate social behavior in monkeys. The concept of a critical period implies that an individual would be unable to develop normal social behaviors if that individual were not exposed to the proper social stimulation during a particular period of its life. The use of a critical period concept is controversial. Many authors have instead supported the use of the notion of a "sensitive period" to describe this phenomenon in primates (Harlow, Gluck, & Suomi, 1972; Immelmann &

Suomi, 1981). A sensitive period implies that an animal may be *more* responsive to certain types of stimulation at specific points in its life, but the same stimuli at other times may still have some affect on the animal.

Long-Term Effects of Isolation

The primate deprivation syndrome induced by social isolation is very long lasting. Most monkeys that have been isolated for 6 months or more following their births display at least some abnormal behaviors throughout their lives. Some forms of abnormality, such as self-orality, decrease in frequency as the isolate matures. However, idiosyncratic stereotyped patterns are often displayed when the animal is under stress throughout adulthood (Suomi, 1982a). In a study of 84 rhesus monkeys, Cross and Harlow (1965) described age changes in the abnormal behaviors of partial and total isolates. Digit sucking, vocalizing, grimacing, self-clasping, crouching, rocking, scratching, and convulsive jerking decreased from ages 1 to 7 years. Self-chewing, self-biting, aggression, pacing, and yawning increased with age.

Isolate-reared monkeys display long-term effects of social behavior as well. Isolates, when placed in a social group, avoid other animals. If they do interact, isolates often display inappropriate responses. Mason (1968) concluded that socially deprived animals do not properly integrate behavior patterns enough to be effectively applied in social situations. They do not send or receive communication signals in an appropriate manner. Isolates tend to be hyperaggressive and may, for example, attack an infant or an animal that is much more dominant than themselves (Mitchell, 1968). Few normal monkeys would direct aggressive behavior toward those types of conspecifics.

Rowland (1964) found that total isolation for 6 to 12 months following birth has a persistent effect on social behavior. These animals are fearful, disturbed, and sexually abnormal when they are 12–20 months old. Partial isolates, when paired with unfamiliar animals at 22–44 months old, demonstrate high degrees of fear, aggression, and idiosyncratic bizarre movements, as well as low levels of environmentally directed orality, little sexual behavior, and little play (Mitchell, Raymond, Ruppenthal, & Harlow, 1966). The 12-month-total isolates are mainly fearful and nonaggressive (although they threaten many attacks), while the 6- month isolates are fearful and physically aggressive. Even at 4½ years of age these total isolates are still socially inactive and fearful (Mitchell, 1968). Aggressive behavior in isolates is generally more frequent, longer in duration, and more severe than is aggressive behavior in feral animals (Mason, 1968). Isolates also have unstable dominance orders when placed in groups (Mason, 1968).

The sexual behavior of isolates is adversely affected. Although their sexual development is normal physiologically, their behavioral expression of sex shows evidence of severe deficits. Isolates' sexual behavior is both unusually low in frequency and abnormal in form (Mitchell, 1968). Male isolates rarely attempt to mount females, and, if they do, their attempted mounts are not properly oriented to facilitate intromission. Female isolates often try to avoid males and may threaten them or collapse under their weight when mounted. Wild-born chimpanzees (pongids) that have been separated from their mothers and then raised in total or partial isolation also do not exhibit normal sexual behavior (Kollar, Edgerton & Beckwith, 1968), even though they were not isolated from birth. It appears that an opportunity to copulate before reaching maturity is necessary for the normal development of sexual behavior in nonhuman primates. However, some of the isolated chimpanzees in a study by Rogers and Davenport (1969) recovered from some of the adverse effects and were able to copulate. This recovery was attributed to the chimpanzees' having less rigid behavior patterns than rhesus monkeys.

The maternal behaviors of adult female isolates are also abnormal. Approximately 75% of these mothers either neglect or abuse their first-born offspring (Seay, Alexander, & Harlow, 1964; Harlow, Harlow, Dodsworth, & Arling, 1966). As a comparison only 5% of mother-reared rhesus monkeys are inadequate mothers (Ruppenthal, Arling, Harlow, Sackett, & Suomi, 1976). The maternal behaviors of many isolates improve after they give birth to a second infant. (See the section "Child Abuse" for a further discussion of this topic.)

Treatment of Isolated Primates

Early attempts at rehabilitating isolate-reared monkeys were generally unsuccessful. Techniques such as behavior modification procedures (Sackett, 1968), systematic desensitization to reduce fear on emergence from isolation (Mitchell & Clark, 1968), and social modeling by socially sophisticated peers (Mitchell, Raymond, Ruppenthal, & Harlow, 1966) were employed. The resulting rehabilitation was minimal and the behavioral improvements did not generalize to other situations.

However, in the early 1960s it became obvious that rhesus isolates responded more positively to younger conspecifics than to agemates or adults, and therapy employing infants was suggested (Mitchell, 1965, 1966, 1970). Later attempts at treatment using infant therapists were indeed more successful. Three-month-old socially normal monkeys have been used as "monkey therapists" (Suomi & Harlow, 1972). These infants were chosen to be paired with the isolates because it was assumed that they would promote physical contact without threatening the isolates. Isolates were placed with the "therapists" for five 2-h periods per week for 6 months. Although the isolates originally withdrew from the infants, by the end of 6 months the two animals were actively playing. Most of the isolates' abnormal self-directed behaviors disappeared during the therapy sessions. These encouraging changes were long-lasting. Isolates even displayed some appropriate sexual behaviors during the 2-year period following the therapy sessions (Cummins & Suomi, 1976). Related studies with animals raised in isolation for 1 year found similar although less complete rehabilitation (Novak & Harlow, 1975; Novak, 1979). A variety of studies have shown that the earlier the treatment is begun, the more effective it is. However, even 17-year-old partial isolate males responded positively to infant therapy (Gomber & Mitchell, 1974; Mitchell, Maple, & Erwin, 1979).

Species Differences in the Effects of Isolation

As stated earlier, the rhesus macaque has been the most widely used primate in studies of social isolation. Early studies of the effects of isolation on stumptailed macaques (*M. arctoides*, another cercopithecine) and chimpanzees (a pongid) generated findings consistent with those on rhesus monkeys. Other cercopithecines like Japanese macaques (*M. fuscata*) and gelada baboons (*Theropithecus gelada*) and cebids like capuchin monkeys (*Cebus apella*) also seem to respond to isolation in a manner similar to that of rhesus monkeys (Anderson & Chamove, 1980; Candland & Mason, 1968). These findings led to the opinion that the primate deprivation syndrome was universal within the primate order and so could be applied to humans as well as apes and monkeys (Harlow, Gluck, & Suomi, 1972).

Further research, though, has challenged the validity of that conclusion. In 1976, Sackett, Holm, and Ruppenthal reported that the cercopithecine pigtailed macaques (*M. nemestrina*) did not respond to isolation in the "expected" manner. They exhibited spontaneous recovery from the effects of 9 months of isolation. They showed relatively little self-directed and stereotyped behavior patterns and were able to easily integrate into new social groups (Sackett *et al.* 1976). These dramatic differences exist despite the fact that rhesus and pigtails have quite comparable early physical and social development and similar maternal care strategies.

Crab-eating macaques (*M. fascicularis*), also cercopithecines, have been shown to spontaneously recover their normal social behaviors on emergence from isolation, although they *do* exhibit abnormal behaviors during the isolation period (Sackett *et al.*, 1976). In a comparative study of isolation effects, rhesus showed the highest levels of self-directed behaviors, crabeaters intermediate levels, and pigtails low levels (Sackett, Ruppenthal, Fahrenbruch, Holm, & Greenough, 1981). Crabeaters and pigtails engaged in relatively high levels of exploration, while rhesus showed low levels. Crabeaters alone showed very high levels of positive social behavior. The important point here is that even these closely related species react very differently to 6 months of total isolation (Capitanio, 1982).

The effects of isolation on apes has not been extensively studied, but there seems to be considerable variation in their responses to social restriction as well. Among the great apes, early isolation does not seem to affect orang-utans later in life, but chimpanzees and gorillas are affected. Chimpanzees subjected to total isolation for the first 2 years of life display a wide range of abnormalities (Davenport & Rogers, 1970). At 6 years of age these chimpan-zees display 25 distinct abnormal behavior patterns, and as they get older this increases to 75 patterns. Even after years of living in social groups these animals continue to exhibit abnormal self-directed behaviors. Their coordi-nation of complex social behaviors, such as grooming and sexual activity, remain deficient. Factors such as the complexity of normal social repertoires and natural social groupings may be important in determining species varia-bility, but these ideas have not yet been thoroughly tested (Suomi, 1982a).

Other Forms of Social Restriction

Mother-Only Rearing

Forms of social deprivation less severe than isolation have also been stud-ied. When a monkey mother and an infant are housed by themselves, each of them is socially deprived. Alexander (1966) found that infants living in these conditions for their first 4 or 8 months of life are initially hostile when exposed to agemates. These mother-only infants also show less bodily con-tact than do control infants that have normal peer experience. Mothers of the infants are present for both of the above two tests. When mothers are *not* present at this first meeting with other infants, mother-only infants do not show an increase in aggression or a decrease in bodily contact (Griffin & Harlow, 1966). Mother-only subjects continue to show abnormally high levels of aggression and are socially deficient even at 6 years of age.

Effects of the environment on infant behavior were studied by housing some mother–infant pairs in bare, soundproof cages and other such pairs in open laboratory cages equipped with toys (Jensen & Bobbitt, 1968; Jensen, Bobbitt, & Gordon, 1967). The stimulus-poor environment intensifies the physical relationship between the mother and infant (as evidenced by more time spent in physical contact with each other) and retards the infants' development (as evidenced by more behavior directed toward themselves and less toward the environment). The environment does not seem to affect the nature of the mother's role as there are no differences in maternal protec-tion or punishment between the two environments. None of these infants display the severe abnormalities seen in isolated monkeys, but they are socially subordinate to control monkeys (who are raised with mothers and peers) at 6 months of age (Jensen & Bobbitt, 1968).

Peer-Only Rearing

Mother-only rearing does not lead to the development of normal infants, and neither does peer-only rearing. Peer-only reared infants show high degrees of clinging and huddling with cage mates and low levels of play (Chamove, 1966). Monkeys housed with more than one peer show more normal play behavior than do those housed with a single cage mate, but they all display prolonged and excessive clinging behavior (Harlow & Harlow, 1962). Peer-only reared monkeys develop more normally than do mother-only reared monkeys, however.

When peer experience is combined with the use of artificial mother surrogates for the first 6 months of life, essentially normal infant behavior is observed (Rosenblum, 1961). The surrogates receive the prolonged clinging that probably would be directed at the other infants were the surrogate not present. Thus, these infants spend time playing instead of just huddling as do the infants of Chamove (1966).

Studies of Social Separation

Many studies of the social separation of nonhuman primates have been carried out in the laboratory. Again, macaques have been the most common subjects. Separation studies have been used as animal models of human depression. Depression has been reported to be the most universally- occurring and costly mental affliction known to humanity (Suomi, 1982c). The most common theoretical explanations of depression incorporate a separation from the loss of an individual or object and the resulting affective disturbance. Since nonhuman primates form strong social attachments to conspecifics, they are a useful model for human depression.

Mother – Infant Separation Studies

The first in a series of studies of monkey mother – infant separation was performed by Seay, Hansen, and Harlow (1962). Mother – infant rhesus pairs housed together for the first 6 months of the infants' lives were separated for 3 weeks such that they could see, hear, and smell each other but could not physically contact one another. Initially, the infants actively protested the separation by an increase in vocalizations, mother viewing, and general activity. After 2 days of this protest behavior the infants' responses changed significantly. Typically, they sat in hunched-over positions and showed little response to their environments. These infants *looked* depressed. Exploration decreased as did peer-directed behaviors. Reactions to the separation disappeared when the mother and infant were united. Almost all of the infants reestablished contact with their mothers immediately when reunited. There was an increase in mother–infant cradling, clinging, and ventral contract. Three weeks after the reunion, all social and nonsocial behaviors had returned to baseline levels, so no long-term effects of separation were implicated. In a later study the mother was removed from visual and auditory contact, as well as from physical contact (Seay & Harlow, 1965). In this case, aggression toward peers increased after the reunion.

Numerous investigations replicated the same phases of infant reaction to separation—an initial protest followed by depressive reactions and the reunion that quickly dissipated the depressed behaviors (Hinde, Spencer-Booth, & Bruce, 1966; Kaufman & Rosenblum, 1967). The pattern of monkey infant behavior displayed at separation is very similar to the behavior patterns exhibited by human infants when they are separated from their mothers (Bowlby, 1960). The humans show protest at the point of separation and later display depressed behaviors. When reunited with their parents most of the children quickly recover their normal behaviors. Some children, however, seem to become resentful and act detached from their parents (Bowlby, 1961). These detached children initially refuse to go to their mothers on reunion and sometimes run from them or direct aggression toward them.

Physiological correlates of stress have been measured following maternal separation. The infants' heart rate, blood pressure, body temperature, and plasma cortisol levels are all elevated and indicate a massive activation of the sympathetic nervous system (Suomi, 1982a) during the protest phase. During the depressive state, physiological responses are less clear and there seems to be a great deal of individual differentiation. Most physiological changes do return to preseparation levels following the reunion. A few long-term physiological effects have been reported (Reite, Short, Seiler, & Pauley, 1981), and they may parallel some long-term behavioral effects noted by some researchers (Mitchell, Harlow, Griffin, & Møller, 1967).

An important study of the effects of repeated separations has been performed by Griffin and Harlow (1966). Three groups of rhesus monkeys were raised with only mothers for 8 months. During this time the groups underwent various series of social separations. A "rotated mother" group of infants was employed in which an infant was repeatedly separated from one mother for 2 h every 2 weeks. After the separation period it was returned to one of the other three mothers. In the "repeated separation" group, the infants were repeatedly separated but were returned to the same mother after each separation. The control group infants were never separated. Separations led to the typical infant protest syndrome. Mothers were overprotective only if the same infant was returned to them each time. Previous separations *increased* the disturbing effects in the infants who were repeatedly separated from the same mother. At 8 months of age these infants were placed together (their mothers were not present). High levels of contact behavior were exhibited by the repeatedly separated infants. The exaggerated separation response of the repeatedly separated infants was still evident when they were 19 months old (Mitchell *et al.*, 1967), a year after their final maternal separation.

Effects of Separation on the Mother

The great majority of separation studies document the infants' responses to separations, but some have also analyzed the effects on mothers. Pigtail macaque mothers separated from their infants became more active and vocal, and these responses further increased during the presentation of infant calls played on a tape recorder (Simons, Bobbitt, & Jensen, 1968). Jensen (1968) found that pigtail monkey mothers showed behavioral evidence of depression 18 days after separation from their infants. However these symptoms were no longer evident 2 months after the separation. The depression exhibited by the pigtail mothers was not as severe as that experienced by the infants. In another study, mothers that had been repeatedly separated from their infants over a period of 8 months showed a greater preference for their own infants than mothers who had not had a history of repeated separations (Sackett, Griffin, Pratt, & Ruppenthal, 1966).

Factors Influencing Reactions to Separations

Although obvious trends in reactions to separations exist, the complete behavioral sequence of protest, depression, and return to normal is not universally observed. Many factors seem to influence the subjects' reactions to maternal separation. There is general agreement that at least some component of the typical separation response is genetically determined (Suomi, 1982b). There is much discussion, however, over exactly which components are so determined. A universal primate reaction to separation from mother has been proposed (Bowlby, 1969, 1973). This reaction is said to involve all stages — protest, depression, and detachment at reunion. Another theoretical explanation is that only the protest and despair components are preprogrammed. The detachment component is attributed to specific environmental influences and is not usually seen in nonhuman primates (Kaufman,

1977). The most recent approach hypothesizes that only the protest phase is universally displayed, and the depression and detachment responses are dependent on particular circumstances (Plimpton & Rosenblum, 1983).

The Plimpton and Rosenblum (1983) approach is supported by many studies in which primate infants fail to display any form of behavioral depression or detachment on maternal separation. A host of factors seem to influence the primate infant's reaction to maternal separation and reunion. The age, sex, and species of the subject are important, as are the nature of the social environment, the quality of its relationship with its mother, the separation duration, the familiarity of the environment, and the demands placed on the infant and mother during separation. Obviously, the phenomenon of social separation in primates is a very complex one.

Species differences in separation response are evident in even closely related species. While pigtail macaques tend to display the typical response pattern including protest and depression, bonnet macaques do not. Bonnet monkey infants only mildly protest when separated and do not exhibit behavioral depression (Rosenblum & Kaufman, 1968). This species difference has been explained in terms of species differences in social structure. Bonnet infants are readily "adopted" by other members of their group when their mother is removed, whereas pigtail infants are usually ignored or punished by other members of their group when their mother is removed. Even bonnet monkeys are not immune to depression following maternal separation, though, as has been demonstrated under some circumstances as when others are not present to adopt them (Plimpton, 1981; Reite & Snyder, 1982).

There is also a considerable degree of within-species variation due to individual differences in subjects. There is the recent suggestion that autonomic reactivity differences in rhesus monkey infants may largely be genetically determined (Suomi, 1982b). Individual differences also exist in human infant responses to maternal separation. As Suomi (1982a) reminds us, only 25% of the human infants described by Spitz in 1946, in his study of anaclitic depression, actually displayed the analclitic depression syndrome—the other 75% did not show any major depressive symptoms.

Separations Other than from Mother

Since most depression observed in humans is not the direct result of the loss of one's mother in childhood, the relevancy of studies of monkey maternal loss to the study of human depression is questionable. For this reason, studies of separations from animals other than mothers have been undertaken. Three-month-old infants that had developed strong attachments to peer groups showed classic protest and depression responses when separated from these peers for a 4-day period (Suomi, Harlow, & Domek, 1970). These infants did not habituate to repeated 4-day separations, and the series of separations seemed to slow normal social development. Monkey infants reared on inanimate surrogates (Novak, 1973; Coe & Levine, 1981) or with adult male conspecifics (Redican, 1975, 1978), even isolate-raised male conspecifics (Gomber & Mitchell, 1974), also reacted negatively to separation from their respective "companions." Obviously, infant monkeys can become strongly attached to individuals other than their mothers and can intensely react to separation from these individuals.

In other studies of separation, older nonhuman primates have been used as subjects. Early findings revealed that juvenile and adolescent rhesus monkeys displayed different forms of behavioral protest than did infants. However, these studies were not designed to produce depression, and none was observed (Erwin, Brandt, & Mitchell, 1973; Maple, Risse, & Mitchell, 1973). Later studies found that these older animals were indeed relatively unaffected by short-term peer separations but that more extensive separations did affect the older monkeys. Suomi, Eisele, Grady, and Harlow (1975) found that 5-year-old subjects separated from the family groups they had been reared with and placed in individual cages *did* exhibit protest and depressive reactions. In contrast, those 5-year-olds that were placed with either familiar peers or with unfamiliar strangers after separation showed only mild behavioral reactions to the treatment.

The long-term effects of early social separations on animals' predispositions to depressive reactions to separations later in life have been examined. Some studies have found that a previous history of separations has led to more severe reactions to later social separations. However, other studies have found no effect of early experience with separations (Young, Suomi, Harlow, & McKinney, 1973; Mineka, Suomi, & DeLizio, 1983). It appears that monkeys that react severely to separation as infants (i.e., showed signs of depression) do tend to react in a similar fashion when separated as older animals (Suomi, Mineka, & DeLizio, 1987). Furthermore, Mitchell et al. (1967) found that rhesus repeatedly separated during the first year of life emitted, at 19 months of age, excessive numbers of calls for social contact *and* showed more subordinate behavior in social pairings (even when not separated) than did nonseparated animals. Once again there are undoubtedly many factors that influence the reactions of these monkeys to separation and other events in later life, and all of these factors have not yet been thoroughly documented.

Treatment of Separation-Induced Depression

The most common "treatment" for depression caused by social separation is the reunion of the separated animals. As has been explained, this

reunion generally dissipates the depressive behaviors. Other efforts at rehabilitation have also been attempted. Antidepressant drugs have been administered, and electroconvulsive shock therapy has been used. (See Suomi,
1982a, for a more complete review of this topic.) Drugs such as imipramine
and MAO inhibitors, such as DMI, which are commonly used for the treatment of depressed humans, have been tested on nonhuman primates. These
drugs have been shown to have modes of action, time courses, and success
rates in depressed monkeys that are very similar to those in depressed
humans. Apparently, useful treatments for human depression are helpful for
depressed monkeys and vice versa. This generalization is strong support for
the validity of the nonhuman primate model for human depression (Suomi,
1982a,c).

Child Abuse

Several models have been proposed as explanations for the existence of
human child abuse. One general category of models emphasizes the *internal*
psychopathological condition and inadequacies of the abusive parent
(Steele, 1977; Spinetta & Rigler, 1972). Another general category of models
emphasizes *external* stresses — typically social and economic pressures — on
the abusive parent. A model labeled the *"social interactional model"* has
been proposed (Burgess, 1979; Vasta, 1982), which emphasizes the influence
of the child's characteristics on the abusive interaction. It incorporates parental, environmental, and offspring variables as dynamic interactants in
abuse (Schapiro & Mitchell, 1983). Many psychologists, anthropologists,
and primatologists studying abuse in nonhuman primates believe that useful
parallels between it and human child abuse exist. Indeed, some striking
similarities between human and nonhuman abuse have been found.

Reite and Caine (1983) have examined 12 years of data on infant abuse in
a colony of pigtailed macaques. They reported that male infants were abused
(i.e., physically injured) more often than were female infants. In addition,
18% of the abused infants were *repeatedly* abused. Most abuse was performed by animals that were otherwise behaviorally normal. All of these
findings are consistent with data on human child abuse. Reite and Caine
concluded that there seemed to be an abuse threshold, which, if exceeded,
resulted in abuse. A variety of factors, including the individual history of the
parent as well as impinging environmental influences, appeared to be involved. Social and biological factors affected the incidence of abuse.

Nadler (1983) suggested that the early social experience of the primate
mother may set the boundaries within which later maternal behavior may
develop. A greater degree of restriction of early social experience would thus
limit the *potential* for the development of normal maternal behavior. The

extensive data dealing with rhesus monkeys indicate that females reared apart from their mothers are inadequate mothers for their own first-born young. However, their maternal behavior improves with successive offspring (Ruppenthal, Arling, Harlow, Sackett, & Suomi, 1976). Peer-raised females are reported to be more adequate mothers than those raised in isolation or with a cloth-covered surrogate (Ruppenthal *et al.*, 1976).

Peer-raised mothers do not behave *indifferently* toward their young as do the two socially deprived groups. However, there is *no* difference in the frequency of infant *abuse* among these three groups of mothers. Sumoi (1978) has suggested that the infant abuse displayed may be related to the common rearing experience of the animals apart from their own mothers and may reflect a "general social incompetence." One component of this social incompetence is inadequate or abusive behavior toward first-born infants. A second component may be improved maternal competency with subsequent offspring. It may be that the mother provides some experience that somehow reduces the chances that her infant would later abuse its own offspring. Parallels of early social stress in humans, such as neglect and abuse by parents, are common in parents that abuse their children (Kempe, Silverman, Steele, Droegemueller, & Silver, 1962; Parke & Collmer, 1975).

Davenport and Rogers (1970) studied the maternal behavior of chimpanzees, some of which had been removed from their mothers at birth and raised in various conditions of social restriction for the first 2 years of their lives. Females reared by their own mothers for more than 18 months displayed maternal behavior that was superior to those that had received less contact with their mothers. The more severely deprived females displayed essentially no solicitous behavior toward their offspring and showed little if any improvement in their maternal behavior with successive infants. In this case then, in contrast to findings described for rhesus monkeys, the early social restriction of chimpanzee mothers-to-be eliminated the ability of the mother to change her behavior after gaining experience with her earlier infants.

The social environment is an extremely important factor in the incidence of abuse. The demands of the human child have been proposed as causal factors in abuse (Burgess, 1979; Vasta, 1982). In many societies, including most nonindustrialized ones, demands of the child on the mother are diluted by the role that the extended family (or even the entire village) plays in child rearing. The pressure on the mother may be relieved by the sharing of child-care tasks. The mother's behavior may also be inhibited through the possible social reaction to abusive behavior she may exhibit. Concurrent with the lack of extended family living in Western societies is the decrease in influence of outsiders in a potentially abusive incident. This may be correlated with high levels of child abuse. Indeed, physical punishment has been found to be the most frequent in mother–child households where a mother can punish a child without other adults being aware of the punishment (Korbin, 1977). Relative social isolation of the parent is typical of human parents who abuse their children (Elmer, 1967; Young 1964).

Social support throughout the entire child-rearing process may be as important to apes as it is to humans. A social group may be important as an ever-changing source of arousal and as a buffer against the stress of isolation (Maple & Warren-Leubecker, 1983). Socially isolated apes are understimulated and may abandon or ignore their young for this reason. Others seem to meticulously overattend to their offspring and may injure them by the removal of hair, nails, or skin (Maple & Warren-Leubecker, 1983). On the other hand, overstimulation due to crowding or to high noise levels may also agitate parents and so may lead to abandonment of young.

Nadler (1983) has proposed that the most significant factor in infant abuse in gorillas has been the absence of a social group at the time of the abusive incident. In one investigation, seven of the eight adequate mothers were housed with a male or with a larger social group at the time of the delivery of the infant and afterward. In contrast, eight of the nine neglectful or abusive mothers were housed with only their infants at the time of the abuse. Observations in the wild have revealed that gorilla mothers do generally raise their infants within a social group and that they tend to spend a relatively large proportion of their time in close proximity to the dominant, silverback male of their troop. Wild gorilla mothers spend the most time near the silverback at the time immediately following parturition, and this early postnatal period is the interval during which the highest frequency of infant neglect and abuse is typically seen in captive gorilla mothers separated from conspecifics.

In a comparative study of three species of macaques living in large social groups, Schapiro and Mitchell (1983) found significant social and biological contributions to infant abuse. The abusing mother was characterized as a reactor to external stress. Mothers stressed by physical injury seemed to be less able to deal with the additional stress of their offsprings' demands. This finding has also been noted in humans, particularly in disabled fathers who are primary caregivers while the mother works (Merrill, cited in Spinetta & Rigler, 1972). Some animals appear to be physiologically predisposed to the effects of stress. Infant abuse could be one manifestation of this relatively low tolerance for stress (Suomi, 1982a).

Many studies have found that human children with "abnormalities" such a prematurity (Weston, 1974), mental retardation (Gil, 1970), and congenital defects (Lynch, 1975) are more susceptible to abuse than normal children. The suggestion is that infants which need special care, and so require more of their mothers' time and energy, are not only disadvantaged because of their physical defects but are also more likely to be abused. As described earlier, however, (see the section "Abnormal Behavior in the Wild") nonhuman primates do *not* appear to react to abnormal infants in a manner similar to many of their human counterparts. Nonhuman primates seem to give additional compensatory care to defective infants. This discrepancy in findings may be explained if one assumes that defective monkey infants do not constitute an additional stress for their mothers as do human infants. In general it appears that macaques living in stable social groups, analogous to extended human families, may experience less stress associated with caring for their offspring than do monkeys living in unstable groups. In turn, social group stability would be expected to decrease the likelihood of physical abuse of young primates.

Research concerning the therapeutic treatment of abusive nonhuman primate parents is in its preliminary stages. Initial data indicate that abusive adult animals may be somewhat improved by the provision of physical and social environments that are conducive to social interaction (Riddle, Keeling, Alford, & Beck, 1982).

While the data on nonhuman primate infant abuse seem to hold significant implications for the understanding and possible treatment of human child abuse, some researchers are not convinced that these apparent parallels are useful. For instance Hrdy (cited in Herbert, 1982) argues that the concept of child abuse as used by public health officials is uniquely human. Hrdy claims that analogies with captive monkeys are not valid, because the motivational factors behind the two types of abuse are different. She states that human child abuse is a learned phenomenon, while nonhuman primate abuse is a manifestation of an adaptive strategy. But all of Hrdy's research has involved infanticide by male, nonhuman primates in the wild. Her conception of the research area may therefore be very different from that of a comparative psychopathologist.

Klopfer (cited in Herbert, 1982) also argues against use of the primate model for human child abuse. He states that human child abuse involves a cognitive response of a mother to her child. He says that invoking this cognitive factor is not necessary to explain abuse in nonhuman primates. Despite these criticisms, many investigators are continuing the study of abuse by monkeys of their infants, some with the intention of directly comparing the findings with human child abuse. It is the opinion of the present authors that the research area continues to be a promising one. Precluding or even discouraging further investigations would be at best premature.

Usefulness of the Nonhuman Primate Data to the Human Field of Study

The study of abnormal behavior in nonhuman primates can be useful on several levels to the area of psychopathology in humans. A comparative approach can help to define the concept of abnormality and to distinguish it from normality. As we have seen, some laboratory studies of aberrations in nonhuman primate behavior have been designed to model specific human conditions. Nonhuman primates have also been used in testing the behavioral effects of new drugs thought to have therapeutic potential.

Studies of social restriction—either through isolation or separation—have also generated fundamental information for human behavior. The significance of early experience in shaping the development of primate behavior in general (including human) has been illuminated. The important roles of tactile contact and movement in infant primate development have been emphasized. Positive treatment of abnormal social behaviors (through the use of socially normal "therapists") has been found to be possible. By combining information from all of these perspectives, we increase the possibility of learning to prevent or even cure some abnormal human behaviors.

There are limitations to the comparative primate approach. A constructive critique of nonhuman primate models of human abnormal behavior has been provided by Dienske and de Jonge (1982). These authors directed their attention to the two most often studied nonhuman primate species (as far as the area of abnormal behavior is concerned). These two species are the rhesus monkey and the common chimpanzee. Dienske and de Jonge have reminded us that, with regard to both normal and abnormal development, rhesus, chimpanzees, and humans seem to be on three distinct levels of complexity and that the three species differ greatly in at least the five following characteristics: (1) *Speed of development*: decreasing from rhesus to chimp to human; (2) *Complexity of mother–infants interaction patterns*: increasing from rhesus to chimp to human; (3) *Behavioral capacities to be developed*; increasing from rhesus to chimp to human; (4) *Number of risk factors and types of social deprivation*: increasing from rhesus to chimp to human; and (5) *Efficacy of peers as substitutes for mothers*: decreasing from rhesus to chimps to humans.

The same authors (Dienske & de Jonge, 1982) also noted the following: (1) There is an increasing amount of eye-to-eye contact between mother and infant, with rhesus showing little, chimps more, and humans by far the most; (2) Stereotyped, apparently preprogrammed grooming movements decrease through the series; (3) Vocal reciprocity between mother and infant is missing in rhesus and chimps; (4) Active "teaching" sessions are absent in rhesus and chimps; (5) Fathers are more important in humans than in the other two species; (6) Peer interactions are delayed in humans; and (7) Instrumental (tool-use) and linguistic abilities are much more salient in *Homo sapiens*. These same authors also correctly point out that the above differences are of grave importance to an understanding of the effects of early social deprivation, separation, and maternal (parental) abuse. They also strongly encourage an emphasis on the wide interindividual or temperamental variation seen in all three species; they note that symptoms stemming from educational deprivation appear to be primarily human in nature; and they remind us that social isolation in rhesus generally affects many behavior classes, is (fortunately) extremely rare in humans, and is therefore of fundamental but not of immediate practical importance to human abnormality.

However, they also stress that the study of human deprivation is hampered by the facts that: (1) the studies must be retrospective, (2) knowledge of early life histories are limited, (3) different risk factors coincide, restricting insight into causal factors, (4) one factor may induce others during development, and (5) ethical considerations are more serious in human research. Most importantly, they conclude their critique of the whole research area with the following prescription, which in our view, portends the future of the field:

> Generally speaking, the process of the development of deviant behavior is insufficiently known. Studies on nonhuman primates that are carefully matched with those on humans with respect to risk factors and measurements of their effects will improve our insight into the sources of disturbed behavior. (p. 515)

References

Alexander, B. K. (1966). The effects of early peer-deprivation on juvenile behavior of rhesus monkeys. Unpublished doctoral dissertation, University of Wisconsin, Madison, WI.

Anderson, J. R., & Chamove, A. S. (1980). Self-aggression and social aggression in laboratory-reared macaques. *Journal of Abnormal Psychology, 89,* 539–550.

Berkson, G. (1967). Abnormal stereotyped motor acts. In J. Zubin & H. F. Hunt (Eds.), *Comparative Psychopathology* (pp. 76–94). New York: Grune & Stratton.

Bowlby, J. (1960). Grief and mourning in infancy and early childhood. *Psychoanalytic Study of the Child, 15,* 9–52.

Bowlby, J. (1961). Separation anxiety: A critical review of the literature. *Journal of Child Psychology and Psychiatry and Allied Disciplines, 1,* 251–269.

Bowlby, J. (1969). *Attachment and loss: Vol. 1. Attachment.* New York: Basic Books.

Burgess, R. L. (1979). A social interactional analysis. In B. B. Lahey & A. E. Kazdin (Eds.), *Advances in clinical child psychology.* New York: Plenum.

Candland, D., & Mason, W. A. (1968). Infant monkey heart rate: Habituation and effects of social substitutes. *Developmental Psychobiology, 1,* 254–256.

Capitanio, J. P. (1982, August). Early experience and abnormal behavior. Paper presented at the IXth Congress of the International. Primatological Society, Atlanta, Georgia.

Chamove, A. S. (1966). The effects of varying infant peer experience on social behavior in the rhesus monkey. Unpublished master's thesis, University of Wisconsin, Madison, WI.

Clark, D. L. (1968). Immediate and delayed effects of early, intermediate, and late social isolation in the rhesus monkey. Unpublished doctoral dissertation, University of Wisconsin, Madison, WI.

Coe, C. L., & Levine, S. (1981). Normal responses to mother–infant separation in nonhuman primates. In D. F. Klein & J. Rubkin (Eds.), *Anxiety: New research and changing concepts* (pp. 401–402). New York: Raven.

Cross, H. A., & Harlow, H. F. (1965). Prolonged and progressive effects of partial isolation on the behavior of macaque monkeys. *Journal of Experimental Research in Personality, 1,* 39–49.

Cummins, M. S., & Suomi, S. J. (1976). Behavioral stability of rhesus monkeys following differential rearing. *Primates, 17*, 42–51.

Davenport, R. K., & Rogers, C. J. (1970). Differential rearing of the chimpanzee: A project survey. In G.H. Bourne (Ed.), *The Chimpanzee,* (Vol. 3, pp. 337–360). Basel: Karger.

Dienske, H., & de Jonge, G. (1982). A comparison of development and deprivation in nonhuman primates and man. *Journal of Human Evolution, 11*, 511–516.

Elmer, E. (1967). *Children in Jeopardy: A Study of Abused Minors and Their Families.* Pittsburgh, PA: Univ. of Pittsburgh Press.

Erwin, J., Brandt, E. M., & Mitchell, G. D. (1973). Attachment formation and separation in heterosexually naive preadolescent rhesus monkeys (*Macaca mulatta*). *Developmental Psychobiology, 6*, 531–538.

Fedigan, L. M., & Fedigan, L. (1977). The social development of a handicapped infant in a free-living troop of Japanese macaques. In S. Chevalier-Skolnikoff & F. E. Poirier (Eds.), *Primate bio-social development: Biological, social, and ecological determinants* (pp. 205–222). New York: Garland.

Fobes, J., King, J. (1982). *Primate Behavior.* New York: Academic Press.

Gil, D.G. (1970). *Violence Against Children.* Cambridge, MA: Harvard Univ. Press.

Gomber, J. M., & Mitchell, G. (1974). Preliminary report on adult male isolation-reared rhesus monkeys caged with infants. *Developmental Psychology, 9*, 419.

Goosen, C. (1981). Abnormal behavior patterns in rhesus monkeys: Symptoms of mental disease? *Biological Psychiatry, 16*, 697–716.

Griffin, G. A., & Harlow, H. F. (1966). Effects of three months of total deprivation on social adjustment and learning in the rhesus monkey. *Child Development , 37*, 533–547.

Harlow, H. F. (1958). The nature of love. *American Psychologist, 13*, 673–685.

Harlow, H. F., Gluck, J. P., & Suomi, S. J. (1972). Generalization of behavioral data between nonhuman and human animals. *American Psychologist, 27*, 709–716.

Harlow, H. F., & Harlow, M. K. (1962). Social deprivation in monkeys. *Scientific American, 207*, 136–146.

Harlow, H. F., & Harlow, M. K. (1969). Effects of various mother–infant relationships on rhesus monkey behaviors. In B. M. Foss (Ed.), *Determinants of infant behavior* (Vol. 4, pp. 15–36). London: Methuen.

Harlow, H. F., Harlow, M. K., Dodsworth, R. O., & Arling, G. A. (1966). Maternal behavior of rhesus monkeys deprived of mothering and peer associations in infancy. *Proceedings of the American Philosophical Society, 110*, 58–66.

Harlow, H. F., & Zimmerman, R. R. (1959). Affectional responses in the infant monkey. *Science, 130*, 421–432.

Hinde, R. A., Spencer-Booth, Y., & Bruce, M. (1966). Effects of 6-day maternal deprivation on rhesus monkey infants. *Nature (London), 210*, 1021–1033.

Herbert, W. (1982). The evolution of child abuse. *Science News, 122,*, 24–26.

Immelmann, K., & Suomi, S. J. (1981). Sensitive phases in development. In K. Immelman, G. Barlow, M. Main, & L. Petrinovich (Eds.), *Issues in behavioral development.* London and New York: Cambridge Univ. Press.

Jensen, G. D. (1968). Reaction of monkey mothers to long-term separation from their infants. *Psychonomic Science, 11*(5), 171–172.

Jensen, G. D., & Bobbitt, R. A. (1968). Monkeying with the mother myth. *Psychology Today, 1*, 44.

Jensen, G. D., Bobbitt, R. A., & Gordon, B. N. (1967). Sex differences in social interaction between infant monkeys and their mothers. *Recent Advances in Biological Psychiatry, 21*, 283–292.

Kaufman, I. C. (1977). Developmental considerations of anxiety and depression: Psychobiological studies in monkeys. In T. Schapiro (Ed.), *Psychoanalysis and contemporary science* (pp. 317–363). New York: International Universities Press.

Kaufman, I. C., & Rosenblum, L. A. (1967). The reaction to separation in infant monkeys: Anaclitic depression and conservation-withdrawal. *Psychosomatic Medicine, 29,* 648–675.

Kempe, C. H., Silverman, F. N., Steele, B. F., Droegemueller, W., & Silver, H. K. (1962). The battered-child syndrome. *Journal of the American Medical Association, 181,* 17–24.

Kollar, E. J., Edgerton, R. B., & Beckwith, W. C. (1968). An evaluation of the ARL colony of chimpanzees. *Archives of General Psychiatry, 19*(5), 580–595.

Korbin, J. (1977). Anthropological contributions to the study of child abuse. In *Child Abuse and Neglect* (Vol. 1, pp. 7–24). Oxford: Pergamon.

Lovejoy, C. O. (1981). The origin of man. *Science, 211,* 341–350.

Lynch, M. (1975). Ill health and child abuse. *The Lancet, 331,* 317–319.

Maple, T., Risse, G., & Mitchell, G. D. (1973). Separation of adult males from adult female rhesus monkeys (*Macaca mulatta*) after a short-term attachment. *Journal of Behavioral Science, 1,* 327–336.

Maple, T. L., & Warren-Leubecker, A. (1983). Variability in the parental conduct of captive great apes and some generalizations to humankind. In M. Reite & N. Caine (Eds.), *Child abuse: The nonhuman primate data* (pp. 119–137). New York: Alan R. Liss.

Mason, W. A. (1960). The effects of social restriction on the behavior of rhesus monkeys: I. Free social behavior. *Journal of Comparative and Physiological Psychology, 53,* 583–589.

Mason, W. A. (1968). Early social deprivation in the nonhuman primates: Implications for human behavior. In D. C. Glass (Ed.), *Environmental Influences* (pp. 70–101). New York: Rockefeller University and Russel Sage Foundation.

Mason, W. A. (1978). Social ontogeny. In J. Vandenberg & P. Marler (Eds.), *Social behavior and communication* (pp. 53–71). New York: Plenum.

Mason, W. A., & Berkson, G. (1975). Effects of maternal mobility on the development of rocking and other behaviors in rhesus monkeys: A study with artificial monkeys. *Developmental Psychobiology, 8*(3), 197–211.

Mason, W. A., & Kenney, M. D. (1974). Redirection of filial attachment in rhesus monkeys: Dogs as mother surrogates. *Science, 183,* 1209–1211.

Mears, C., & Harlow, H. F. (1975). Play: Early and eternal. *Proceedings of the National Academy of Sciences, 72,* 1878–1882.

Mineka, S., Suomi, S. J., & DeLizio, R. D. (1983). Multiple separations in adolescent monkeys: An opponent-process interpretation. *Journal of Experimental Psychology: General, 110,* 56–85.

Missakian, E. A. (1969). Reproductive behavior of socially deprived male rhesus monkeys. *Journal of Comparative and Physiological Psychology, 69,* 403–407.

Mitchell, G. (1965). Long-term effects of total social isolation upon the behavior of rhesus monkeys. Unpublished master's thesis, University of Wisconsin, Madison, WI.

Mitchell, G. (1966). A follow-up study of total social isolation in the rhesus monkey. Unpublished doctoral dissertation, University of Wisconsin, Madison, WI.

Mitchell, G. (1968). Persistent behavior pathology in rhesus monkeys following early social isolation. *Folia Primatologica, 8,* 132–147.

Mitchell, G. (1970). Abnormal behavior in primates. In L. A. Rosenblum (Ed.), *Primate behavior* (Vol. 1, pp. 195–249). New York: Academic Press.

Mitchell, G, & Clark, D. L. (1968). Long term effects of social isolation in nonsocially adapted rhesus monkeys. *Journal of Genetic Psychology, 113,* 117–128.

Mitchell, G., Harlow, H. F., Griffin, G. A., & Møller, G. W. (1967). Repeated maternal separation in the monkey. *Psychonomic Science, 8,* 197–198.

Mitchell, G., Maple, T., & Erwin, J. (1979). Development of attachment potential in captive rhesus monkeys. In J. Erwin, T. Maple and G. Mitchell (Eds.), *Captivity and behavior* (pp. 59–112). New York: Alan R. Liss.

Mitchell, G., Raymond, E. J., Ruppenthal, G. C., & Harlow, H. F. (1966). Long term effects of total social isolation upon behavior of rhesus monkeys. *Psychological Reports, 18*, 567–580.

Nadler, R. D. (1983). Experiential influences on infant abuse of gorillas and some other nonhuman primates. In M. Reite and N. Caine (Eds.), *Child abuse: The nonhuman primate data* (pp. 139–150). New York: Alan R. Liss.

Novak, M. A. (1973). Fear-attachment relationships in infant and juvenile rhesus monkeys. Unpublished doctoral dissertation, University of Wisconsin, Madison, WI.

Novak, M. A. (1979). Social recovery of monkeys isolated for the first year of life: II. Long-term assessment. *Developmental Psychology, 15*, 50–61.

Novak, M. A., & Harlow, H. F. (1975). Social recovery of monkeys isolated for the first year of life: I. Rehabilitation and therapy. *Developmental Psychology, 11*, 353–365.

Parke, R. D., & Collmer, C. W. (1975). Child abuse: An interdisciplinary analysis. In E. M. Hetherington (Ed.), *Review of Child Development Research* (Vol. 5, pp. 509–590). Chicago: Univ. of Chicago Press.

Plimpton, E. H. (1981). Environmental variables and the response to maternal loss. Unpublished doctoral dissertation, State University of New York (Downstate Medical Center), New York.

Plimpton, E. H., & Rosenblum, L. A. (1983). Detachment-avoidance responses to mother following a separation: A comparative perspective. In H. F. Harlow, L. A. Rosenblum, & S. J. Suomi (Eds.), *Advances in the study of primate social development.* New York: Academic Press.

Redican, W. K. (1975). A longitudinal study of behavioral interactions between adult male and infant rhesus monkeys (*Macaca mulatta*). Unpublished doctoral dissertation, University of California, Davis, CA.

Redican, W. K. (1978). Adult male-infant relations in captive rhesus monkeys. In D. Chivers & J. Herbert (Eds), *Recent advances in primatology* (Vol. 1, pp. 36–48). New York: Academic Press.

Reite, M, & Caine, N. (Eds.). (1983). *Child abuse: The nonhuman primate data.* New York: Alan R. Liss.

Reite, M., Short, R., Seiler, C., & Pauley, J. D. (1981). Attachment loss and depression. *Journal of Child Psychology and Psychiatry and Allied Disciplines, 22*, 141–169.

Reite, M., & Snyder, D. (1982). Physiology of maternal separation in a bonnet macaque infant. *American Journal of Primatology, 2*, 115–120.

Riddle, K. E., Keeling, M. E., Alford, P. L., & Beck, T. F., (1982). Chimpanzee holding, rehabilitation and breeding. Facilities design and colony management. *Laboratory Animal Science, 32*(5), 525–533.

Rogers, C. M., & Davenport, R. K. (1969). Effects of restricted rearing on sexual behavior of chimpanzees. *Developmental Psychology, 1*, 200–204.

Rosenblum, L. A. (1961). The development of social behavior in the rhesus monkey. Unpublished doctoral dissertation, University of Wisconsin, Madison, WI.

Rosenblum, L. A., & Kaufman, I. C. (1968). Variations in infant development and response to maternal loss in monkeys. *American Journal of Orthopsychiatry, 38*, 418–426.

Rowland, G. L. (1964). The effects of total social isolation upon learning and social behavior in rhesus monkeys. Unpublished doctoral dissertation, University of Wisconsin, Madison, WI.

Ruppenthal, G. C., Arling, G. L., Harlow, H. F., Sackett, G. P., & Suomi, S. J. (1976). A 10-year perspective on motherless mother monkey behavior. *Journal of Abnormal Psychology, 85*, 341–349.

Sackett, G. P. (1965). The effects of rearing conditions upon monkeys (*Macaca mulatta*). *Child Development, 36*, 855–868.

Sackett, G. P. (1968). Abnormal behavior in laboratory reared rhesus monkeys. In M. W. Fox (Ed.), *Abnormal behavior in animals* (pp. 293–331). Philadelphia, PA: Saunders.

Sackett, G. P., Griffin, G. A., Pratt, C. L., & Ruppenthal, G. C. (1966). Mother-infant and adult female choice behavior in rhesus monkeys after various rearing experiences. Paper presented at the Midwestern Psychological Association Meeting, Chicago.

Sackett, G. P., Holm, R., & Ruppenthal, G. C. (1976). Social isolation rearing: Species differences in behavior of macaque monkeys. *Developmental Psychology, 10*, 283–288.

Sackett, G. P., Ruppenthal, G. C., Fahrenbruch, C. E., Holm, R. A., & Greenough, W. T. (1981). Social isolation rearing effects in monkeys vary with genotype. *Developmental Psychology, 17*, 313–318.

Schapiro, S., & Mitchell, G. (1983). Infant-directed abuse in a semi-natural environment: Precipitating factors. In M. Reite & N. Caine (Eds.), *Child abuse: The nonhuman primate data* (pp. 29–48). New York: Alan R. Liss.

Seay, B. M., Alexander, B. K., & Harlow, H. F. (1964). Maternal behavior of socially deprived rhesus monkeys. *Journal of Abnormal and Social Psychology, 69*, 345–354.

Seay, B. M., Hansen, E. W., & Harlow, H. F. (1962). Mother-infant separation in monkeys. *Journal of Child Psychology and Psychiatry, 3*, 123–132.

Seay, B. M., & Harlow, H. F. (1965). Maternal separation in the rhesus monkey. *Journal of Nervous and Mental Disease, 140*, 434–441.

Simons, R. C., Bobbitt, R. A., & Jensen, G. D. (1968). Mother monkeys (*Macaca nemestrina*) responses to infant vocalizations. *Perceptual and Motor Skills, 27*, 3–10.

Spinetta, J. J., & Rigler, D. (1972). The child abusing parent: A psychological review. *Psychological Bulletin, 77*, 296–304.

Spitz, R. A. (1946). Anaclitic depression. *Psychoanalytic Study of the Child, 2*, 313–347.

Steele, B. F. (1977). Child abuse and society. *Child Abuse and Neglect, 1*, 1–6.

Suomi, S. J. (1978). Maternal behavior by socially incompetent monkeys: Neglect and abuse of offspring. *Journal of Pediatric Psychology, 3*, 28–34.

Suomi, S. J. (1982a). Abnormal behavior and primate models of psychopathology. In J. Fobes & J. King (Eds.), *Primate behavior* (pp. 171–215). New York: Academic Press.

Suomi, S. J. (1982b). Genetic, maternal, and environmental influences on social development in rhesus monkeys. In B. Chiarelli & R. Corriccini (Eds.), *Primate behavior and sociobiology* (pp. 81–87). Berlin and New York: Springer-Verlag.

Suomi, S. J. (1982c). Animal models of human psychopathology relevance for clinical psychology. In P. Kendall & J. Butcher (Eds.), *Handbook of research methods in clinical psychology* (pp. 249–271). New York: Wiley.

Suomi, S. J., Collins, M. J., Harlow, H. F., & Ruppenthal, G. C. (1976). Effects of maternal and peer separations on young monkeys. *Journal of Child Psychology and Psychiatry, 17*, 101–112.

Suomi, S. J., Eisele, C. J., Grady, S. A., & Harlow, H. F. (1975). Depression in adult monkeys following separation from nuclear family environment. *Journal of Abnormal Psychology, 84*, 576–578.

Suomi, S. J., & Harlow, H. F. (1972). Social rehabilitation of isolate-reared monkeys. *Development Psychology, 6*, 487–496.

Suomi, S. J., & Harlow, H. F. (1978). Early experience and social development in rhesus monkeys. In M. E. Lamb (Ed.), *Social and personality development* (pp. 252–271). New York: Holt.

Suomi, S. J., Harlow, H. F., & Domek, C. J. (1970). Effect of repetitive infant-infant separation of young monkeys. *Journal of Abnormal Psychology, 76*, 161–172.

Suomi, S. J., Mineka, S., & DeLizio, R. D. (1987). Consistency of individual differences among juvenile rhesus monkeys in response to repetitive peer separations. Manuscript in preparation.

Vasta, R. (1982). Physical child abuse: A dual component analysis. *Developmental Review* 3, 87–96.

Weston, J. T. (1974). The pathology of child abuse. In R. E. Helfer & C. M. Kempe (Eds.), *The battered child* (pp. 61–86). Chicago: Univ. of Chicago Press.

Young, L. (1964). *Wednesday's children: A study of child neglect and abuse.* New York: McGraw-Hill.

Young, L. D., Suomi, S. J., Harlow, H. F., & McKinney, W. T. (1973). Early stress and later responses to separation. *American Journal of Psychiatry, 130*, 400–405.

3

Evolution and Pregnancy:
A Biosocial View of
Prenatal Influences

JAMES S. CHISHOLM and GAEL D. HEATH

The field of prenatal influences on infant constitution and behavior is ancient and its literature voluminous, yet it remains, in the words of one of its leading researchers, "a 'grey area' of modern science" (Stott, 1973, p. 770). The reason for the largely unproductive and slightly disreputable nature of research on prenatal influences is the virtual absence of theory and hence the absence of any basis for hypothetico-deductive reasoning. Or as Chalmers (1982) concluded in his review of prenatal influences, " . . . the paucity of theoretical models in this predominantly empirical field is sufficient evidence in itself that the nature of the research is generally uncoordinated and seemingly patternless" (1982, p. 329). The purposes of this chapter are thus two. First, we will review advances in evolutionary theory that may provide a basis for productive model building and testing. Second, we will review selected empirical studies of prenatal influences whose conclusions are at least consistent with the evolutionary approach outlined. Further, we will argue in a general way that progress in the field of prenatal influences is likely to depend on the abandonment of traditional disciplinary boundaries and on an appreciation that "explanations" of prenatal influences offered by different disciplines are incomplete, but not necessarily wrong, and especially that they are complementary and not mutually exclusive. We will also argue that complete explanations of prenatal influences will include analyses of the social–cultural environment of the pregnant woman. Finally, in conclusion, we suggest some of the implications for a variety of areas of theory and research that would follow from an evolutionary approach to the question of prenatal influences.

Conceptual Issues in the Study of Prenatal Influences

Reasons for the unproductive and vaguely disreputable nature of research on prenatal influences include conceptual issues that are related to, but go beyond, the obvious problem of the lack of a theoretical basis for model building and hypothesis testing. The problem, as Chalmers (1982) noted, is not one of a dearth of empirical studies. On the contrary, there are a great many studies showing a correlation between a variety of prenatal events and conditions and particular peri- or postnatal outcomes (see, for example, reviews by Chalmers, 1982; Ferreira, 1965, 1969; Grimm, 1967; Joffe, 1969; Kopp & Parmalee, 1979; McDonald, 1968; Montagu, 1962; Pasamanick, Rodgers, & Lilienfeld, 1956; Pasamanick & Knobloch, 1966; Sameroff & Chandler, 1975; Stott, 1973). The problems, of course, arise from the troublesome fact that too few of the "demonstrations" of prenatal effects can be replicated and from the widespread failure to demonstrate the precise mechanisms whereby the effects are transmitted from the mother's environment to the mother and thence to the fetus. The upshot is that it becomes very difficult to work inductively when prenatal events sometimes have consequences and sometimes do not and, even when they do, to show how they have been exerted.

There are ways to begin getting around the problems, however. First, we cannot allow gestation and childbirth to continue acting as conceptual and disciplinary barriers to a fuller understanding of the determinants of infant behavior. Too often developmental psychologists are ignorant of embryology, fetal neuroendocrine development, and maternal–placental–fetal physiology, and too often there seems to be the silent assumption that for all practical purposes development and epigenesis begin at birth. At the same time, however, obstetricians, human embryologists, developmental neurologists, and physiologists specializing in maternal–fetal exchange, even though they have a better potential grasp of the mechanisms of prenatal effects, are traditionally most concerned with clinical outcomes, and except for obvious teratogenic agents, they too often treat the maternal–fetal unit and the process of gestation as a closed system and too often see childbirth as the culmination of development. Progress in the field of prenatal influences has depended on the adventurous few who have crossed the conceptual barriers of gestation and childbirth, but the history and sociology of science still conspire to keep too separate studies or pre- and postnatal developmental change and continuity.

A second way to begin getting around the problems of research on prenatal influences is to broaden our concepts of the nature of explanations of behavior. One observation that can be made about the vague and frequently contradictory nature of reports of prenatal influences is that researchers too often seem to confuse levels of explanation or, worse, seem unaware that different — *but not mutually exclusive* — levels of explanation even exist. At the most simple level, for example, many developmental neurobiologists may be skeptical of prenatal maternal psychological influences on fetal development and infant behavior because they feel that no *cause* has been adduced. This logical mistake simply confuses proximate causes (some neuroendocrine causal pathway) with more distal ones (e.g., maternal psychosocial stress). The failure to appreciate the interaction of multiple levels of causation is exacerbated by the "soft science" (e.g., psychology) — "hard science" (e.g., developmental neurobiology) dichotomy, which is only another manifestation of the nature – nurture dichotomy, and by disciplinary boundaries, which prevent the extension of thought past the conceptual barrier of childbirth (or outside the mother's body, if not outside the developing fetal brain, or at least the placenta). These conceptual blocks make it impossible to employ either a behavioral ecological or an evolutionary perspective in the study of prenatal influences and thus preclude one promising avenue toward a basis for hypothetico-deductive reasoning.

The failure to appreciate the different but complementary levels of the causation of behavior and the failure to extend research across disciplinary boundaries are both more serious and more complex than the simple failure to distinguish between proximate causes (mechanisms) and more distal ones. Still missing is consideration of two additional levels of causation: what has been called "ultimate causation" (natural selection) and human phylogeny or evolutionary history. In evolutionary biology, zoology, developmental psychobiology, and biosocial anthropology, it is becoming increasingly apparent that attempts to explain any behavior must include considerations of causes of that behavior at a minimum of four separate, but complementary and not mutually exclusive, levels of analysis. The most elegant formulation of this explanatory approach has been set forth by Tinbergen (1951, 1963) and more recently by Blurton Jones (1972, 1982), Daly and Wilson (1983), and Konner (1982). The essence of this explanatory approach requires that when we ask why a behavior occurs we have to ask four different kinds of question. The first set of questions are those about immediate or proximate causes and include specific questions about the neuroendocrinology of perception, motivation, response thresholds, reflexes, and more. The second set of questions are those about ontogeny or development and include such specific questions as what factors of growth and development, maturation, experience, and "prepared learning" (e.g., critical or sensitive periods) may underlie the organism's capacity to show the behavior in question. The third set of questions are those about ultimate causation or natural selection and include questions about whether and how the behavior in question might maintain or increase the organism's reproductive success or inclusive fitness. These are questions about ultimate causation or natural selection, because even if an organism has only the general *capacity* for a behavior or only the general *capacity* to be affected by early experience, the only way that that capacity can exist is by virtue of information contained in DNA; and the primary way that genetic information affecting these capacities becomes represented in an organism's genotype is through the process of adaptation by natural selection that effects change in gene frequencies in a population from one generation to the next. Finally, the fourth set of questions are those about phylogeny or evolutionary history. Questions at this level of causation involve considerations about how members of a species evolved the capacity to perform the particular behavior of interest; these are questions about phylogenetic inertia, preadaptation, and adaptive modes characteristic of taxa above the species level.

Armed thus with a broad conception of how behavior is caused by a multitude of factors operating at different levels of explanation, researchers will not so easily be caught up in disciplinary boundaries or the nature–nurture dispute. Failing to accept that explanations of behavior at each of these levels are separate but not mutually exclusive is the major conceptual mistake underlying the very existence of the futile nature–nurture debate. Research on prenatal influences will benefit from this approach to the multiple level causation of behavior, because without such a perspective there can be little appreciation of *why* prenatal influences might exist at all and, even more, of why they exist when they do. Without such an appreciation of why they exist there can be little basis for hypothetico-deductive reasoning. With no basis (other than an empirical one) for expecting prenatal influences or for expecting them under certain conditions, there can be little incentive for searching for the mechanisms or causal pathways whereby such influences are actually exerted and even less theoretical basis for narrowing and focusing the search for these mechanisms. Finally, of course, when neither proximate, developmental, nor ultimate mechanisms can be hypothesized, the field will revert to vague, contradictory, "uncoordinated and seemingly patternless" empirical nit-picking.

There already exists in developmental psychology, however, a theoretical paradigm for attempting to understand why it is that early experience affects later behavior under some conditions but not others. Many of the implications of the evolutionary approach to questions about the separate but complementary causes of behavior sketched above are similar to those of what have been called "transactional" models of development in developmental psychology (Sameroff, 1975; Sameroff & Chandler, 1975). Put simply, the crux of such transactional models is that the infant may have a significant effect on its own development, perhaps in a goal-corrected way, by virtue of the infant's influence on the behavior of its caregivers, which, however, depends not only on individual differences in children but also on the environment of early interaction with caregivers. Transactional models of development have arisen specifically to account for the troublesome inconsistency in reports of the effects of early experience (including prenatal experiences) on later behavior (e.g., Sameroff & Chandler, 1975), on logical arguments about the direction of effects in early infant–caregiver interaction (e.g., Bell, 1968; Lewis & Rosenblum, 1974), and on arguments from attachment theory about the biological survival value of certain infant behaviors (e.g., Bowlby, 1969). Some of these similarities between the arguments and implications of the evolutionary approach outlined above and transactional models of development will become apparent in the following section in which the evolutionary biological rationale for expecting prenatal influences will be spelled out.

Phylogenetic Considerations: Evolution, Pregnancy, and Developmental Plasticity

There are three areas of theory in evolutionary biology that are immediately relevant to questions about prenatal influences on infant behavior and outcome. The first deals broadly with questions about the fourth level of causation (phylogeny), i.e., questions about the evolutionary history of developmental patterns, the natural selection for behavioral–developmental plasticity, and the phylogeny of hominid pregnancy. The second and third deal with questions about the third level of causation (natural selection or "ultimate causation"); the second, with facultative adaptation in utero, and the third, with the related concepts of inclusive fitness, parental investment, kin selection, and parent–offspring conflict in utero.

Evolutionary biologists and biologically minded developmental psychologists have recently begun to appreciate that developmental plasticity (the genotypical capacity to develop the optimum phenotype in a wide variety of developmental environments) may be especially characteristic of humans and may be biologically adaptive in the ultimate sense; they have also begun to work out how this developmental plasticity may have been selected for. This new appreciation has a number of roots. One is the increasing evidence in developmental psychology that early experience is likely to affect later behavior only under the most stable environmental circumstances (e.g., Bateson, 1976, 1982; Chisholm, 1983; Dunn, 1976; Kagan, Kearsley, &

Zelazo, 1980; Kagan, 1980, 1981; Sameroff, 1975; Sameroff & Chandler, 1975). Another source has been the resurgence of interest in the evolution of ontogenetic patterns. This interest has blossomed because of research in comparative zoology and behavioral ecology showing broad similarities in species' ontogeny according to two different modes of natural selection called r- and K-selection (MacArthur & Wilson, 1967; Pianka, 1970; Wilson, 1975). The principles of r- and K-selection will be dealt with in more detail shortly, but it is worth mentioning here that the concepts of r- and K-selection, along with the concept of life history strategies (e.g., Gadgil & Bossert, 1970; Stearns, 1976; Horn, 1978) and a dissatisfaction with explanations of behavior formulated only in terms of the genotype, have independently led to exciting new approaches to the evolutionary significance of developmental patterns (e.g., Bateson 1982; Burghardt & Bekoff, 1978; Plotkin & Odling-Smee, 1979, 1981; Gould, 1977).

A more far-reaching source of interest in developmental plasticity and the relations between ontogeny and phylogeny comes, however, from theoretical analyses of the most basic evolutionary rationale for such plasticity. This theoretical rationale holds that the genotypical basis for the ontogenetic capacity to develop the optimum phenotype in a variety of developmental environments represents natural selection for increasingly complex, sophisticated, and finely tuned "environmental tracking mechanisms" and that such natural selection is also an example of "an optimal strategy of evolution" (Slobodkin & Rapoport, 1974). Environmental tracking is the process whereby natural selection works to produce the ubiquitous "good fit" between organism and environment. Put simply, Slobodkin and Rapoport argue that there will tend to be natural selection for better environmental tracking because organisms with more environmental tracking mechanisms, and more sophisticated tracking mechanisms, will have more *ways* of responding to the environment and will thus be more "adaptable." In the process of environmental tracking, organisms are seen as responding to the environment in terms of multiple, hierarchically interconnected response mechanisms. These response mechanisms begin with bio- and electrochemical responses at the level of individual cells then proceed to specific neural nets (e.g., those involved in perception and the activation of reflexes and "instincts" such as innate releasing mechanisms and fixed action patterns). Next, the response mechanisms advance through slower but more pervasive or longer-lasting learning and/or endocrine responses, and ultimately, when the environmental perturbation is long lasting and affects large numbers of individual organisms, the response mechanisms progress to population responses in demographic and gene pool characteristics. The immediate and quick responses, when called into play frequently and/or for long periods of time in large numbers of individuals, serve to trigger the slower responses, which in turn may reset the response thresholds of the quicker responses. The slowest responses are the most costly responses, because they have so many effects on the potential effectiveness of all responses above them in the response hierarchy.

Behavior, especially social behavior, is the best example of an environmental tracking device. Behavioral responses to the environment have been selected for in evolution because they provide a high degree of response flexibility that protects or conserves the slower and more costly potential response capacity latent in the gene pool. Slobodkin and Rapoport conceive of natural selection for increasingly sophisticated environmental tracking mechanisms, because such sophistication or complexity provides "an optimal strategy of evolution." The essense of this strategy is that responses to the environment are more-or-less appropriately scaled to the impact and scope of the environmental perturbation. The quickest, least costly, and lowest stake responses are made first, and if the perturbation to which they are the response is short, of little impact, or unique and if the responses are successful in alleviating stress to the organism, then the organism's capacity to respond successfully or adaptively to future perturbations is not endangered. If the initial response is not successful, because the perturbation is more severe and/or long-lasting, then these quick and easy responses may be called into play more frequently, and may then trigger deeper, slower, and potentially more costly response mechanisms. In the long run, Slobodkin and Rapoport argue, plasticity, flexibility, or adaptability in immediate behavioral responses to the environment will tend to be selected for, because this tends to protect or conserve the flexibility and adaptability of the slower, deeper, and more costly physiological, demographic, and populational genetic adaptive mechanisms. These latter responses are ultimately the *least* flexible ways of responding to the environment, because they depend for their adaptive potential on mutation or recombination making available just the right set of new genetic material for the process of natural selection to operate on. This evolutionary trend toward greater response plasticity enables organisms to respond phenotypically to relatively short-term environmental changes (e.g., those occurring within the lifetime of an individual), while reserving genotypical response capacity for "tracking" long-term environmental changes (e.g., those occurring over several generations). Thus, there will tend to be natural selection for an "essential indeterminancy" (Waddington, 1968) in the ontogenetic effect of the genotype on the phenotype, because the genotype will be altered only when the phenotypical responses (especially the behavioral ones) made at each higher level in the response hierarchy have been shown to be at least partially effective. This is because stress is itself a sort of evidence that the response was effective, for the experience of stress is, in a manner of speaking, an indicator of continued life and is also information that deeper and slower response mechanisms can "use" to alter their values. For example, the phenotypical behavioral response of, say, running away from a predator (which depends on the successful operation of even quicker and less costly perceptual response mechanisms) allows natural selection to be focused on aspects of the organism's phenotype, such as heart size and pumping capacity, blood chemistry, or muscle size, that bear a more direct relation to information contained in the organism's genotype. This short-term plasticity not only gives natural selection *more time* to weed out the truly unfit (as opposed to the simply unlucky), it also focuses selection pressure on those parts of the phenotype that bear a closer and more direct relation to the genotype. It will be an interesting question for historians of science why this notion of natural selection for behavioral/developmental plasticity has lain dormant for so many years, for it seems to be a logical implication of what biologists have called "the Baldwin effect" since 1896 (Baldwin, 1896).

Closely related to this abstract theoretical conceptualization of natural selection for behavioral/developmental plasticity, and to some extent growing out of it, are the more concrete concepts of life history strategies in general and the ontogenetic patterns associated with r- and K-selection in particular. The relatively new wing of evolutionary biology concerned with life history strategies had as its primary impetus the realization that while most evolutionary models were based on how many copies of one's genes were passed into the next generation, in order for this to be possible at all, the organism first had to survive and then grow before it could successfully reproduce (e.g., Gadgil & Bossert, 1970). Thus, natural selection could not be expected to maximize reproductive potential at the expense of simple survival and ontogenetic preparation for reproduction, and there should be, in any given environment, measurable trade-offs between adaptations for survival, growth and development and learning, and reproductive rate.

The concept of r- and K-selection describes what some of these trade-offs are and how they may have been selected for. r- and K-selection represent opposite ends of a continuum of natural selection or two modes in the operation of natural selection. In unpredictable environments (or environments where some predictable major perturbation has a periodicity greater than the life span of the individuals) there are often catastrophic mortality rates (rabbits are a good familiar example) in which large numbers of individuals die not so much because they are unfit but because they are unlucky (i.e., mortality is not directed; the difference between survival and mortality does not depend on genotypical or phenotypical differences). When selection is thus so undirected it is "unfocused" and cannot work to produce a more efficient phenotype but, instead, can work only to produce a reproductive strategy based on transmitting as *many* copies of parental genes as possible into the next generation as *fast* as possible. The evolutionary payoff here is obvious: Individuals able to reproduce more rapidly and/or in greater numbers are disproportionately represented in future generations by virtue of their head start in filling available niche space. This is the essence of what is called the r-strategy. On the other hand, as an adaptation to the high levels of intraspecific competition that is characteristic of populations at carrying capacity in more constant or predictable environments, the essence of the K-strategy is to ensure that at least *some* copies of parental genes make it into the next generation. Because there is no evolutionary payoff in having large numbers of offspring in rapid succession (for this would increase the already high rates of intraspecific competition and endanger the survival of any offspring at all), the selection pressures are for increased efficiency in the exploitation of scarce resources.

A valid quick conceptualization of K-selection is natural selection for "fewer and better offspring." The most common interpretation of "better" is increased efficiency in the exploitation of scarce resources, but another is that one aspect of "better" includes more sophisticated, complex, and finely tuned environmental tracking mechanisms. This is because with a more constant and predictable environment, high intraspecific competition, and more directed mortality, natural selection is less random and individuals are likely to be selected against because of some functional inefficiency in the way that they respond to environmental perturbations.

Selection for more efficient responses to the environment, for more finely tuned environmental tracking mechanisms, is achieved in K-selection primarily through natural selection for retarded development. Retarded development is selected for through the favoring of regulator genes delaying the switching on of structural genes which code for the production of endocrine substances which determine the onset, rate, and period of physical growth and development processes and sexual maturation processess (at least according to theory; cf. King & Wilson, 1975; Gould, 1977; Brown, 1981). Retarded development maintains or increases reproductive success or inclusive fitness, because with a long period of infant or juvenile dependency and delayed sexual maturity, individuals become more efficient in exploiting resources and more reproductively competitive by virtue of having more time to learn about their environments before they themselves reproduce. An increased capacity for learning constitutes perhaps the most adaptively significant and phenotypically plastic environmental tracking device known.

At the same time that there is selection for retarded development there is also selection for the other hallmark of K-selection, increased parental investment. This is because with each increase in "quality" ("better," or more efficient offspring, i.e., increased survivorship) there is a corresponding decrease in quantity (*numerical* reproductive success). By observation and definition (Trivers, 1972), as parental investment goes up, the parent's ability to invest in *other* offspring (even if only potential) goes down. But because there is always at least a residue of accidental death (i.e., random, undirected mortality), this creates a positive feedback cycle: continued selection for efficiency and more finely tuned environmental tracking mechanisms. This is because as investment increases, the number of potential offspring goes down, exerting even more selection for both increased investment by parents and increased efficiency in offspring. Parents must also simply be vigilant for longer and longer periods as they continue to have offspring who are continuously more retarded in their development and who take progressively more time to learn about their environments.

Individuals who develop slowly have more time to learn about the environments in which they lay their reproductive potential on the line, and they are likely to be better *able* to learn as well. This is because by retarding the rate of somatic development (and/or extending its period), neural structures are given more time to differentiate. Growth is not a unidimensional increase in size but obviously also includes development, differentiation, and an increase in organizational complexity. Because organisms with retarded somatic development develop for longer periods of time, morphological, neurological, endocrine, and (ultimately) behavioral organization can proceed farther in descendant forms than they did in ancestral forms. This increase in organizational complexity by itself tends to increase adaptive potential (behavioral–developmental plasticity), because the organism is presented to its developmental environment for longer periods of time in each succeeding generation in a physiological–neuroendocrine state that is initially more plastic, more sensitive, or more responsive to environmental influences (which is the entire adaptive point behind selection for increasingly complex and sophisticated environmental tracking mechanisms). It is a characteristic of immature neurons that they are more "plastic" than mature neurons, better able to establish new neuronal connections and to modify existing ones (Jacobson, 1969). It is also a characteristic finding of all developmental sciences that, as in embryology, early forms are less "canalized" than more developed forms (e.g., Waddington, 1968, 1975). And in developmental neurobiology " . . . the most dramatic examples of nervous system flexibility [have been] found in immature animals" (Lynch & Gall, 1979).

Not only is there fossil evidence of progressive retardation in the ontogeny of ancestral hominid forms (see Leutenegger, 1972; Holt, Cheek, Mellit, & Hill, 1975; Mann, 1975), there are reasons to believe that some portion of the evolutionary success of the early hominids was due to selection for a new life history strategy involving that portion of life spent in the mother's womb. In other words, not only does the rate of hominid postnatal development (especially in the brain) seem to have been progressively retarded (and/or its period extended), so too may hominid prenatal development have been affected by K-selection and other factors. Thus, while essentially nothing is known about early hominid gestation, when some old and more recent data and hypotheses are juxtaposed, at least the significance of the evolution of hominid gestation becomes clear.

To explore the topic of the evolution of hominid gestation it is useful first to suggest the intensity of selection pressures on the pregnant female and especially on the fetus. The period from conception to birth has probably always been the single most dangerous part of the hominid life span. Accurate data on fetal wastage are notoriously difficult to acquire, but some general points can be made. Howell (1979) notes that among the !Kung San, a modern hunter–gatherer society, the *known* incidence of fetal wastage was 55/500, that is, out of every 10 pregnancies 1 resulted in spontaneous abortion or stillbirth. Howell also notes that she has "no doubt" that the actual figure is "much higher" (1979, p. 138f). French and Bierman (1962) report an incidence of fetal mortality of 99/1000 on the Hawaiian island of Kauai, a figure remarkably similar to Howell's !Kung rate of 55/500, which is interesting for they were dealing with a Westernized population with good nutrition and access to modern medical care. Rates even higher have been reported for other populations (Santow, 1978), however, and Henry (1976) reanalyzed French and Bierman's data, using a model to predict actual incidence of fetal wastage, and suggests that their figure of 99/1000 is likely to be underestimated by a factor of more than two. Henry suggests that according to his model, the actual incidence was probably closer to 237/1000.

It is probably futile to spend much effort on deriving rates of fetal wastage for almost any population, especially extinct ones; these data are mentioned here simply to suggest that the prenatal period is a period of intense natural selection, even today, where perhaps as many as 50% of all pregnancies may not result in live birth (Wasser & Barash, 1983). Accurate figures, of course, are virtually impossible to obtain, even for modern populations, because the mother very often may not even know she was pregnant and lost the conceptus. It has been estimated, for example, that 50% of all spontaneous abortions occur in the first few weeks of pregnancy (Kerr, 1971). It has also been estimated that virtually all of these spontaneous abortions (which the mother probably notices only as a late period) involve problems in embryogenesis (Kerr, 1971; Santow, 1978). Kerr (1971) has also reported empirical data showing that fully 36% of clinically recognized abortuses have a chromosome anomaly.

The point is that even today there is a selection funnel during gestation and that anywhere from 25–50% of all conceptions do not result in live birth.

(Roberts and Lowe [1975] suggest that in some populations the figure may reach 78%). Even if we do not assume that fetal wastage was higher in early hominid populations, this rate of fetal wastage multiplied by thousands of generations will have been a significant selection pressure. The theory of evolution by natural selection provides us, therefore, with the rationale for asking in what particular ways the fetus was adapted to the environment of pregnancy, i.e., maternal physiology (we will ask later about adaptation to the factors that affect maternal physiology and about maternal adaptation to the fetus).

In evolutionary terms the placenta itself (an organ developing from the embryo—hence, a fetal organ) is an adaptation to the environment of pregnancy. Higher primate and perhaps especially hominid gestation can be understood in part as a complex of maternal and fetal adaptations for promoting fetal neurobiological development. Starting only with the fact of an evolutionary increase in brain size, it is possible to argue for a high degree of fetal sensitivity to maternal physiology during pregnancy. The evolutionary increase in hominid brain size, of course, is well documented, and there are a plethora of theories as to why such an evolutionary trend occurred. Part of it may be due to the effects of K-selection: With retarded development organ systems are simply given more time to grow and hence grow larger (e.g., Gould, 1977). A variety of not mutually exclusive theories emphasize more direct selection for large (adult) brain size as a function of (adult) environmental factors, including, for example, locomotion in three dimensions, multimodal sensory systems, emphasis on vision, and a long period of social learning (Eisenberg, 1981). It is not necessary here, however, to specify why hominid brains increased in size so much, only to suggest that the placenta and maternal–fetal exchange and mutual sensitivity were crucial adaptations *permitting* the development of the big brain. In other words, regardless of the selection pressures for increased brain size, they could not operate unless embryological and fetal adaptations provided the optimum developmental environment.

One of the most vital constraints on the development of a big brain is an adequate oxygen supply, especially during periods of rapid brain growth (e.g., Dobbing, 1974). At least in adults, for example, while the brain amounts to only 2% of body weight, it consumes in the neighborhood of 18% of the total oxygen budget (Blinkov & Glezer, 1968). Goodman (1963) noted this point several years ago and argued that the evolution of the more efficient higher primate hemochorial placenta was a prerequisite for the ontogenetic development of the large hominid brain, for the neocortex especially is easily damaged by fetal hypoxia. Goodman argues thus that the appearance of the more efficient hemochorial placenta could have engendered additional selection pressures in the development of the higher primate fetus. This is because the more primitive epitheliochorial placenta is less efficient than the hemochorial placenta in that the former maintains a greater separation between the maternal and fetal circulations, while the latter achieves its greater efficiency (in oxygenation, among other things) by bringing maternal and fetal circulations into closer contact. Luckett (1974), in his review of placental function among the primates, notes that the trophoblast achieves the maximal level of invasiveness of the uterine wall in Hominoidea. Selection may thus have favored fetuses who could simply take more oxygen from their mothers' circulations by developing more efficient placentas. Goodman notes too, however, that no adaptation is ever perfect and solving one problem often leads to the appearance of new problems: The closer contact between maternal and fetal circulations in the progressively bigger-brained higher primates and hominids could well have brought the maternal immune system into play more frequently and thus could have constituted a new range of prenatal environmental factors to which fetus (and mother) would have to respond. Goodman concentrates on only one aspect of the new intrauterine environment that would likely follow from the selection for a more efficient placenta: The maternal immune system might be activated more frequently because any new genetic material, from whatever source, would result in new fetal proteins coming into closer contact with the maternal circulation because of the greater efficiency of the placenta. When this occurred the survival and normal development of the fetus would be increasingly problematic because of maternal rejection of fetal antigens. Goodman suggests that this could lead to natural selection for reduced genetic heterogeneity in early hominid populations through the agent of maternal rejection (spontaneous abortion) of new fetal genetic material. He suggests further another selection pressure toward shortened gestation (which in any event seems to have occurred — but not necessarily because of the "obstetric dilemma" presented by the demands of restructuring the pelvis for bipedal locomotion [Lindburg, 1982]), since shortened gestation would permit the speedier expression (postconception) of new genetic material. Finally, he suggests too that retarded development might have been selected for in the fetus since postponing the expression of new genetic material until after birth would not antagonize the maternal immune system.

In addition to maternal–fetal oxygen transport, straightforward nutritive transport is also a function of a placenta, and Martin (1981, 1983; Lewin, 1982) has argued implicitly that maternal–fetal nutritive transport is a prerequisite for the development of big brains. Noting that metabolic rates correlate very significantly with brain size in a large number of species, Martin suggests that "It is the mother's energetic potential that determines the brain size of the developing fetus" (quoted in Lewin, 1982, p. 840). To be sure, this energetic throughput depends on maternal factors, but selection for the development of a more efficient placenta would be another route to the adaptation of high energy transfer from mother to fetus. With a more efficient placenta the fetus is better able to "elicit" increased parental investment from its mother—by simply taking more energy from her blood stream.

While we remain woefully ignorant of the details, Goodman's arguments about oxygen transport and Martin's arguments about nutritive transport both point to the placenta as an evolutionary adaptation which *permits* the development of the large hominid brain. Regardless of the ultimate causes of (selection pressures for) the large hominid brain, the full phenotypical expression of the DNA *potential* for such a large brain (and hence its adaptive significance) would seem to be dependent on the more "generous" fetal developmental environment made possible by the increased efficiency of the placenta.

This brief examination of broad trends in the evolution of developmental patterns and of hominid pregnancy points out the relevance of questions about the fourth level of causation (phylogenetic history) to an understanding of prenatal influences. Summarizing quickly, the argument is that perhaps the major avenue through which natural selection achieves increased behavioral–developmental plasticity (and hence increased adaptability through more sophisticated environmental tracking mechanisms) is through the alteration of life history strategies. Among primates, generally, and hominids, specifically, this has resulted in a long evolutionary history of K-selection and its concomitants, neoteny and increased parental investment. The increased behavioral–developmental plasticity of the hominids, made possible by the dramatic increase in brain size and associated learning capacities, may have been crucially dependent on the evolution of a placenta efficient enough to permit the ontogenetic development of such a big brain. A placenta with such efficiency in maternal energy throughput and oxygen transport would likely have the simultaneous, epiphenomenal effect of increasing the developing fetus's sensitivity to quantitative and qualitative variability in a wide variety of uterine environmental factors. No adaptation is ever perfect, and all adaptations seem to represent a compromise between two or more different, if not opposing, selection pressures (cf. Tinbergen, 1965). In other words, the full and adaptive ontogenetic *expression* of genetic maternal underlying the adult hominid brain seems to have depended on the phylogenetic development of new ontogenetic patterns: the development of a highly efficient placenta. Actually achieving this developmental efficiency, however, may have included the price of exposing the fetus to more uterine environmental perturbations.

Natural Selection for Prenatal Influences

Having outlined in general terms how and why the evolution of the higher primate placenta might expose the fetus to more uterine environmental perturbations, it is now possible to move on to the more detailed discussions of possible ultimate causes of the fetus's sensitivity to prenatal influences that follow. That is, having suggested how and why the fetus might have become exposed to such intrauterine developmental perturbations (explanations at the fourth level of causation, phylogenetic history), it is now possible to discuss how and why these evolutionarily new uterine influences might have constituted naturally selective forces (explanations at the third level of causation, adaptation by natural selection). An appreciation of these potentially selective prenatal environmental factors might provide a basis for developing useful theoretical models of prenatal influences. Before outlining some of the ways in which natural selection might operate in utero, however, it is necessary first to review some of the empirical data on prenatal influences in humans.

Evidence for Prenatal Effects

Beginning at a physiological level, there is no longer any doubt that psychological stress (i.e., personal, subjective feelings of anxiety, tension, depression, etc.) has a real and measurable neuroendocrine component and that the "stress response" is likely a phylogenetically extraordinarily old adaptive mechanism for "fight or flight" (see reviews by Selye, 1956; Stone, 1975; Rose, 1980). Nor is there any doubt that the maternal neuroendocrine response to environmental stressors can affect the fetus, although many particular pathways remain to be fully worked out. The major way in which the maternal stress response affects the fetus is that when maternal adrenocortical stress hormones enter the fetal circulation through the placenta they become part of the fetal pituitary–adrenal system and cause a reduction in fetal adrenocorticotrophin release (for a review of maternal hormone affects on the fetus see Joffe, 1978). Besides direct placental transfer of maternal stress hormones, however, the fetus may be affected by (at least) two other routes: Vigorous vestibular stimulation of the fetus may elicit the fetal stress response by itself (Rosenblatt, 1967), and any cause of reduced uteroplacental blood flow (e.g., hypertension in the mother) may reduce the flow of oxygen or nutrients to the fetus (e.g., Chisholm, Woodson, & da Costa Woodson, 1978). The opportunity for research on human fetal developmental neurobiology is necessarily limited, and the precise developmental effects of maternal stress hormones and reduced uteroplacental blood flow on the developing fetal neuroendocrine system are not well understood. This fact must surely account for many of the inconsistent results in studies of prenatal effects on postnatal behavior; Dobbing (1974), for example, has shown that the developing fetal brain is quite differentially sensitive to environmental insult at different developmental stages.

Having sketched the general physiological mechanisms whereby maternal psychosocial stress may be transferred to the fetus, it is appropriate to continue with data on the effects of such stress on those aspects of infant physiology closely related to infant behavior. For example, two independent studies have shown a relationship between maternal prenatal anxiety and newborn APGAR scores. Jones and Dlugokinski (1978) found a significant inverse relationship between newborn APGAR scores and maternal prenatal anxiety as measured on the Holmes and Rahe (1967) life change index, and Crandon (1979) found a similar significant inverse relation between APGAR score and prenatal maternal anxiety measured on the IPAT scale. Sontag has not only reported a relationship between prenatal maternal anxiety and increased fetal activity (1944), he has also consistently found a relationship between prenatal maternal anxiety and infant behavior he characterizes as "irritable" and "hyperactive" (1941, 1966). These infants had more gastrointestinal problems, increased heart rates, increased vasomotor irritability, and more variability in respiration. Jost and Sontag (1944) reported that mothers with the highest levels of ANS activity (respiration and heart rate) regularly had more active fetuses. In a somewhat similar study, Smith and Steinschneider (1975) found that newborns (24–48-h old) born to mothers with the lowest heart rates fell asleep faster, slept longer, and cried less than did high maternal heart rate children. Both Turner (1956) and Dodge (1972) have reported a positive relationship between measures of prenatal maternal anxiety and gastrointestinal problems (excessive vomiting and pyloric stenosis) in the newborn, as did Falorni, Furnasarig, & Stefanile (1979), who also noted EEG perturbations in infants of mothers suffering high levels of pregnancy anxiety. Turner (1956), Falorni et al. (1979), Ottinger and Simons (1964), Stott (1973), and Sontag (1966) have also all reported significantly greater irritability (frequency and/or duration of crying) in newborns born to mothers especially anxious during pregnancy.

Longer-term follow-up of the effects of prenatal maternal anxiety has also suggested that these effects may not be transient, although clearly environmental interactions of augmentation, maintenance, and suppression are to be expected (e.g., along the lines of a transactional model [cf. Sameroff & Chandler, 1975] or a more explicitly biologically based epigenetic model [cf. Gottlieb, 1976; Bateson, 1976]). Huttenen and Niskanen (1978), for example, in one of the more dramatic studies of long-term effects, found an increased incidence of adult schizophrenia and criminality in a large sample who had lost their fathers prenatally compared to a control sample who lost their fathers during the first year of life. The authors suggest that the stress effects on the mother of losing her husband during pregnancy were transferred to the fetus, and they specifically implicate stress effects on the developing fetal hypothalamus during the middle of pregnancy. Additional intriguing evidence for long-term effects of prenatal maternal anxiety comes from the research of Mednick and his colleagues (Mednick, 1970; Mednick, Mura, Schulsinger, & Mednick, 1971). Mednick's sample consisted of 207 children at risk for the development of schizophrenia because of presumed familial genetic factors. Twenty of these children later developed severe behavior problems and were compared to the other high risk children who did not (or had not yet developed them). The mothers of the children developing behavior problems suffered disproportionately from "very severe environmental stress" during pregnancy and a higher incidence of pregnancy and birth complications (e.g., bleeding during the last half of pregnancy, pregnancy hypertension, preeclampsia, etc.). The behavior-problem children also were more likely to evidence poorly controlled and hyperresponsive electrodermal activity patterns. Mednick suggests that the hippocampus and Purkinje cells of the cerebellum may be particularly sensitive to developmental hypoxia and that inhibitory brain centers are thus damaged, leading to poor ANS modulation in later life. In partial support to this interpretation, Mednick notes that rats with hippocampal lesions are typically hyperreactive and that biochemical changes in the hippocampus can be detected immediately after an hypoxic episode, whereas such changes in other areas of the brain are not detectable for hours. Beginning thus with "very severe environmental stress," Mednick outlines a causal pathway whereby maternal anxiety might affect the developing fetal nervous system and thus postnatal physiology and behavior and, at least in this high-risk sample, the subsequent increased likelihood of the full expression of whatever genetic factors may underlie schizophrenic behavior. In this context, and given the relationships between ANS activity and arousal or apprehension and reports of a relationship between prenatal maternal anxiety and increased fetal activity, it is interesting to note that Sontag (1963) also found that individuals who were more active as fetuses were more likely to score high on a measure of "social apprehension" at 2½ years (although the relationship was not as strong for girls as for boys).

To strengthen the case for a possible systematic relationship between prenatal maternal anxiety and postnatal behavior – developmental problems (or at least differences) in the child, it is worth briefly reviewing some additional studies which, although they do not examine the prenatal maternal anxiety – postnatal behavior link directly, do examine either the relationship between prenatal maternal anxiety and the incidence of pregnancy – birth complications (PBCs) or the relationship between PBCs and postnatal behavior or constitution. Beginning with the evidence for a link between prenatal maternal anxiety and PBCs, an early study by Coppen (1958) compared 50 primiparous women who developed preeclampsia (i.e., hypertension, proteinuria, and edema) to 50 matched controls who did not. The 50 preeclamptic women revealed significantly more psychiatric symptoms (which also increased in severity during the course of pregnancy more than did the fewer symptoms of the normal women). The preeclamptic women also suffered more heartburn and vomiting than did the normals, reported more marital problems and less satisfying sexual relations with their husbands, and more emotionally disturbing major life changes during pregnancy than did the normals. Analogous findings in prospective studies employing better measures have been reported by Davids, DeVault, & Talmadge (1961), McDonald and Christokos (1963), Gunter (1963), Spielberger & Jacobs (1978), and Crandon (1979). Each of these studies (using, respectively, the Manifest Anxiety Scale, the MMPI and the MAS, the Cornell Medical Index, and the IPAT) reports a positive and significant association between prenatal maternal anxiety and such PBCs as preeclampsia, prolonged or precipitate labor, bleeding, polyhydramnios, abruptio placentae, and lower APGAR scores. Gunter (1963) also found a higher incidence of premature and small-for-gestational-age infants born to those women scoring highest on prenatal anxiety; these women, in addition, were determined to have been deserted or neglected by their own mothers more than the women with fewer PBCs and to have less satisfactory relations with their husbands. McDonald (1968) provides a useful review and critique of studies of prenatal maternal anxiety and PBCs up to the late 1960s; authors of the more recent research reviewed below appear to have been responsive to McDonald's criticisms.

Nuckolls, Cassel, & Kaplan, (1972), for example, noting that perceived psychosocial stress is likely to be a function of the interaction between number and severity of stressors and the pregnant woman's capacity for coping (e.g., social support networks), measured both and found that while neither life change events (measured on the Holmes and Rahe, 1967, scale) nor "psychosocial assets" by themselves predicted the incidence of PBCs, when the two measures were combined, they did so significantly. In a similar vein, recognizing the necessity of separating more-or-less permanent "trait" anxiety from more-or-less transient "state" anxiety, Edwards and Jones (1970) found that prenatal measures of trait anxiety were unrelated to the incidence of PBCs but that women with PBCs differed from those without in the patterns of change in measures of state anxiety during the last trimester. Gorsuch and Key (1974), measuring both state and trait anxiety and major life changes (on the Holmes and Rahe scale) also found no relationship between trait anxiety and incidence of PBCs but did find more PBCs related to increased state anxiety in the middle of pregnancy, and they found that women with more PBCs also reported more stressful life events during the second and third trimesters.

Related, although somewhat contradictory, findings are reported in studies of the incidence of PBCs in mentally ill and healthy pregnant women. Sameroff and Zax (1973), for example, compared normal, neurotically depressed, and schizophrenic women and found that both the neurotically depressed and schizophrenic women had significantly more PBCs than normals (and that the infants born to the troubled women had significantly more EEG perturbations than those born to normal mothers). Sameroff and Zax also report that the chronicity of the mental disorder was more strongly related to the incidence of PBCs than was any particular psychiatric diagnosis. Cohler, Gallant, Grunebaum, Weiss, & Gamer (1975), on the other hand, in a similar study, found that psychiatric illness per se was not related to the incidence of PBCs but that the number of PBCs was greater in women suffering acute, rather than chronic, disturbances.

Finally, concentrating on the link between prenatal maternal anxiety and labor–delivery complications specifically, Davids and DeVault (1962), Kelly (1962), Klusman (1975), Lederman, Lederman, Work, & McCann (1978), and Friedman, Essman, & Fisichelli (1979) have all shown a positive association between several measures of maternal anxiety during pregnancy and such labor–delivery complications as perceived pain, uterine activity, and length of labor (either precipitate or prolonged).

Whether or not maternal anxiety or untoward emotional state is considered as a complication of pregnancy, there is no question that PBCs in general constitute a risk factor for normal delivery and normal fetal development. The early work of Lillienfeld, Pasamanick, and Rogers (1955), Pasamanick and Knobloch (1966), Kawi and Pasamanick (1959), and Drillien and his colleagues (e.g., Drillien & Wilkinson, 1964; Drillien, Ingram, & Wilkinson, 1966), for example, established the statistically significant role of PBCs in the etiology of a wide range of birth defects and behavioral abnormalities (including cerebral palsy, epilepsy, mental deficiency, reading problems, cleft lip and palate, Down's syndrome, and more). Besides noting that early severe and prolonged prenatal emotional stress appeared to differentiate between Down's syndrome children and children developing other disorders, Stott (1971) also suggested that the increase in birth defects observed in England and Germany during WWII might have been related to the severe psychosocial stresses associated with the bombing of civilian populations (a suggestion similar to one made years earlier by Sontag, 1944). Torrey, Hersh, & McCabe (1975) and Deykin and MacMahon (1980) have also implicated prenatal maternal anxiety and a high incidence of PBCs in the etiology of early autism.

Taken together, these studies indicate, as Sameroff and Chandler (1975) also concluded in their important review, that "women with high levels of anxiety, stress, or psychiatric disorder have been found to have a greater proportion of pregnancy complications and a greater proportion of physical anomalies in their offspring" (1975, p. 46). High rates of PBCs, however, have been implicated in the development of more than these relatively obvious and major physical anomalies; they have also been related to minor abnormalities and simple, normal individual differences. Zeskind and Lester (1978), for example, showed that clinically normal newborns whose mothers had higher rates of PBCs could be reliably distinguished from matched infants whose mothers had no PBCs on the basis of their cries, both by sound spectrograph, and by naive judges (who ranked the high PBC infant cries as more aversive, grating, sick, urgent, or distressing). Barnes (1975) and Richards (1979) report that in their prospective study infants born to high PBC mothers (including those who had as few as only one diastolic blood pressure reading during pregnancy that was ≥90 mmHg) were more likely to be judged as irritable and fussy, of "difficult temperament," having more sleep problems, engaging in more solitary play, and difficult to discipline. Hall (1977) notes too that women suffering even "mild toxemia" (one or more diastolic blood pressure readings ≥90 mmHg any time during pregnancy) gave birth to infants who scored lower on the alertness and social responsiveness items on the Brazelton Scale (NBAS, Brazelton, 1973).

Suggestive as they are, these empirical data on prenatal influences in humans have been difficult to interpret in a coherent way (i.e., Stott's [1973] "gray area" of modern science). To date, the most coherent approach has been that of Sameroff and his colleagues (Sameroff, 1975; Sameroff & Chandler, 1975), whose concept of the "continuum of reproductive-caretaking casualty" was developed largely to make sense of the fact that prenatal factors do not always have clear later effects. In an attempt to construct a developmental model that could meaningfully incorporate these inconsistencies, Sameroff and Chandler have argued that "the *constants* in development are not some set of traits but rather the processes by which these traits are maintained in the transactions between organism and environment" (1975, p. 70, original emphasis). The theme to be developed in the following section is that one process perhaps slighted by the transactional approach is the process of adaptation by natural selection in utero. Sameroff and Chandler also argue (from an evolutionary point of view, correctly):

> The human organism appears to have been programmed by the course of evolution to produce normal developmental outcome under all but the most adverse of circumstances. Any understanding of deviancies in outcome must be seen in the light of this self-righting and self-organizing tendency which appears to move children toward normality in the face of pressure toward deviation. (1975, p. 71)

This "self-righting" tendency that Sameroff and Chandler speak of as a product of evolution is analogous to the concept of "natural selection for behavioral–developmental plasticity" discussed in the previous section of this chapter (although in this context behavioral–developmental "elasticity" is a better word). In the following section we will develop the hypothesis that natural selection could operate in utero to make fetuses sensitive to certain uterine environmental influences because the fetus's sensitivity to these influences might constitute part of the process whereby "children move toward normality," i.e., that one class of prenatal influences might exist because the developmental effect of the uterine influence is part of the "self-righting" process, an adaptive response by the fetus to some uterine environmental perturbation.

In the second section below we will develop the notion that the transactional model of developmental may have focused too much on the developing fetus by itself. While current thinking in the evolutionary biology of development finds the concept of "self-righting" tendencies which "move children toward normality" attractive, current thinking in evolutionary biology also demands that we recognize the concept of *inclusive* fitness — which opens the possibility of conflict between the individual fitness interests of mother and fetus. That is, while recognizing the hypothetical existence of "self-righting" processes in the fetus and/or maternal–fetal interaction, we must also recognize that natural selection does not "care" *only* about any particular fetus "moving toward normality" but also about the *mother* moving toward normality so that she may conceive and bear *future* children and rear them or already existing children to maturity. Recognizing the concept of inclusive fitness allows us also to make statements about one of Sameroff and Chandler's unanswered questions. They say:

> Psychosomatic factors do appear to increase sharply the risk of complications and of physical anomalies in the fetus. An unanswered question, however, is whether these pregnancy and delivery complications are a part of a causal chain leading to later disorder, or whether both are parallel disorders resulting from the poor psychological state of the mother. (1975, p. 73)

Working within the framework of their "continuum of reproductive-care-taking casualty" model but with the addition of current thinking in evolutionary biology, it will be possible to argue why the latter option may be more likely.

Facultative Adaptation in Utero

Since the primary way that maternal effects can be directly transmitted to the fetus is through the placenta, by bringing the fetal and maternal circulations into more intimate contact, the advent of the more efficient higher primate placenta exposed the developing fetus to evolutionarily new uterine environmental influences. With the increasing neurobiological complexity of the evolving hominid brain, the impact of these new uterine influences might also be expected to increase. A major component of an evolutionarily based model of prenatal influences rests on the fact that (with exceptions and limitations to be discussed in the next section) whenever the developmental effect of these new uterine environmental influences increased the fetus's or infant's inclusive fitness, there would result natural selection for increased fetal sensitivity to these influences. To put it another way, one class of prenatal influences on infant behavior might be the result of natural selection *for* fetal sensitivity to certain uterine environmental factors. The relevant evolutionary principle here is that of facultative adaptation. In the context of prenatal influences, facultative adaptation would occur when the response of the fetus to some uterine factor conferred some added fitness to the fetus, i.e., when the developmental effect of the prenatal influence increased the fetus's or infant's chances of survival, growth and development, learning, and ultimate reproduction.

One way in which the prenatal influences might confer some added fitness on the infant is by "preadapting" the fetus to aspects of the postnatal environment into which he or she is *going to be born*, i.e., when the uterine environment facilitates or entrains the appearance of some behavior or behavioral predisposition in utero (for example, by altering postnatal response thresholds) which achieve their adaptive significance only in some particular postnatal environment. We already know that prenatal development prepares the fetus for postnatal life, at least in a general way (e.g., Woodson, 1983), but the possibility of facultative adaptation in utero might be especially likely when maternal environmental factors impinge on the fetus directly without involving uteroplacental transfer (e.g., noise or vestibular stimulation) or when there exist some regularities in the effect of the maternal environment (physical or psychosocial) on the quantity and/or quality of nutrients, oxygen, or endocrine substances crossing the placenta.

The simple review of studies of prenatal effects whose conclusions are consistent with an interpretation of facultative adaptation in utero obviously does not constitute any test of the hypothesis of such adaptation but may at least suggest how prenatal natural selection might favor fetal sensitivity to certain uterine environmental factors, whether or not direct placental transfer is involved. Selected examples of such studies are discussed below only to show how facultative adaptation in utero might work.

Among the many animal studies of prenatal effects consistent with a facultative adaptation interpretation, a particularly clear example comes from the work of Reppert and Schwartz (1983), who showed that an "entrainable" circadian clock is present in the suprachiasmatic nuclei of fetal rats. The mother acts as a "transducer" between her environment and the fetal brain, and her circadian rhythm coordinates that of her pups. Reppert and Schwartz suggest that without this prenatal entrainment the pups' circadian rhythms would be uncoordinated in the early postnatal period, placing them at some increased risk during this vulnerable time. Perhaps the paradigmatic example of facultative adaptation in utero, however, comes from Gottlieb's work on species recognition in birds. Gottlieb showed that when duck embryos are denied the prehatching experience of hearing normal duck vocalizations there was a posthatching reduction in ducklings' responsiveness to their mothers' calls (Gottlieb, 1971). It is a safe assumption that heightened posthatching responsiveness to maternal vocalizations would confer a survival and/or reproductive advantage to the duckling through the role of this responsiveness in the imprinting process; the posthatching survival – reproductive advantage in turn suggests the possibility of prehatching natural selection for sensitivity to these sounds, perhaps through the establishment of neural mechanisms which lower the duckling's response threshold as a function of prehatching auditory experience with them.

The existence of a similar phenomenon in humans is not impossible and could be tested. It has long been known that the human fetus can hear, at least by midgestation, and maternal reports of sudden fetal movements after loud noises are common. Furthermore, it has been shown that newborn infants will display greater motor activation to the human voice than to other sounds (Hofer, 1981), that infants of only 12 h will respond preferentially to a recording of mother's voice over that of a stranger (DeCasper & Fifer, 1980), and that infants of only 2 days will synchronize their limb movements with the sound segments of adult speech (Condon & Sander, 1974). To be sure, it is not known whether, or to what extent, these newborn behaviors are contingent on prenatal auditory experience. Their very early appearance implicates significant prenatal maturation of the neural mechanisms involved, and the parallel with prehatching facultative adaptation in ducklings is intriguing, but the relevant research has not been done. It would thus be interesting to compare these early behaviors in infants born to normal parents with those in infants born to mute parents. Given the importance of mutual sensitivity and response – contingency in early mother – infant interaction for language development and the attachment process, fetuses possessing the neurobiological equipment making them sensitive to these uterine auditory experiences may have enjoyed some postnatal selective advantage.

Another, somewhat analogous phenomenon in humans, which likewise may not involve direct placental transfer, has been reported by Ando and Hattori (1970). They report that Japanese infants whose parents moved close to the Osaka airport after the fifth month of pregnancy or after birth were significantly more likely to be awakened by the noise of jet aircraft passing overhead than infants whose parents lived close to the airport prior to conception or who moved there prior to the fifth month of pregnancy. They conclude that early prenatal exposure to the noise of the jets conferred greater postnatal adaptability through the operation of neural developmental processes which increased habituation capacity prenatally. This example obviously does not suggest prenatal natural selection for decreased responsiveness to the noise of jet aircraft, or even perhaps to loud noises in general, but might still suggest selection for neural developmental processes permitting prenatal habituation in general.

Another potential example of facultative adaptation in utero in humans involves the apparent motor precocity of infants who showed high levels of activity as fetuses. Richards and Newberry (1938) seem to have been the first to investigate this question, finding that 6-month-old infants who had high fetal activity scores (according to mothers' reports) in the last 3 months of pregnancy (although fetal vestibular sensory neurons are functional as early as the end of the first trimester) indeed also scored higher on the Gesell motor development scales. Replicating these findings, Walters (1965) showed that greater fetal· activity in the last trimester was positively and significantly associated with performance on the Gesell scales at 12, 24, and 36 weeks, with the best single correlation being that between fetal activity in the ninth month of pregnancy and Gesell scores at 36 weeks. By themselves these data do not argue for uterine facultative adaptation, for the prenatal–postnatal correlations might indicate only continuity in individual differences in a motor activity dimension. In combination with other studies of determinants of fetal activity, however, the hypothesis of facultative adaptation in utero becomes more attractive. For example, Sontag (1944, 1963; Sontag & Wallace, 1935) has reported consistent correlations between maternal fatigue and fetal activity. Harris and Harris (1946) also noted a relationship between maternal activity and fetal activity and suggested that common reports by pregnant women of greater fetal activity in the evening might be explained by the fact that greater maternal activity during the day would usually lead to greater fatigue in the evening. Finally, vestibular stimulation of preterm infants has been shown to improve their sensorimotor functioning over nonstimulated controls (Masi, 1979).

Together, these studies suggest the possibility that not only may fetal activity be related to postnatal motor development but also that postnatal motor development may be influenced by prenatal maternal activity. If additional research were to confirm these apparently interrelated findings, the interpretation of facultative adaptation in utero would be an attractive one. On the assumption that for over 5 million years of hominid evolution the most common maternal prenatal activity was walking and on the assumption that relatively advanced motor development would facilitate infantile adjustment to being carried (i.e., for habituation to vestibular stimulation, for grasping, or for postural adjustment), if not also to locomotion itself, then infants born to mothers who walked a lot during pregnancy might be "preadapted" for high levels of maternal locomotion after birth. Exploring briefly the second level of explanation (proximate developmental causes), it is not immediately obvious what neuroendocrine mechanisms might underlie the elicitation of fetal activity by maternal activity. Whatever the proximate cause of such fetal activity, however, there is evidence suggesting a mechanism whereby the effects of this fetal activity might facilitate motor development and, thus, at least part of a mechanism whereby selection for fetal responsiveness to maternal activity could entrain relatively precocial motor development. This evidence is the finding that fetal alcohol syndrome infants typically show a much reduced range of limb movements because of the contraction of soft tissues in and around the joints. One function of fetal movements seems to be the prevention of the fetus literally ossifying in the fetal position. Super (1976) has already pointed out how the infant's opportunity to practice motor behaviors may be related to cases of apparent precocial motor development; the studies reported here suggest that future studies of precocial motor development might usefully include measures of the *fetus's* opportunity to practice motor skills.

The last example of potential facultative adaptation in utero to be discussed here focuses on the possibility of developmentally adaptive prenatal influences on postnatal temperament. The general hypothesis is that prenatal maternal stress may systematically affect the fetal neuroendocrine system such that fetal development is "canalized" along some new developmental pathway leading to postnatal behavioral predispositions (temperament) which confer some selective advantage in the very environment that elicited the maternal stress response in the first place. In the extensive animal research on prenatal effects the best apparent example of what might be interpreted as facultative adaptation in utero are the widespread reports that psychological stressors applied to pregnant females lead to greater emotionality in their offspring (for a review of these studies see Rosenblatt, 1967). The neuroendocrine mechanisms involved have been well investigated (e.g., Rosenblatt, 1967; Joffe, 1978).

At first glance these results might be considered suggestive of facultative adaptation in utero because of the possible adaptiveness of predispositions toward greater emotionality and fearful responses in an environment already "proven" to be stressful by the mothers' responses to it. Things are not, however, so straightforward, for while the animal research data seem clearly to indicate that prenatal maternal stress *can* affect the behavior of offspring, there is a frustrating inconsistency in the *direction* of these effects. Not only does the direction and precise nature of prenatal effects depend on the genotype of both mother and infant (Joffe, 1978), so too may there be interactions between the maternal and fetal genotypes and the timing, intensity, frequency, and duration of the prenatal stressors on the mother. Finally, in order for an interpretation of facultative adaptation to be possible, it must be demonstrated that the offspring's postnatal behavior in fact really does confer some advantage in the environment which elicited the maternal stress response. Since virtually all animal studies of prenatal effects are laboratory studies, not naturalistic, and since so many use the technique of cross-fostering to control for postnatal environmental effects, these studies are inadequate for testing the notion of the adaptiveness of prenatal influences on postnatal behavior. Cross-fostering after birth, for example, makes it impossible to test the hypothesis that the neonatal temperamental effects of prenatal maternal stress may be adaptive in the way they better enable the infant to elicit parental investment from or become attached to a stressed mother.

Thus, even for the limited goal of simply outlining what the hypothetical process of facultative adaptation in utero might be and how it might work, the experimental animal research data are of little immediate relevance. There are, however, relevant data on prenatal influences on neonatal temperament in humans which are at least illustrative of some possibilities that could be investigated.

Barnes's (1975) and Richards's (1979) finding of an association between "elevated blood pressure" (among other PBCs) and normal individual differences in infant irritability has led to more detailed investigations of the specific relationship between pregnancy blood pressure and newborn behavior. These studies are especially relevant to the possibility of facultative adaptation in utero because they all focus explicitly on normal (i.e., normotensive) pregnancy and normal individual differences in newborn behavior. In addition, they raise the possibility of group differences in newborn behavior as a function of group differences in the distribution of prenatal environmental factors related to individual differences in development. Chisholm (1983; Chisholm et al., 1978) found, for example, as did Freedman (1974), that newborn Navajo infants were quieter and less irritable (on the NBAS) than newborn Anglo-American infants. While the Anglo-American sample was not large enough for examining the maternal blood pressure – neonatal irritability relationship, the Anglo-American women did have higher blood pressure during pregnancy than the Navajo women (in spite of expectations to the contrary, for the Navajo women were both significantly older and of significantly higher parity, two factors that ordinarily are associated with higher blood pressure during pregnancy). Moreover, among the Navajo there was a positive correlation between maternal blood pressure during the second trimester of pregnancy and newborn irritability. Korner and her colleagues (Korner, Gabby, & Kraemer, 1980), using an electronic activity recorder to more objectively measure infant irritability, provided a replication of these findings by showing that normal maternal blood pressure during pregnancy (although third trimester instead of second) was the best predictor of newborn irritability even after controlling for a variety of other pre- and perinatal factors. In another cross-cultural study, with larger samples and more pregnancy blood pressure data, Chisholm (1981) showed again that maternal blood pressure during pregnancy (also the second trimester) was positively related to newborn irritability (on the NBAS) among Aboriginal and white Australian mothers and infants. The Aboriginal women tended to have lower pregnancy blood pressure than the white Australian women, and the Aboriginal infants also were significantly quieter and less irritable than the white Australian infants. Moreover, multiple regression analyses showed that maternal blood pressure during pregnancy was the best predictor of newborn irritability even after controlling for population genetic factors (i.e., race) and other potentially confounding pre- and perinatal factors. Woodson (cf. Chisholm et al., 1978; Woodson, Blurton Jones, da Costa Woodson, Pollack, & Evans, 1979) has arrived at generally similar conclusions about the effects of elevated maternal pregnancy blood pressure on newborn irritability in a variety of racial and ethnic groups.

While we remain ignorant of the details, a general mechanism for transferring the effects of elevated maternal pregnancy blood pressure to the fetus has been outlined. Because the distinction between normotension and hypertension is relatively arbitrary (i.e., blood pressure follows a normal distribution and there is no obvious cutoff point for diagnosing hypertension), the mechanisms affecting uteroplacental blood flow in pregnancy hypertension are also likely to be operative in normotensive pregnancies as well, if at reduced levels. As mentioned, an increase in blood pressure during pregnancy causes a reduction in uteroplacental blood flow; Browne and Veall (1953), for example, showed that normal placental blood flow in the last few weeks of pregnancy was 600 ml/min but that in preeclamptic and chronically hypertensive women this was reduced to only about 200 ml/min. Pregnancy hypertension has also been shown to reduce total placental mass in humans (Myerscough, 1974), rats (Wigglesworth, 1966), and rhesus monkeys (Myers, Hill, Holt, Scott, Mellits, & Cheek, 1971; Hill, 1975). Moreover, infants of hypertensive mothers are commonly reported to be irritable and hyperactive. Schulte, Schrempf, and Minze (1971), for example, in a study of infants born to clinically toxemic women (who were *also* below the 10th percentile for intrauterine growth), found that although on average these infants were hypotonic and apathetic, a large minority were hypertonic, irritable, and hyperactive. Because blood pressure increases with altitude, the work of Saco-Pollitt (1981) is especially interesting here. She compared the Brazelton scale performance of infants born to women living above 8000 ft in the Peruvian Andes to those born at lower altitudes along the Peruvian coast. Among other differences, the high-altitude babies were less responsive to social stimulation and were poorer in state control and self-quieting.

Returning to the determinants of Navajo–Anglo-American and Aboriginal–white Australian group differences in blood pressure, we can rule out altitude differences, because each group in the paired comparisons lived at the same altitude. We can largely rule out population differences in the genetic substrates for adult blood pressure because of the low level of heritability of blood pressure (estimates as low as .20; Kass, Rosner, Zinner, Margolius, & Lee, 1977). The most attractive explanation for these population differences in blood pressure (and thus for differences in neonatal irritability) is group differences in environmental stressors that elicit an increase in blood pressure as part of the normal human stress response. Not only is there a vast literature on the relationship between psychosocial stress and elevated blood pressure in individuals (e.g., Selye, 1956; Kaplan, 1978), there is also considerable evidence of a positive relationship between the specific stressor of culture contact or acculturation and group differences in blood pressure (e.g., Page, 1976; Scotch, 1960; Kaminor and Lutz, 1960; Dressler, 1982). Moreover, there is evidence of a relationship between the stressor of culture contact and elevated blood pressure specifically among the Navajo (Alfred, 1970) and among a number of Aboriginal Australian groups (Abbie & Schroeder, 1961; Casley-Smith, 1958; Edwards, Wise, Thomas, Murchland, & Craig, 1976). In these latter studies it was shown that Navajos living on the Navajo reservation had lower blood pressure than Anglo-Americans and other Navajos living off the reservation and that Aboriginal Australians with little or no contact with white Australian society had lower blood pressure than Aborigines or white Australians living in Australian towns or large urban centers. These and similar studies do not necessarily mean that traditional tribal life in rural areas is not stressful; they do suggest that coping mechanisms inherent in large, intact, traditional social support networks are likely to reduce *perceived* stress. In this context it is worth pointing out as an example that in Chisholm's (1981) study of the relationship between prenatal maternal blood pressure and newborn irritability among Aboriginal Australians, 11 of the 51 Aboriginal women in the sample did not live on Aboriginal reserves but spent their pregnancies in Darwin, a white Australian city of 50,000. These 11 women had pregnancy blood pressures significantly higher than those women who spent their entire pregnancies in bush settlements. On the other hand, the white Australian woman with the highest pregnancy blood pressure was married to a missionary and was living in one of the most remote bush settlements, far away from family and friends. There was a strong tendency for the infants of all these women to be irritable at birth.

The possibility of group differences in diet cannot be ruled out, but both the Navajo and Aboriginal blood pressure studies cited just above cast doubt on this hypothesis. Furthermore, recent evidence suggests that dietary factors as an explanation of differences in blood pressure are either unlikely or only partially relevant. Light, Koepke, Obrist, and Willis (1983), for example, noting that abnormal sodium retention has long been considered a major cause of hypertension, found that at least among males at risk for hypertension (because of one or two hypertensive parents), experimentally induced psychological stress can operate to increase blood pressure through the mechanism of altering renal excretory function.

There is reason to believe that elevated blood pressure by itself may raise the threshold for the perception of stimuli as noxious or aversive; individuals under chronic psychosocial stress may actually learn to increase their blood pressure as a psychological adaptation through a biofeedback process (Dworkin, Filewich, Miller, Craigmyle, & Pickering, 1979). Finally, since high levels of physical activity tend to reduce blood pressure over the long run, group differences in maternal activity during pregnancy cannot be entirely ruled out as an explanation of group differences in pregnancy blood pressure. This may be unlikely, however, given that the normal activities of pregnant women even in technologically very simple societies seem insufficient to produce the high heart rate and blood pressure levels required for this effect to work over time.

In sum, since facultative adaptation in utero seems to occur in animals, since there seem to be regularities in the effect of maternal prenatal anxiety on maternal physiology, since there are known hormonal and hemodynamic mechanisms whereby maternal physiological states may be transferred to the fetus, and since many normal infants born to women experiencing pregnancy stress are relatively irritable, the hypothesis of facultative adaptation to maternal stress in utero among humans is worthy of consideration. A concrete prediction of this evolutionarily based hypothesis is that when mothers experience at least some kinds of stress or anxiety during pregnancy and have relatively more irritable infants as a consequence, then this relatively irritable temperament of the infant should somehow be adaptive in the larger postnatal environment which caused the maternal anxiety in the first place. One way a relatively irritable temperament might be adaptive is to elicit more parental investment. For example, if maternal anxiety is a function of the mother's concerns about infant mortality or resources for child care, newborn irritability might elicit greater maternal proximity and attempts to quiet the baby (through feeding, cuddling, etc.). In support of this possibility, LeVine (1977) observes that in societies with high infant mortality parents seem to have simple survival and health as their primary concern. LeVine characterizes child care in such societies in this way: closer mother–infant proximity throughout the day, very rapid response to crying, which soon becomes less frequent than in Western societies, very frequent feeding, especially in response to crying, and little concern with fostering emotional responsiveness. Note here how maternal responsiveness to infant crying makes the crying adaptive in a biological sense and at the same time shows how the child's social environment may *prevent* continuities in behavior (cf. Bell & Ainsworth, 1972; Woodson, 1983).

An irritable or reactive temperament could conceivably be biologically adaptive (in the life history strategy sense of fostering learning) in another way. Regardless of the nature of the stressors which cause maternal prenatal anxiety, the dearth of close emotional support during pregnancy may exacerbate perceived stress. If there is a continuation of this dearth of support for the mother after delivery, the child's irritable–reactive temperament could be adaptive by increasing the frequency and/or duration of social interactions with anyone. For example, the Navajo infants in Chisholm's (1983) research had lower levels of irritability and reactivity from the very beginning and throughout the first year of life continued to show lower levels of crying, vocalizing, mutual gazing with mother, approaching mother, and more. They also lived in dense social environments, with an average of 6.5 more adults and older children around them than the Anglo-American children, who typically spent the day alone with their mothers. In order for the Anglo-American children to have any interactions at all, they had to "work harder" than the Navajo infants, and the isolated Anglo-American mother–infant pairs engaged in more frequent and longer and more intense social interactions than did the Navajo mother–infant pairs. The Navajo children, however, interacted much more (for higher totals) with other caretakers besides mother. Conversely, the lower levels of irritability–reactivity in the Navajo infants might also be adaptive in fostering relaxed and quiet social interactions in a dense social environment where the state of one individual is more likely to affect the state of another and where so many potential social interactors might otherwise tend to keep the infant in high levels of arousal.

Whatever advantages might conceivably accrue to the infant with an irritable temperament, his or her very irritability is likely to be stressful to the mother. Thus, it might be argued that natural selection should never favor irritable infants, especially if the infant's irritability added to the mother's anxiety which entrained the infant irritability in the first place. Kin selection theory, however, shows how natural selection might be expected to favor infants who can elicit parental investment even when parents are unwilling (Trivers, 1972). If the infant's irritable temperament makes the mother seek help in child care and/or simple support from her family or friends, then infant irritability might prove additionally adaptive. Crockenberg (1981), for example, showed that infants who were highly irritable developed secure attachments to their mothers when the mothers also had high levels of social support.

It remains to be shown how higher (or lower) levels of irritability or reactivity in the newborn are in fact adaptive. The speculations offered here are just that, but they illustrate how the hypothetical process of facultative adaptation in utero might operate. At the very least, the evolutionary approach embodied in this hypothesis suggests that research on prenatal influences must focus on more than the presence or absence of newborn behavioral effects of prenatal influences, but it must also examine the nature of these behavioral effects in relation to the sources of prenatal maternal anxiety or stress, especially in relation to the effects of these sources of prenatal maternal anxiety on maternal postnatal behavior and the infant's larger developmental environment. If the newborn behavioral effects of prenatal maternal anxiety in any way foster survival, growth and development and learning, or even ultimate reproduction in this environment, the interpretation of facultative adaptation in utero or prenatal behavioral canalization would be attractive.

Parent – Offspring Conflict and Kin Selection in Utero

Besides raising the possibility of facultative adaptation in utero, there is another way in which evolutionary biological thinking might contribute to the development of more useful models of prenatal environmental influences. The evolutionary biological principles relevant here are those of parent – offspring conflict and kin selection, both applied in utero. They are discussed together here because of their joint relevance to the larger principle of inclusive fitness, that is, the representation of an individual's genes in subsequent generations through direct reproduction *and/or* investment in the offspring of *other* individuals with whom one shares a high proportion of genes identical by common descent. The concept of facultative adaptation in utero is not unrelated to questions about inclusive fitness, but it emphasizes the *individual* fitness interests of the fetus as it adapts to its uterine environment and thus, presumably, to the environment into which it is going to be born. The concepts of parent – offspring conflict in utero and kin selection in utero, however, focus on the mother and her unborn child as two separate individuals who are closely (but not perfectly) related genetically. The concept of inclusive fitness may prove to be especially relevant to questions about prenatal influences because it is only during the gestational phase of the human life cycle that correct kin recognition between two individuals is absolutely guaranteed.

The concept of parent–offspring conflict was first developed by Trivers (1974) who, starting with the assumption that natural selection tends to maximize individual organisms' inclusive fitness (cf. Hamilton, 1964), concluded that conflict between parents and offspring was an inescapable consequence of the evolution of sexual reproduction. This is because the inclusive fitness interests of parents and offspring, while similar, are not identical (or as many sociobiologists put it, while offspring are 100% "related to themselves," they are only 50% related to their parents). Thus, Trivers argues, because parents are 50% related to all of their offspring they will tend to invest equally in each one, but the offspring will tend to attempt to elicit more than their "fair share" of parental investment. The classic example of parent–offspring conflict is weaning, where it is evident that the offspring of many mammals attempt to prolong nursing while their mothers appear to resist continuing this investment, usually because they are preparing to invest in their next offspring. Alexander (1974), on the other hand, has taken the position that rather than parent–offspring conflict, outright parental *manipulation* of offspring is a better concept. He argues that natural selection should always favor parents in any sort of inclusive fitness dispute, because any adaptation that permits an offspring to gain more than its "fair share" of parental investment could not evolve, since any genetic substrate for successful "cheating" by offspring would be passed on to the "cheater's" offspring, to the detriment of the "cheater's" inclusive fitness. While the relative explanatory power of these two approaches is not yet clear, both provide evolutionary biological grounds for expecting parent–offspring "conflict" (even if the parent always wins).

In any event, there is no reason why parent–offspring conflict or parental manipulation of offspring could not occur in utero. Indeed, given the endocrine and hemodynamic pathways connecting mother and fetus and the kin recognition certainty that mother and fetus share, their existence in utero seems likely. A possible example of parent–offspring conflict in utero has already been suggested by Blurton Jones (1978). Observing that in the great majority of human populations the mean birthweight is less than the optimum birthweight (i.e., that birthweight where neonatal and infant mortality and morbidity rates are the lowest) and that natural selection might otherwise be expected to optimize infants' chances of survival by selecting for intrauterine weight gain to place them at the optimum birthweight, he suggests that the difference between the mean and optimum birthweights may represent parent–offspring conflict in utero. In other words, if natural selection cared only about the infants' inclusive fitness it might be expected to select for birth at the optimum birthweight, but if the mothers' inclusive fitness interests are also considered, then we might expect parent–offspring conflict over how much parental investment the mother will make in the last few weeks of pregnancy. The infant's fitness will manifestly increase if gestation is prolonged, but there is a point of diminishing returns for the mother. Continued gestational investment by the mother after the infant's postnatal survival and capacity for successful growth are reasonably well assured will tend to decrease the mother's inclusive fitness — through increased uterine depletion, potential reduction of body fat stores, and even increased interbirth interval. Thus, Blurton Jones suggests the fact that there is typically a difference between mean and optimum birthweights might constitute indirect evidence of an intrauterine compromise between the different fitness interests of mother and infant.

In addition to providing new insights into the otherwise puzzling difference between mean and optimum birthweights, the concept of parent–offspring conflict in utero may prove relevant to a variety of other questions about prenatal influences. At the level of simple logic, for example, recognizing that the inclusive fitness interests of mother and fetus are not identical provides an evolutionary theoretical basis for expecting considerable variability in the continuity of prenatal influences. That is, when maternal inclusive fitness interests are seen as distinct from those of the fetus, we are forced to also consider all those other demographic and environmental factors which may also impinge on the mother's inclusive fitness. Gestation is not just a biological phenomenon but a biosocial phenomenon, and much of the vague and contradictory nature of reports of prenatal influences may be due to the failure to consider the potential for maternal–fetal conflict and how maternal inclusive fitness interests are affected by life historical, demographic and social–cultural as well as physical environmental factors. The following discussion of these general points will provide additional potential examples of parent–offspring conflict in utero and will also suggest why pregnancy and delivery complications *and* later infant disorders are likely often to be "parallel disorders resulting from the poor psychological state of the mother" (i.e., our position on Sameroff and Chandler's [1975, p. 73] "unanswered question," [see p. 61]).

In Blurton Jones's example of parent–offspring conflict in utero, the mother and fetus seemed to reach a compromise on the fetus's ultimate birthweight. In the most severe and dramatic cases of parent–offspring conflict, however, the fetus would be aborted. While the existence of a spontaneous abortion mechanism in humans has been suggested by several researchers (e.g., Stott, 1971; Ferreira, 1969; Drillien & Wilkinson, 1964; Davids *et al.*, 1961), only Bernds and Barash (1979) have provided an evolutionary theoretical rationale for expecting natural selection for such a mechanism. Briefly, their argument is that natural selection would favor mammalian mothers who were able to "detect" (through unspecified proximate physiological mechanisms) abnormal fetuses and then terminate further investment by aborting them. This is because an abnormal fetus is not likely to contribute to the mother's inclusive fitness and indeed is likely to detract from it by reducing the amount of investment she might bestow on normal offspring already born or to be born in the future. They note that the mother's inclusive fitness interests are best served by termination of investment in the defective offspring at the earliest possible moment, but following Dawkins and Carlisle (1976), they also note that mechanisms for even very late termination of investment would be selected for because amount of prior investment is not relevant to the cost – benefit ratio — only the amount of future investment weighed against the probability of increased inclusive fitness. Bernds and Barash make a persuasive theoretical argument for the evolution of a spontaneous abortion mechanism in humans and other mammals by citing numerous studies whose conclusions are consistent with the hypothesis that such prenatal termination of parental investment may increase maternal inclusive fitness.

The significance of Bernds and Barash's evolutionary model of the early termination of pregnancy for questions about prenatal influences in general may be extended, however, by noting that their notion of the early termination of pregnancy may be just one example of the broader evolutionary biological principle of female choice (Trivers, 1972). This concept refers to the basic reproductive strategy of female organisms. In evolutionary terms, because females invest more in offspring than do males (through production of the larger gamete and, in mammals at least, also through gestation, parturition, lactation, and primary responsibility for other forms of postnatal care), they are expected to be more choosy and discriminating in their mating behavior than males. That is, because of their greater investment, the number of offspring that most mammalian females may bear is lower than the number that most mammalian males may father. According to evolutionary reasoning this sex difference in potential reproductive success, because of the sex difference in parental investment, means that females have more to lose from mating with an inappropriate male. Most models of female choice have focused primarily on the adaptive significance of females choosing mates from the right species, of the right sex, and of the right age, but Trivers (1972) has extended the concept to include the female's subtle discrimination of male worth in terms of genetic material and his potential for male parental investment.

The concept of female choice, however, may be usefully extended beyond the female's relatively circumscribed decision to mate or not, for while she may be choosing a mate, a more encompassing view is that she is choosing to *initiate* investment in an offspring. Bernds and Barash's notions of evolved mechanisms for the maternal evaluation of the fetus and for the termination of investment in the fetus (i.e., abortion) are examples of the female choosing whether to *continue* investing in an offspring. If female choice then is more about initiating and maintaining her investment in an offspring, we might expect females to be highly discriminating not only about the quality of the father and the quality of the unborn offspring but also about the environment in which gestation takes place and *into which* the offspring will be born. Thus, even when the quality of the male is high and all indications are that the quality of the unborn offspring is high, we might still expect the female to terminate investment in an unborn offspring when she judges the environment of pregnancy or the environment into which her child is *going to be* born as nonoptimum for the child's growth, development, learning, or ultimate reproductive capacity — and hence nonoptimum for the mother's own inclusive fitness. The environment of pregnancy and the environment into which her child is going to be born both include the child's father, however, so females might also be expected to be *continuously* gauging their mates' potential for parental investment, at least until some point of diminishing returns is reached.

Expressed as a general principle and building on the ideas of both Bernds and Barash and Dawkins and Carlisle, we expect mammalian females, including humans, to be *continuously* gauging not only the quality of a mate and an unborn child but all those factors which reduce the probability that future investment in any given child (born or unborn) will increase the mother's inclusive fitness. The concept of female choice is thus expanded to a female's basic "decision" as to whether any given child (not yet conceived, unborn, or already delivered) represents a greater contribution to her inclusive fitness than an existing child or a future child. Female choice is thus a continuum from the choice of whether or when to mate, with whom to mate, and whether to continue an investment already initiated. Because females may make bad "choices" and because social or physical environmental conditions may change, the "choice" of whether to continue an investment ranges from whether to abort a conceptus, through the "decision" to abort a fetus at any stage of development, and through the "decisions" to nurture a newborn, to commit infanticide, to give the child away, to neglect the child, or to invest differentially in one offspring over another. At each stage in this continuum of "choices," the factors affecting whether investment should be continued will vary, but a partial list would include not only estimates of the child's viability and probability of ultimate reproductive success and the probability of future investment by the child's father but also estimates of investment by others (relatives or nonrelatives), social and economic conditions the child is likely to face, how many offspring the mother already has and how many she might expect to bear in the future, her own health, and perhaps even the number of offspring her close relatives have or might have in whom she might also invest. Her own age and parity are two especially important factors a pregnant woman should "consider" in estimating the probability that any given unborn child will contribute to her inclusive fitness. Age is crucial because it so closely determines the probability of conceiving another child in the future (i.e., being able to initiate a new investment). If a woman is young and has her entire reproductive career ahead of her, maintaining investment in an unborn child who has a low probability of contributing to her inclusive fitness (because of the child's constitution and/or because the expected environment of development is nonoptimum) would usually be unwise from an evolutionary perspective. On the other hand, if she is old enough to be unlikely to be able to conceive again, she might do better to maintain the investment in this child even though it may be unlikely to contribute much to her inclusive fitness. At the same time, however, she must consider her reproductive history: If she is of high parity and her children have survived but still require some care from her, she might do better to terminate investment in the existing fetus because continuing such investment might detract from her capacity to invest in her other children. Similar arguments have been made by Wasser & Barash (1983).

Before providing some examples from the literature that are generally consistent with the hypothesis of spontaneous abortion as an evolved mechanism for female choice (in our broader sense of the concept), we must emphasize that such "manipulation" will not necessarily result in the mother's complete termination of all investment. This means that the concept of female choice may be relevant not only to studies of spontaneous abortion but also to the entire continuum of reproductive–caretaking casualty, i.e., it may also be relevant to studies of prenatal influences on the constitution and behavior of living infants. Reasons for postulating a graded continuum of effects of maternal manipulation include, first, the potential for parent–offspring conflict in utero: Regardless of a mother's "decision" to abort, her unborn child might be expected, under certain circumstances, to resist the mother's attempts at abortion. Second, the mother's "decisions" about continuing investment in an unborn child do not have to be dichotomous, "either-or" decisions but may instead match some degree of investment against some probability of the child contributing to her inclusive fitness. Finally, we recognize that no adaptation is ever perfect, that pathology exists, that human perceptual capacities (unconscious as well as conscious) are fallible, and that even if an evolved abortion mechanism exists, it may not always function perfectly. Thus, our reasons for discussing spontaneous abortion here are that spontaneous abortion may represent only one end of the continuum of reproductive–caretaking casualty, that it may be only one kind of prenatal influence (albeit the most extreme), and that the demographic and environmental correlates of spontaneous abortion may provide clues in understanding the outcome of nonlethal prenatal influences.

The literature on spontaneous abortion in humans is at least as much a "grey area" of modern science as is the literature on less extreme prenatal influences. Bernds and Barash (1979) and Wasser and Barash (1983) have begun to make sense of this literature with the notion that pregnant women should be sensitive to indicators of the likelihood that an unborn child will contribute to their inclusive fitness more or less than an already existing child or some future child. In addition, however, there exist several spontaneous abortion studies whose results might have been predicted on the basis of our hypothesis that female choice during pregnancy may include the pregnant woman's "decision" about whether to *maintain* investment in a fetus according not only to the quality of the fetus but also to the quality of the environment into which the child will be born and the probability of obtaining a better developmental environment for some future child by postponing the initiation of investment.

One component of the environment into which children are born that is likely to have a major impact on how they will develop and thus the probability that they will contribute to their mothers' inclusive fitness is the amount of investment they receive from other adults besides their mother. The usual conceptualization of female choice is limited to females' preconception estimates of a male's genetic contribution to their children and the amount of parental investment these males may provide the child after birth. Regardless of a male's genetic contribution to her unborn child, however, if he should become unavailable for any postnatal investment, a pregnant woman might increase her inclusive fitness by terminating investment in a fetus and postponing the initiation of investment in a subsequent child until she perceives a higher probability of sufficient investment by another male. This evolutionarily based hypothesis about the social environmental correlates of spontaneous abortion receives some support from intriguingly common reports of the untoward effects of disharmonious marital relations or loss of spousal support on the course of pregnancy and/or neonatal outcome. Milne (1971), for example, found an increased incidence of spontaneous abortion in illegitimate pregnancies (in which the father is less likely to be supporting the mother) than in legitimate ones. Mann (1956, 1959), Berle and Javert (1954), and Weil and Stewart (1957), in their studies of habitual aborters, all stress the increased risk for abortion attendant on low levels of support from husbands (including the husband's loss of job during pregnancy). While noting the excessive incidence of PBCs and prenatal and neonatal mortality among teenage mothers, Niswander and Gordon (1972), with data from the massive Collaborative Perinatal Project, note that teenage girls who are *not* subject to the "special stresses" of being young mothers (e.g., lack of support from the baby's father) have even more uneventful pregnancies than do older women. Emmanuel (1972) cites a study conducted in California military hospitals where there was an inverse correlation between the incidence of perinatal mortality and father's rank. Berle and Javert (1954) concluded their report with this apt summary: "The threat of greatest significance in the majority of cases appeared to be uncertainty concerning the husband" (1954, p. 305).

Moving up the continuum of reproductive–caretaking casualty, the relation between disharmonious marital relations or loss of spousal support and nonlethal prenatal influences is also apparent. The work of Huttunen and Niskanen (1978) has already been mentioned: Focusing only on the long–term effects of prenatal loss of father versus loss of father in the first postnatal year, they found a significantly higher incidence of psychiatric disorder in the prenatal-loss group. Stott (1973), in his longitudinal study of prenatal maternal anxiety and later infant outcome, concluded that "stresses involving severe, continuing personal tensions (*in particular marital discord*) [emphasis added] were closely associated with child morbidity in the form of ill-health, neurological dysfunction, developmental lag, and behaviour disturbance" (1974, p. 785). Gorsuch and Key (1974), in their study of the relationship between specific life change events during pregnancy and the incidence of PBCs, found that death of spouse was one of the most consistent predictors of abnormalities of pregnancy and delivery and in the newborn. Everett and Schechter (1971), in a comparative study of prenatal anxiety in married and unmarried pregnant women, found significantly higher levels of state anxiety in the unwed women. Analogous findings are reported by Nilson and Almgren (1970), Gruenberg (1967), Gunter (1963), and Cox (1979), whose study is especially interesting because of its focus on non-Western women; his study showed significantly more psychiatric–emotional problems in Ganda women who were separated from their husbands during pregnancy.

While these data on the role of disharmonious marital relations and/or loss of spousal support in the incidence of spontaneous abortion, PBCs, and poor infant outcome are generally consistent with our notion of *continuous* female choice about maintaining investment, it should be obvious that additional factors must also be considered. One is the likelihood that women should be sensitive not only to the source of support (i.e., husbands) but, even more, simply to the probability of receiving any support at all. This is because there are cultural differences in how much fathers are expected to invest in their children and cultural differences in how much support a pregnant woman may expect to receive from family, friends, or social service agencies. We thus expect low levels of spousal support to be most clearly associated with the continuum of reproductive–caretaking casualty in

Western societies, in which nuclear families predominate and wide geographical separation of family members is common. We further expect this relationship to be strongest among the lower socioeconomic groups within Western societies, in which pregnant women are least able to expect "investment" in their children from any source. The role of poverty in spontaneous abortion, PBCs, and poor infant outcome is, of course, already well documented (e.g., Osofsky & Kendall, 1973; Illsley, 1967; Werner, Bierman, & French, 1971; Sameroff & Chandler, 1975). The role of social–emotional support for pregnant women in alleviating reproductive–caretaking casualty is implicit in the majority of studies of the causes of prenatal maternal anxiety cited throughout this chapter and is becoming better documented; one study, for example, has shown that the presence of a supportive companion during labor, even if a complete stranger, can shorten labor and reduce delivery complications (Sosa, Kennel, Klaus, Robertson, & Urratia, 1980).

Other factors impinging on *continuous* female choice about maintaining investment in an unborn offspring are, as mentioned above, maternal age and parity. Epidemiological studies of the incidence of various components of the continuum of reproductive–caretaking casualty typically show a U-shaped curve, with the youngest and oldest women and those of lowest and highest parity suffering the highest incidence. MacGillivray (1958) and Pritchard and MacDonald (1976), for example, both note that the incidence of preeclampsia and eclampsia is highest in young, nulliparous women, with a secondary peak among women at the end of their reproductive careers who have already had many pregnancies. They also note that preeclampsia and eclampsia may well be different phenomena in the two age–parity groups, for while predisposing conditions (primarily renal disease) are commonly identified in older women of higher parity, typically *no* predisposing factor can be identified in young women of low parity. Notwithstanding the possible contribution of a relatively immature reproductive system to the incidence of spontaneous abortion, PBCs, and poor infant outcome in the very youngest teenage mothers, the shape of this distribution curve is difficult to interpret except from an evolutionary perspective, for the youngest women are expected to be the strongest and most healthy. Indeed, as mentioned above, Niswander and Gordon (1972) showed that when the "special [psychosocial] stresses" of being a young mother are factored out, young, nulliparous women indeed do have less eventful pregnancies/deliveries than older women. It is thus attractive to speculate that young, nulliparous women, with their entire reproductive careers ahead of them, may be "deciding" to abort because maintaining the investment already begun could detract from their capacity to invest in future children who are perhaps more likely to be born into a more supportive environment. The oldest, multiparous women, however, with their reproductive careers largely behind them, may be "deciding" to abort because maintaining the investment already begun might detract from their capacity to invest in already existing children — especially if the current unborn child is at risk for nonoptimum fetal growth and development because of an aged or well-used reproductive system (e.g., renal disease effects on placental transfer, the effects of a "depleted uterus," or the effects of age-induced elevated blood pressure). Whatever the reasons and mechanisms, women who have most frequently been pregnant are most likely to abort (Warburton & Fraser, 1964), and the incidence of numerous abnormalities of the newborn is well known to increase with maternal age and/or parity.

While preeclampsia and eclampsia are not the only reasons for spontaneous abortion, additional data on the nature and incidence of this syndrome may be relevant to discussions about the possibility of a mechanism for the *late* termination of pregnancy in humans. First, it is interesting to note that preeclampsia–eclampsia (PE/E) may be unique to humans; Pritchard and MacDonald state that "the syndrome of preeclampsia–eclampsia is unique to pregnant or puerperal women and has not been identified in animals to occur spontaneously nor has it been experimentally reproduced" (1976, p. 552). Second, in spite of the very great number of theories, there is no commonly accepted cause, and PE/E remains of unknown etiology. Third, there are strong suspicions nonetheless that psychosocial factors play a major role. As early as 1952, for example, Dieckman provided a summary of his work that is largely supported by more recent evidence: "[preeclampsia–eclampsia] are diseases of culture and civilization, probably because of mental strain and changes in diet and habits" (1952:55).

Coppen (1958), in a retrospective comparison of 50 women who developed PE/E and 50 women of the same age and parity who did not, found significantly more psychiatric–emotional problems in the PE/E group, who in addition were more likely to report problems or low levels of satisfaction in sexual relations with their husbands. Salerno (1958) reports that fully 70% of the incidence of PE/E is accounted for by girls 14–19-years-old but adds that this figure is much reduced among young girls who are married. Salerno also cites a European study which showed an incidence of 1.53/1000 for PE/E among married women but an incidence of 3.38/1000 among unmarried women. He reports further that the incidence of PE/E is especially high among young schizophrenic women, even before their first psychotic episode. Pritchard and MacDonald (1976) report an overall rate for PE/E between 5 and 15% of all pregnancies but report that it is typically higher among poor women and that among American black women rates as high as 25% have been reported. Soichet (1959), arguing for the role of psychosocial factors in PE/E, makes the observation that while PE/E is more common among American blacks than whites, it is rare among African blacks. Bell and Wilk (1955) argue for psychosocial factors in the development of PE/E by noting that among native Fijians the PE/E rate was only 1.8% but that among Indian migrants to Fiji the rate was 8.5%. In a similar cross-cultural study, but with a concentration on within-group socioeconomic differences as a source of psychosocial stresses, Llewellyn-Jones (1965) reported a PE/E rate of 3.8% for the better-off group but a rate of 6.5% for the more impoverished group. Thus, given that no underlying organic cause for PE/E can ordinarily be shown, it is tempting to speculate that psychosocial stress itself may be the underlying cause and that PE/E may represent a mechanism for the termination of investment in a fetus late in pregnancy, when the mother begins to experience high levels of anxiety about the developmental effects of the environment into which her child will be born.

Whether or not PE/E itself is a mechanism for the late termination of pregnancy in humans, the broad association between maternal psychosocial stress during pregnancy and the increased risk for spontaneous abortion, PBCs, and poor infant outcome is well documented. This association makes sense in terms of the evolutionary biological concepts of female reproductive strategy and "female choice in utero." Arguing from this evolutionary approach to Sameroff and Chandler's (1975) "unanswered question" about the continuum of reproductive–caretaking casualty, we suspect that *both* pregnancy and delivery complications *and* physical anomalies in the fetus represent "parallel disorders resulting from the poor psychological state of the mother" (1975, p. 73), at least when the mother's "poor psychological state" is a result of her perceptions about the environment into which the child will be born. While we require much more detailed knowledge of the psychophysiological mechanisms involved, especially in the termination of pregnancy (successful or not), we also require much more detailed knowledge about the determinants of the mother's "poor psychological state," especially since this state may be an accurate and evolutionarily adaptive reflection of a poor *environmental* state, i.e., one that is not optimal for bearing and rearing children.

We also recognize the likelihood, however, that the mother's "poor psychological state" may owe as much to the state of the fetus as the state of the environment into which the child will be born. Gorsuch and Key (1974), Drillien and Wilkinson (1964), and Davids et al. (1961), for example, have all raised the possibility that the presence of abnormalities in the fetus may (through unspecified proximal mechanisms) engender feelings of anxiety in the mother. Although they do not discuss this possibility, it is consistent with the notions of Bernds and Barash (1979), who emphasize the evolutionary adaptive functions of maternal assessment of the quality of her fetus. In this view of the relation between maternal prenatal anxiety and a hypothetical abortion mechanism, maternal prenatal anxiety would still be part of the abortion mechanism itself. Stott (1971), however, raises the interesting possibility that the reason there is such a strong correlation between birth defects and prenatal maternal anxiety is that this maternal anxiety actually *interferes* with the operation of an evolved abortion mechanism.

The possibility that various abnormalities of the fetus might be causally related to the operation of a spontaneous abortion mechanism (or the incidence of PBCs if it operated imperfectly), whether or not maternal prenatal anxiety is involved, may be worth some further consideration here, if only to cover a logical possibility stemming from an additional prediction of evolutionary theory. This prediction is that spontaneous abortion might not always be the mother's "decision" and that under some circumstances an unborn child might increase its inclusive fitness by "aborting itself." This is the notion of "fetal altruism" (kin selection) raised by Bernds and Barash (1979) in connection with data showing that in cases of both MZ and DZ twin pregnancies, it is more likely that only one twin will be stillborn, rather than both. Further, they note that there is a tendency for the living twin to be born first and that among living newborn twins, the perinatal mortality rate is higher for the second one. Recent data on the outcome of twin pregnancies makes the hypothesis of fetal altruism even more intriguing. New research using ultrasound is suggesting that not only is the rate of twinning higher than had been suspected, the prenatal mortality rate for one of a set of twins is much higher than had been appreciated; one estimate is that up to 78% of all twin pregnancies produce only one live birth, with the other twins having been completely resorbed or delivered (second) as *foeti papyracei* (Landy, Keith, & Keith, 1982). Because the uterus acts as an infallible kin-recognition mechanism in twin pregnancies and because twins are thus correctly guaranteed either 50% (DZ twins) or 100% (MZ twins) of their genes in common, any mechanism for the mutual assessment of viability by each twin and for the self-abortion by one in favor of the other would theoretically stand a good chance of being selected for. On the other hand, the same logic could be used to predict fetal sibling competition, in which instead of the less viable twin aborting itself, the stronger twin manages to accrue all of the uterine developmental resources for itself. While the logic of these evolutionary biological arguments may be sound, however, and while data on the outcome of twin pregnancies generally suggest that one twin may very often survive while the other dies, or is at least less viable, it goes without saying that these are logical possibilities only and that there appears to be no direct evidence for the existence of such mechanisms.

Continuing briefly in the realm of logical possibilities, and notwithstanding difficulties in specifying the proximate physiological mechanisms involved, it may nonetheless be worthwhile to speculate a bit further on implications of the notion of kin selection in utero. In twin (or multiple) pregnancies each inhabitant of the uterus is guaranteed correct kin recognition, which has to be (for practical purposes) either 50% or 100%. In successive singleton pregnancies, however, inhabitants of the uterus are still guaranteed correct kin recognition, even if the degree of guaranteed relatedness drops to only 25% (i.e., successive inhabitants of a uterus must be at least half sibs). Even this reduced degree of relatedness, however, because it is always guaranteed to be correct, might make it adaptive in inclusive fitness terms for a singleton fetus to "assess" its own viability and/or the environment into which it can expect to be born (through the effects of this environment on maternal physiology) and to "decide" that a future inhabitant of the uterus (who has to be at least a half sib) might have a better chance for ultimate reproductive success.

Summary and Conclusions

Taken together, the arguments and data presented here indicate that the development of useful models of prenatal influences will include considerations of evolutionary biology. Such considerations provide, first, a phylogenetic basis for expecting prenatal influences and, second, the hypothetico-deductive basis for generating hypotheses about the specific processes involved. Our brief review of life history strategies and of the evolution of hominid developmental patterns and the higher primate placenta suggests that natural selection for increased behavioral–developmental plasticity exposes the developing hominid fetus to phylogenetically new uterine environmental factors. Having been exposed to a new developmental environment, the process of adaptation by natural selection can be expected to have favored those effects of the new uterine environment which conferred some inclusive fitness benefits on the developing fetus and/or its mother. One way that adaptation by natural selection in utero might favor the inclusive fitness of both mother and fetus is through the process of facultative adaptation in utero, i.e., natural selection for the capacity of the fetus to respond to uterine environmental influences such that its postnatal survival and optimum development are better assured. This process of the uterine entrainment of prenatal development for postnatal survival and/or optimal development has been identified and described in animals, and there is evidence of similar prenatal influences in humans that is consistent with such an interpretation. The notion of facultative adaptation in utero thus provides a productive specific basis for generating new hypotheses about prenatal influences.

Adaptation by natural selection in utero might also lead to a range of prenatal influences through the process of parent–offspring conflict in utero, i.e., natural selection for mechanisms whereby the pregnant woman may (a) evaluate the viability of the fetus; (b) evaluate the environment into which her child will be born and its potential impact on her child's reproductive success; (c) evaluate the relative contribution to her own inclusive fitness of investing in the present fetus against investing in children already born and the probability of successfully bearing and rearing future children; and (d) terminate investment in the present fetus when any of the above evaluations indicate a low return in inclusive fitness points for her investment. However, because of the fact that mother and fetus share only 50% of their genes in common, we might expect mothers and their unborn children to disagree about the amount of investment by the mother. This disagreement could be expected to lead to selection for mechanisms whereby the fetus may elicit more or continued maternal investment. Further, because of the possibility that selection might favor maternal matching of some degree of investment against some probability of inclusive fitness return, we might expect that complete termination of investment to occur in only the most extreme cases. Finally, even if there has been natural selection for an abortion mechanism, such a mechanism may be imperfect in its operation. For these reasons parent–offspring conflict in utero need not be relevant only to spontaneous abortion but may be equally relevant to the entire continuum of reproductive casualty. Numerous studies of prenatal influences in humans showed conclusions that were at least consistent with the implications of parent–offspring conflict in utero.

While the results of many studies of prenatal influences are intriguingly consistent with the hypothesis of facultative adaptation and parent–offspring conflict in utero, the fallacy of affirming the consequence remains a potential problem. What remains to be accomplished is the specification of proximate mechanisms and causal pathways whereby facultative adaptation and parent–offspring conflict in utero can be shown to operate. Bringing evolutionary biology to the study of prenatal influences will aid this endeavor in at least two ways: first by providing a rationale for expecting such mechanisms and, second, by helping to narrow the search for them. An evolutionary approach to prenatal influences will help to narrow the search for the mechanisms of such influences by focusing researchers' attention on those aspects of maternal, fetal, and placental physiology affected by the joint interaction of indicators of fetal viability, of maternal reproductive history, of the maternal environment of pregnancy, and of maternal perceptions of the environment into which her child is going to be born. An evolutionarily based study of prenatal influences thus demands a synthesis of the methods and data of such disparate fields as human physiology (especially reproductive and stress physiology), obstetrics, gynecology, and pediatrics, developmental psychology and neurobiology, psychophysiology of perception, and social and cultural anthropology, which are well suited for describing the social organization of pregnancy, social support networks, coping mechanisms, belief and value systems, and cultural differences in patterns of perception and cognition.

Synthesizing the methods and data of these fields in the study of prenatal influences might have valuable reciprocal implications for areas of special interest to each. For example, researchers in developmental psychology are recently renewing their interest in the concept of temperament — the characteristic pattern of response by children to a wide range of stimuli that is relatively consistent and stable and that is held to be influenced by genetic and/or prenatal variables. An evolutionary approach to temperament would suggest in general that temperamental differences might be biologically adaptive, but the notion of facultative adaptation in utero might suggest how these early individual differences were adaptive. The concept of facultative adaptation in utero might similarly be useful for researchers in cross-cultural studies of child development, in which consistent ethnic group differences in newborn behavior have been identified and there are indicators of corresponding differences in the experience of pregnancy. An evolutionarily based study of prenatal influences could also have implications for clinical obstetrics and pediatrics in the way it might suggest or further delineate maternal and fetal risk factors. Our extension of the evolutionary concept of female choice, for example, provides a theoretical rationale for why low levels of spousal support is so often implicated in pregnancy and delivery complications. The inclusion of at least implicit or potential inclusive fitness considerations in the determination of risk factors might improve prediction and prevention efforts.

Finally, a synthesis of the methods and data of these several disciplines in the study of prenatal influences may provide a model for other evolutionary biological studies of human behavior that investigate the significance of proximate mechanisms. The mechanisms of maternal–fetal communication are complex and subtle, but this does not imply they are unaccessible. Maternal–fetal communication is a good place to search for the environmental (social and cultural as well as physical) causes and physiological effects involved in the proximate mechanisms which may — or may not — make human behavior adaptive in the ultimate sense.

References

Abbie, A. A., & Schroeder, J. (1961). Blood pressure in Arnhem Land Aborigines. *Medical Journal of Australia, 2*, 493–496.

Alexander, R. D. (1974). The evolution of social behavior. *Annual Review of Ecology and Systematics, 5*, 325–383.

Alfred, B. M. (1970). Blood pressure changes among male Navajo migrants to an urban environment. *Canadian Review of Sociology and Anthropology, 7* (3), 289–300.

Ando, Y., & Hattori, H. (1970). Effects of intense noise during fetal life upon postnatal adaptability. *Journal of the Acoustical Society of America, 47* (4), 1128–1130.

Baldwin, J. M. (1896). A new factor in evolution. *American Naturalist, 30,* 441–451.

Barnes, F. (1975). Accidents in the first three years of life. *Child: Care, Health, and Development, 1,* 421–433.

Bateson, P. P. G. (1976). Specificity and the origins of behaviors. In J. S. Rosenblatt, R. A. Hinde, E. Shaw, & C. Beer, (Eds), *Advances in the Study of Behavior* (Vol. 6, pp. 1–20). New York: Academic Press.

Bateson, P. P. G. (1982). Behavorial development and evolutionary processes. In King's College Sociobiology Study Group, Cambridge. *Current Problems in Sociobiology.* London and New York: Cambridge Univ. Press.

Bell, M. E., & Wilk, L. (1955). Racial differences in incidence of pre-eclampsia and eclampsia in Fiji. *Journal of Obstetrics and Gynecology of the British Empire, 621,* 917–928.

Bell, R. Q. (1968). A reinterpretation of the direction of effects in studies of socialization. *Psychological Review, 75,* 81–95.

Bell, S. M., & Ainsworth, M.D.S. (1972). Infant crying and maternal responsiveness. *American Journal of Orthopsychiatry, 19,* 342–350.

Berle, B. B., & Javert, C. T. (1954). Stress and habitual abortion. *Obstetrics and Gynecology, 3,* 298–312.

Bernds, W. P., & Barash, D. H. (1979). Early termination of parental investment in mammals, including humans. In N. Chagnon & W. Irons (Eds.), *Evolutionary Biology and Human Social Behavior,* (pp. 487–506). North Scituate, Massachusetts: Duxbury Press.

Blinkov, S., & Glezer, I. (1968). *The Human Brain in Figures and Tables: A Quantitative Handbook.* New York: Plenum.

Blurton Jones, N. G. (1972). Characteristics of ethological studies of human behavior. In N. G. Blurton Jones (Eds.), *Ethological Studies of Child Behavior* (pp. 3–33). London and New York: Cambridge Univ. Press.

Blurton Jones, N. G. (1978). Natural selection and birthweight. *Annals of Human Biology, 5* (5), 487–489.

Blurton Jones, N. G. (1982). Origins, functions, development, and motivation: Unity and disunity in the study of behavior. *Journal of Anthropological Research, 38,* 333–349.

Blurton Jones, N. G., & Sibly, R. M. (1978). Testing adaptiveness of culturally determined behavior: Do Bushmen women maximize their reproductive success by spacing births widely and foraging seldom? In N. G. Blurton Jones & V. Reynolds (Eds.), *Human Behavior and Adaptation* (pp. 135–157). London: Taylor and Francis.

Bowlby, J. (1969). *Attachment and Loss: Vol. 1. Attachment.* London: Hogarth Press.

Brazelton, T. B. (1973). *Neonatal Behavioral Assessment Scale.* London: Spastics International Medical Publications.

Brown, D. D. (1981). Gene expression in eukaryotes. *Science, 211,* 667–674.

Browne, J. C. M., & Veall, N. (1953). The maternal placental blood flow in normotensive and hypertensive women. *Journal of Obstetrics and Gynecology of the British Empire, 60* (2), 141–147.

Burghardt, G. M., & Bekoff, M. (1978). *The Development of Behavior: Comparative and Evolutionary Aspects.* New York: Garland STPM Press.

Casley-Smith, W. W. (1958). Blood pressure in Australian Aborigines. *Medical Journal of Australia, 1,* 627–633.

Chalmers, B. (1982). Psychological aspects of pregnancy: Some thoughts for the eighties. *Social Science Medicine, 16,* 323–331.

Chisholm, J. S. (1981). Prenatal influences on Aboriginal—white Australian differences in neonatal irritability. *Ethology and Sociobiology, 2,* 67–73.

Chisholm, J. S. (1983). *Navajo Infancy: An Ethological Study of Child Development.* Hawthorne, New York: Aldine Publishing Co.

Chisholm, J. S., Woodson, R. H., & da Costa Woodson, E. (1978). Maternal blood pressure in pregnancy and newborn irritability. *Early Human Development, 2* (2), 171–178.

Cohler, B. J., Gallant, D. H., Grunebaum, H. U., Weiss, J. L., & Gamer, E. (1975). Pregnancy and birth complications among mentally ill and well mothers and their children. *Social Biology, 22,* 269–278.

Condon, W. S., & Sander, L. W. (1974). Neonate movement is synchronized with adult speech: Interactional participation and language acquisition. *Science, 183,* 99–101.

Coppen, A. J. (1958). Psychosomatic aspects of pre-eclamptic toxaemia. *Journal of Psychosomatics, 2,* 241–265.

Cox, J. L. (1979). Psychiatric morbidity and pregnancy: A controlled study of 263 semi-rural Ugandan women. *British Journal of Psychiatry, 134,* 401–405.

Crandon, A. J. (1979). Maternal anxiety and neonatal well-being. *Journal of Psychosomatic Research, 23,* 113–115.

Crockenberg, S. B. (1981). Infant irritability, mother responsiveness, and social support influences on the security of infant-mother attachment. *Child Development, 52,* 857–865.

Daly, M., & Wilson, M. (1983). *Sex, Evolution and Behavior* (2nd ed.). Boston: Willard Grant Press.

Davids, A., & DeVault, S. (1962). Maternal anxiety during pregnancy and childbirth abnormalities. *Psychosomatic Medicine, 24,* 464–470.

Davids, A., DeVault, S., & Talmadge, M. (1961). Anxiety, pregnancy and childhood abnormalities. *Journal of Consulting and Clinical Psychology, 25,* 74–79.

Dawkins, R., & Carlisle, R. J. (1976). Parental investment, mate desertion and a fallacy. *Nature, (London), 262,* 131–132.

DeCasper, A. J., & Fifer, W. P. (1980). Of human bonding: Newborns prefer their mother's voices. *Science, 208,* 1174–1176.

Deykin, E. Y., & MacMahon, B. (1980). Pregnancy, delivery and neonatal complication among autistic children. *American Journal of Diseases of Children, 139* (9), 860–869.

Dieckman, W. J. (1952). *The Toxemias of Pregnancy,* St. Louis, MO: C. V. Mosby.

Dobbing, J. (1974). Prenatal nutrition and neurological development. In J. Cravioto, L. Hambraeus, & B. Vahlquist (Eds.), *Early Malnutrition and Mental Development,* Uppsala: Swedish Nutrition Foundation.

Dodge, J. A. (1972). Psychosomatic aspects of infantile pyloric stenosis. *Journal of Psychosomatic Research, 16,* 1–19.

Dressler, W. (1982). *Hypertension and Culture Change.* New York: Redgrave Publishing Co.

Drillien, C. M., Ingram, T. T. S., & Wilkinson, E. M. (1966). *The Causes and Natural History of Cleft Lip and Palate.* Edinburgh: Livingston.

Drillien, C. M., & Wilkinson, E. M. (1964). Emotional stress and mongoloid births. *Developmental Medicine and Child Neurology, 6,* 140–143.

Dunn, J. (1976). How far do early differences in mother-child relations affect later development? In P. P. G. Bateson & R. A. Hinde (Eds.), *Growing Points in Ethology* (pp. 481–496). London and New York: Univ. of Cambridge Press.

Dworkin, B. R., Filewich, R. J., Miller, N. E., Craigmyle, N., & Pickering, T. C. (1979). Baroreceptor activation reduces reactivity to noxious stimulation: Implications for hypertension. *Science, 205,* 1299–1301.

Edwards, F. M., Wise, P. H., Thomas, D. W., Murchland, J. B., & Craig, R. J. (1976). Blood pressure and electrocardiography findings in the South Australian Aborigines. *Australian and New Zealand Journal of Medicine, 6,* 197–205.

Edwards, K. R., & Jones, M. R. (1970). Personality change related to pregnancy and obstetric complications. In *Proceedings of the 78th Annual Convention of the American Psychological Association,* 341–342.

Eisenberg, J. F. (1981). *The Mammalian Radiations: An Analysis of Trends in Evolution, Adaptation, and Behavior.* Chicago: Univ. of Chicago Press.

Emmanuel, I. (1972). Some preventive aspects of abnormal intrauterine development. *Postgraduate Medicine, 51,* 144–148.

Everett, R. B., & Schechtor, M.D. (1971). A comparative study of prenatal anxiety in the unwed mother. *Child Psychiatry and Human Development, 2* (2), 89–91.

Falorni, M. L., Furnasarig, A. F., & Stefanile, L. (1979). Research about anxiety effects on pregnant woman and her newborn child. In L. Carenza & L. Zichella (Eds.), *Emotion and Reproduction* (pp. 1147–1154). New York: Academic Press.

Ferreira, A. J. (1965). Emotional factors in prenatal environment. *Journal of Nervous and Mental Disease, 141,* 108–118.

Ferreira, A. J. (1969). *Prenatal Environment.* Springfield, IL: Thomas.

Freedman, D. G. (1974). *Human Infancy: An Evolutionary Perspective.* Hillsdale, NJ: Lawrence Earlbaum Associates.

French, F. E., & Bierman, J. M. (1962). Probabilities of fetal mortality. *Public Health Reports, 77,* 835–847.

Friedman, D. D., Essman, W. B., & Fisichelli, V. (1979). Plasma catecholamines during pregnancy and parturition: A new approach to their relationship. In L. Carenza & L. Zichella (Eds.), *Emotion and Reproduction* (pp. 741–748). New York: Academic Press.

Gadgil, M., & Bossert, W. M. (1970). Life historical consequences of natural selection. *American Naturalist, 104,* 1–24.

Goodman, M. (1963). Man's place in the phylogeny of the primates as reflected in serum proteins. In S. L. Washburn (Ed.), *Classification and Human Evolution* (pp. 204–234). Chicago: Aldine.

Gorsuch, R. L., & Key, M. K. (1974). Abnormalities of pregnancy as a function of anxiety and life stress. *Psychosomatic Medicine, 36* (4), 352–362.

Gottlieb, G. (1971). *Development of Species Identification in Birds: An Inquiry into the Prenatal Determinants of Perception.* Chicago: Univ. of Chicago Press.

Gottlieb, G. (1976). The roles of experience in the development of behavior and the nervous system. In G. Gottlieb (Ed.), *Neural and Behavioral Specificity. Studies on the Development of Behavior and the Nervous System* (Vol. 3, pp. 25–59). New York: Academic Press.

Gould, S. J. (1977). *Ontogeny and Phylogeny.* Cambridge, MA: Harvard Univ. Press.

Grimm, E.R. (1967). Psychological investigation of habitual aborters. *Psychosomatic Medicine, 24,* 369–378

Gruenberg, E. M. (1967). On the psychosomatics of the not-so-perfect fetal parasite. In S. A. Richardson & A. F. Guttmacher (Eds.), *Childbearing — Its Social and Psychological Aspects* (pp 53–74). Baltimore, MD: Williams & Wilkins, 1967.

Gunter, L. H. (1963). Psychopathology and stress in the life experience of mothers of premature infants. *American Journal of Obstetrics and Gynecology, 86,* 333.

Hall, F. (1977). Pre-natal events and later infant behavior. *Journal of Psychosomatic Research, 21,* 253–257.

Hamilton, W. D. (1964). The evolution of social behavior. I and II. *Journal of Theoretical Biology, 24,* 1–52.

Harris, D. B., & Harris, E. S. (1946). A study of fetal movements in relation to mother's activity. *Human Biology, 18,* 221–237.

Henry, L. (1976). *Population: Analysis and Models.* New York: Academic Press.

Hill, D. E. (1975). Placental insufficiency and brain growth of the fetus. In D. B. Cheek (Ed.), *Fetal and Postnatal Cellular Growth: Hormones and Nutrition* (pp. 133–140). New York: Wiley.

Hofer, M. A. (1981). *The Roots of Human Behavior.* San Francisco, CA: Freeman.

Holmes, T. M., & Rahe, R. M. (1967). The social readjustment rating scale. *Journal of Psychosomatic Research, 11,* 213–218.

Holt, A. B., Cheek, D. B., Mellit, E. D., & Hill, D. E. (1975). Brain size and the relation of the primate to the nonprimate. In D. B. Cheek (Ed.), *Fetal and Postnatal Cellular Growth: Hormones and Nutrition* (pp. 23–44). New York: Wiley.

Horn, H. (1978). Optimal tactics of reproduction and life history. In J. R. Krebs & L. B. Davies (Eds.), *Behavioral Ecology* (pp. 411–429). Oxford: Blackwell.

Howell, N. (1979). *Demography of the Dobe !Kung.* New York: Academic Press.

Huttenen, M. D., & Niskanen, P. (1978). Prenatal loss of father and psychiatric disorders. *Archives of General Psychiatry, 35,* 429–431.

Illsley, R. (1967). The sociological study of reproduction and its outcome. In S. A. Richardson & A. F. Guttmacher (Eds.), *Childbearing — Its Social and Psychological Aspects.* Baltimore, MD: Williams & Wilkins.

Jacobson, M. (1969). Development of specific neuronal connections. *Science, 163,* 543–547.

Joffe, J. M. (1969). *Prenatal Determinants of Behavior.* Oxford: Pergamon.

Joffe, J. M. (1978). Hormonal mediation of the effects of prenatal stress on offspring behavior. In G. Gottlieb (Ed.), *Studies on the Development of Behavior and the Nervous System: Vol. 4. Early Influences* (pp. 107–144). New York: Academic Press.

Jones, F., & Dlugokinski, E. (1978). *The relationship of stress during pregnancy to perinatal status and maternal readiness.* Paper presented at the first biennial meeting of the International Conference on Infant Studies, Providence, RI.

Jost, H., & Sontag, L. W. (1944). The genetic factor in autonomic nervous system function. *Psychosomatic Medicine, 6,* 308–310.

Kagan, J. (1980). Perspectives on continuity. In O. G. Brim & J. Kagan (Eds.), *Constancy and Change in Human Development* (pp. 26–74). Cambridge, MA: Harvard Univ. Press.

Kagan, J. (1981). Universals in human development. In R. H. Munroe, R. L. Munroe, & B. B. Whiting (Eds.), *Handbook of Cross-cultural Human Development* (pp. 53–62). New York: Garland STPM Press.

Kagan, J., Kearsley, R. B., & Zelazo, P. R. (1980). *Infancy: Its Place in Human Development.* Cambridge, MA: Harvard Univ. Press.

Kaminor, B., & Lutz, W. (1960). Blood pressure in Bushmen of the Kalahari desert. *Circulation, 22,* 289–295.

Kaplan, N. M. (1978, September). Stress, the sympathetic nervous system, and hypertension. *Journal of Human Stress, 4* (3), 29–34.

Kass, E. M., Rosner, B., Zinner, S. H., Margolius, H. S., & Lee, Y-H. (1977). Studies on the origins of human hypertension. In D. Barltrop (Ed.), *Pediatric Implications for Some Adult Disorders* (pp. 145–150). London: Fellowship of Postgraduate Medicine.

Kawi, A. A., & Pasamanick, B. (1959). Prenatal and perinatal factors in the development of childhood reading disorders. *Monographs of the Society for Research in Child Development, 24* (4), 576–581.

Kelly, J. V. (1962). Effect of fear upon uterine motility. *American Journal of Obstetrics and Gynecology, 83,* 576–581.

Kerr, M. (1971). Prenatal mortality and genetic wastage in man. *Journal of Biosocial Science, 3,* 223–237.

King, M. C., & Wilson, A. C. (1975). Evolution at two levels in humans and chimpanzees. *Science, 188,* 107–116.

Klusman, L. E. (1975). Reduction of pain in childbirth by the alleviation of anxiety during pregnancy. *Journal of Consulting Clinical Psychology, 43,* 162–169.

Konner, M. (1982). *The Tangled Wing: Biological Constraints on the Human Spirit.* New York: Holt.

Kopp, C. B., & Parmelee, A. H. (1979). Prenatal and perinatal influences on infant behavior. In J. D. Osofsky (Ed.), *Handbook of Infant Development* (pp. 29–75). New York: Wiley.

Korner, A. F., Gabby, T., & Kraemer, H. G. (1980). Relation between prenatal maternal blood pressure and infant irritability. *Early Human Development, 4,* 35–39.

Landy, H. J., Keith, L., & Keith, D. (1982). The vanishing twin. *Acta Genetica Medica Gemellogica, 31,* 179–194.

Lederman, R. P., Lederman, G., Work, B., & McCann, D. S. (1978). The relationship of maternal anxiety, plasma catecholamines and plasma cortisol in labor. *American Journal of Obstetrics and Gynecology, 132,* 495–500.

Leutenegger, W. (1972). Newborn size and pelvic dimensions of Australopithecus. *Nature (London), 240,* 568–569.

LeVine, R. A. (1977). Childrearing as cultural adaptation. In P. H. Leiderman, S. R. Tulkin, & A. Rosenfeld (Eds.), *Culture and Infancy* (pp. 15–28). New York: Academic Press.

Lewin, R. (1982). How did humans evolve big brains? *Science, 216,* 840–841.

Lewis, M., & Rosenblume, L. (Eds.). (1974). *The Effect of the Infant on Its Caregiver.* New York: Wiley.

Light, K. C., Koepke, J. P., Obrist, P. A., & Willis, P. W. (1983). Psychological stress induces sodium and fluid retention in men at risk for hypertension. *Science, 220,* 429–431.

Lillienfeld, R. M., Pasamanick, B., & Rogers, M. (1955). Relationship between pregnancy experience and the development of certain neuro-psychiatric disorders in childhood. *American Journal of Public Health, 45,* 637–643.

Lindburg, D. G. (1982). Primate obstetrics: The biology of birth. *American Journal of Primatology,* Supplement, *1,* 193–199.

Llewellyn-Jones, D. (1965). The effects of age and social status on obstetric efficiency. *Journal of Obstetrics and Gynecology of the British Commonwealth, 72,* 196–202.

Luckett, W. P. (1974). Comparative development and evolution of the placenta in primates. *Contributions in Primatology, 3,* 142–234.

Lynch, G., & Gall, C. (1979). Organization and reorganization in the central nervous system: evolving concepts of brain plasticity. In F. Falkner & J. Tanner (Eds.), *Human Growth: Vol. 3, Neurobiology and Nutrition* (pp. 125–144). New York: Plenum.

MacArthur, R. H., & Wilson, E. O. (1967). *The Theory of Island Biogeography.* Princeton, NJ: Princeton Univ. Press.

MacGillivray, I. (1958). Some observations on the incidence of pre-eclampsia. *Journal of Obstetrics and Gynecology of the British Empire, 65,* 536–539.

Mann, A. (1975). Paleodemographic aspects of the South African australopithecines. *University of Pennsylvania Publications in Anthropolgy, 1,* 171–175.

Mann, E. C. (1956). Psychiatric investigation of habitual abortion; preliminary report. *Obstetrics and Gynecology, 7,* 589–601.

Mann, E. C. (1957, April). The role of emotional determinants in habitual abortion. *Surgical Clinics of North America,* 447–458.

Mann, E. C. (1959). Habitual abortion. *American Journal of Obstetrics, 77,* 706–718.

Martin, R. D. (1981). Relative brain size and basal metabolic rate. *Nature (London), 293,* 57–60.

Martin, R. D. (1983). Human brain evolution in an ecological context. *Fifty-second James Arthur Lecture on the Evolution of the Human Brain.* American Museum of Natural History, New York.

Masi, W. (1979). Supplemental stimulation of the premature infant. In T. M. Field, A. M. Sostek, S. Goldberg, & H. H. Shuman (Eds.), *Infants Born at Risk* (pp. 369–387). New York: Scientific Publications.

McDonald, R. L. (1968). The role of emotional factors in obstetric complications: a review. *Psychosomatic Medicine, 30,* 222–237.

McDonald, R. L., & Christakos, A. C. (1963). Relationship of emotional adjustment during pregnancy to obstetric complications. *American Journal of Obstetrics and Gynecology, 86,* 341–348.

Mednick, S. A. (1970). Breakdown in individuals at high risk for schizophrenia: Possible predispositional perinatal factors. *Mental Hygiene, 54,* 50–63.

Mednick, S., Mura, A., Schulsinger, F., & Mednick, B. (1971). Perinatal conditions and infant development in children with schizophrenic parents. *Social Biology, 18* (Suppl.), 5103–5113.

Milne, G. (1971). Spontaneous and septic abortions in the city of Aberdeen. *Journal of Biosocial Science, 3,* 93–95.

Montagu, M. F. A. (1962). *Prenatal influences.* Springfield, IL: Thomas.

Myers, R. E., Hill, D. E., Holt, A. B., Scott, R. E., Mellits, E. D., & Cheek, D. B. (1971). Fetal growth retardation produced by experimental placental insufficiency in the rhesus monkey; I-Body weight, organ size. *Biologica Neonatorium, 18,* 373–394.

Myerscough, P. R. (1974). Normal pregnancy and antenatal care. In W. Passmore & J. Robson (Eds.), *A Companion to Medical Studies* (pp. 39.1–39.17). Oxford: Blackwell.

Nilsson, A., & Almgren, P. E. (1970). Para-natal emotional adjustment. *Acta Psychiatrica Scandinavica, 220,* 9–141.

Niswander, K. R., & Gordon, M. (Eds.). (1972). *The Collaborative Perinatal Study of the National Institute of Neurological Diseases and Stroke: The Women and Their Pregnancies.* Philadelphia, PA: Saunders.

Nuckolls, K. B., Cassel, J., & Kaplan, B. M. (1972). Psychosocial assets, life crisis and prognosis of pregnancy, *American Journal of Epidemiology, 95,* 431–441.

Osofsky, H. J., & Kendall, N. (1973). Poverty as a criterion of risk. *Clinical Obstetrics and Gynecology, 16* (1), 103–119.

Ottinger, D. R., & Simons, J. E. (1964). Behavior of human neonates and prenatal maternal anxiety. *Psychological Reports, 14,* 391–394.

Page, L. B. (1976). Epidemiological evidence on the etiology of human hypertension and its possible prevention. *American Heart Journal, 91,* 527–534.

Pasamanick, B., & Knobloch, H. (1966). Retrospective studies on the epidemology of reproductive casualty: Old and new. *Merrill-Palmer Quarterly, 12,* 7–26.

Pasamanick, B., Rodgers, M., & Lillienfeld, A. M. (1956). Pregnancy experience and the development of behavior disorder in children. *American Journal of Psychiatry, 112,* 613.

Pianka, E. R. (1970). On r- and K-selection. *American Naturalist, 104,* 592–597.

Plotkin, H. C., & Odling-Smee, F. J. (1979). Learning, change, and evolution. *Advances in the Study of Behavior, 10,* 1–41.

Plotkin, H. C., & Odling-Smee, F. J. (1981). A multiple-level model of evolution and its implications for sociobiology. *The Behavioral and Brain Sciences, 4,* 225–268.

Pritchard J. A., & MacDonald, P. C. (1976). *William's Obstetrics.* New York: Appleton.

Reppert, S. M., & Schwartz, W. J. (1983). Maternal coordination of the fetal biological clock in utero. *Science, 27,* 969–971.

Richards, M. P. M. (1979). Conception, pregnancy, and birth—a perspective from developmental psychology. In L. Carenza & L. Zichella (Eds.), *Emotion and Reproduction—Proceedings of the Serono Conference (Vol. 20)* (pp. 1125–1130). New York: Academic Press.

Richards, T. W., & Newberry, H. (1983). Studies in fetal behavior, Ill. Can performance on test items at 6 months postnatally be predicted on the basis of fetal activity? *Child Development, 9,* 79–86.

Roberts, C. J., & Lowe, C. R. (1975). Where have all the conceptions gone? *Lancet, 1* (7905), 498–499.

Rose, R. M. (1980). Endocrine responses to stressful psychological events. *Psychiatric Clinics of North America, 3* (2), 251–276.

Rosenblatt, J. S. (1967). Social-environmental factors affecting reproduction and offspring in infra-human mammals. In S. A. Richardson & A. F. Guttmacher (Eds.), *Childbearing— Its Social and Psychological Aspects* (pp. 245–301). Baltimore, MD: Williams & Wilkins.

Saco-Pollitt, C. (1981). Birth in the Peruvian Andes: Physical and behavioral consequences in the neonate. *Child Development, 52* (3), 839–846.

Salerno, L. J. (1958). Psychophysiologic aspects of the toxemias of pregnancy. *American Journal of Obstetrics and Gynecology, 76,* 1268–1273.

Sameroff, A. (1975). Early influences on development: Fact or fancy? *Merrill-Palmer Quarterly, 21* (4), 267–294.

Sameroff, A., & Chandler, M. (1975). Reproductive risk and the continuum of caretaking casualty. In F. A. Horowitz, H. Hetherington, S. Scarr-Salapatek, & G. Siegal (Eds.), *Review of Child Development Research (Vol. 4,* pp. 187–244). Chicago: Univ. of Chicago Press.

Sameroff, A. J., & Zax, M. (1973). Perinatal characteristics of the offspring of schizophrenic women. *Journal of Nervous and Mental Disease, 157,* 191–199.

Santow, G. (1978). *A Simulation Approach to a Study of Human Fertility.* Leiden: Netherlands International Demographic Institute.

Schulte, F., Schrempf, G., & Minze, G. (1971). Maternal toxemia, fetal malnutrition, and motor behavior. *Pediatrics, 48,* 871–882.

Scotch, N. (1960). A preliminary report on the relations of sociocultural factors to hypertension among the Zulu. *Annals of the New York Academy of Science, 94,* 1000–1009.

Selye, H. (1956). *The Stress of Life,* New York: McGraw-Hill.

Slobodkin, L., & Rapoport, A. (1974). An optimal strategy of evolution. *Quarterly Review of Biology, 49,* 181–200.

Smith, C. R., & Steinschneider, A. (1975). Differential effects of prenatal rhythmic stimulation on neonatal arousal states. *Child Development, 46,* 578–579.

Soichet, S. (1959). Emotional factors in toxemia of pregnancy. *American Journal of Obstetrics and Gynecology, 77,* 1065–1073.

Sontag, L. W. (1941). The significance of fetal environmental differences. *American Journal of Obstetrics and Gynecology, 42,* 996.

Sontag, L. W. (1944). War and fetal maternal relationship. *Marriage and Family Living, 6,* 1–5.

Sontag, L. W. (1963). Somatophysics of personality and body function. *Vita Humanae, 6,* 1–10.

Sontag, L. W. (1966). Implications of fetal behavior and environment for adult personalities. *Annals of the New York Academy of Science, 134,* 782–786.

Sontag, L. W., & Wallace, R. F. (1935). The effect of cigarette smoking during pregnancy upon the fetal heart rate. *American Journal of Obstetrics and Gynecology, 29,* 77–82.

Sosa, E., Kennel, J., Klaus, M., Robertson, S., & Urratia, L. (1980). The effects of a supportive companion on perinatal problems, length of labor and mother-infant interaction. *New England Journal of Medicine, 303,* 597–600.

Spielberger, C. D., & Jacobs, G. A. (1978). Stress and anxiety during pregnancy and labor. In L. Carenza, P. Pancheri, & L. Zichella (Eds.), *Clinical Psychneuroendocrinology of Reproduction* (pp. 261–269). New York: Academic Press.

Stearns, S. C. (1976). Life-history tactics: A review of the data. *Quarterly Review of Biology, 51,* 3–47.

Stone, E. A. (1975). Stress and catecholamines. In A. J. Freidhoff (Ed.), *Cathecholamines and Behavior: 2, Neuropsychopharmacology*, (pp. 31–32). New York: Plenum.

Stott, D. H. (1971). The child's hazards in utero. In J. C. Howells (Ed.), *Modern Perspectives in International Child Psychiatry* (pp. 19–60). New York: Bruner/Mazel.

Stott, D. H. (1973). Follow-up study from birth of the effects of prenatal stress. *Developmental Medicine and Child Neurology, 15*, 770–787.

Super, C. M. (1976). Environmental effects on motor development: The case of African infant precocity. *Developmental Medicine and Child Neurology, 18*, 561–567.

Tinbergen, N. (1951). *The Study of Instinct*. London and New York: Oxford Univ. Press.

Tinbergen, N. (1963). On the aims and methods of ethology. *Zeitschfrift für Tierpsycologie, 20*, 410–433.

Tinbergen, N. (1965). Behavior and natural selection. In J. A. Moore (Ed.), *Ideas in Modern Biology* (Vol. 6 of Proceedings of the XVI International Zoological Congress, Washington, 1963).

Torrey, E. F., Hersh, S. P., & McCabe, K. N. (1975). Childhood psychosis and bleeding during pregnancy. *Journal of Autism and Childhood Schizophrenia, 5*, (4), 287–298.

Trivers, R. L. (1972). Parental investment and sexual selection. In B. Campbell (Ed.), *Sexual Selection and the Descent of Man*, (pp. 136–179). Chicago: Aldine.

Trivers, R. L. (1974). Parent-offspring conflict. *American Zoologist, 249–264*.

Turner, E. K. (1956). The syndrome in the infant resulting from maternal emotional tension during pregnancy. *The Medical Journal of Australia, 43*, 221–222.

Waddington, C. H. (1968). The theory of evolution today. In A. Koestler & J. Smythies (Eds.), *Beyond Reductionism*, (pp. 357–395). New York: Macmillan.

Waddington, C. H. (1975). *The Evolution of an Evolutionist*. Edinburgh: Edinburgh Univ. Press.

Walters, C. E. (1965). Prediction of postnatal development from fetal activity. *Child Development, 36*, 801–808.

Warburton, D., & Fraser, F. C. (1964). Spontaneous abortion risks in man: Data from reproductive histories collected in a medical genetics unit. *American Journal of Human Genetics, 161*, 1–25.

Wasser, S. K., & Barash, D. P. (1983). Reproductive suppression among female mammals: implications for biomedicine and sexual selection theory. *Quarterly Review of Biology, 58*, 513–538.

Weil, R. J., & Stewart, L. C. (1957). The problem of spontaneous abortion. III Psychomatic and interpersonal aspects of habitual abortion. *American Journal of Obstetrics and Gynecology, 73*, 322–328.

Werner, E. E., Bierman, J., & French, F. (1971). *The Children of Kauii*. Honolulu, HI: Univ. of Hawaii Press.

Wilson, E. O. (1975). *Sociobiology: The New Synthesis*. Cambridge, MA: Harvard Univ. Press.

Wigglesworth, J. S. (1966). Foetal growth retardation. *British Medical Bulletin, 22*, 13–15.

Woodson, R. H. (1983). Newborn behavior and the transition to intrauterine life. *Infant Behavior and Development, 6*, 139–145.

Woodson, R. H., Blurton Jones, N. G., da Costa Woodson, E., Pollack, S., & Evans, M. (1979). Fetal mediators of the relationship between increased pregnancy and labour blood pressure and newborn irritability. *Early Human Development, 3*, 127–139.

Zeskind, P. S., & Lester, B. M. (1978). Acoustic features and auditory perceptions of the cries of newborns with prenatal and perinatal complications. *Child Development, 49* (3), 580–589.

4

Sudden Infant Death Syndrome: An Anthropological Hypothesis

MELVIN J. KONNER AND CHARLES M. SUPER

Considerable research effort has been focused on the Sudden Infant Death Syndrome (SIDS), a problematic diagnosis that is now the most frequently identified "cause" of death in infancy in the United States (Kelley & Shannon, 1982; Merritt & Valdes-Dapena, 1984) and England (Murphy, Newcombe, & Sibert, 1982). The incidence is about 2/1000 live births, or about 10,000/year (Bergman, Ray, Pomeroy, Wohl, & Beckwith, 1972; Guntheroth, 1977; Zebal & Friedman, 1984). Cases of suffocation and other obvious differential diagnoses are not included in the category of SIDS or are subtracted from calculations of incidence (Bergman, *et al.,* 1972). Factors proposed to be causally related to at least some of these unexplained deaths vary widely. They include:

Chronic hypoxia (Baker & McGinty, 1977; Cornwell, 1979; Jeffery, Rahilly, & Read, 1983; Naeye, 1974, 1976, 1977; Naeye, Ladis, & Drage, 1976; Shannon, Kelly, & O'Connell, 1977);

Acute hypoxia resulting from sleep apnea or specifically "upper airway apnea" (Guilleminault, Peraita, Souquet, & Dement, 1975; Guilleminault, Ariagno, & Korobkin, 1979; Guilleminault, Ariagno, Souquet, & Dement, 1976; Steinschneider, 1972);

Cardiac conduction disorders (Guilleminault *et al.*, 1976);

Botulism (Marx, 1978; Pottgen & Hillegass, 1977);

Hypoglycemia resulting from pancreatic islet cell hyperplasia (Polak & Wigglesworth, 1976; Cox, Guelpa, & Terrapon, 1976) or impaired gluconeogenesis (Cornwell, 1979);

The Role of Culture
in Developmental Disorder

Undetected respiratory viral infections, especially during the growth of active immunity (Carpenter, Gardner, Pursall, McWeeny, & Emery, 1979; Guntheroth, 1977);

Overheating (Stanton, Scott, & Downham, 1980);

Maternal prenatal drug addiction (Chavez *et al.*, 1979);

Allergy, including hypersensitivity to cow's milk (Guntheroth, 1977);

Gastroesophageal reflux (Jeffery, Raphilly, & Read, 1983; MacFadyen, Hendry, & Simpson, 1983);

Hyperextension of the atlanto-occipital joint leading to acute damage of brain stem respiratory centers (Gilles, Bina, & Sotrel, 1979;);

Autonomic instability (Guilleminault *et al.*, 1976);

Overactive endogenous opioid system (Kuich & Zimmerman, 1981);

Intrinsic chronic hypotonia (Korobkin & Guilleminault, 1979);

Delay in the normal disappearance of fetal brown fat cells (Gadson & Emery, 1976; Naeye, 1974);

Damage to or abnormality of the central nervous system (Anderson-Huntington & Rosenblith, 1976; Naeye, Ladis, & Drage, 1976; Quattrochi, Baba, Liss, & Adrion, 1980);

Characteristics of infant temperament such as low activity and responsiveness (Naeye, Messmer, Specht, & Merritt, 1976);

Inadequate adaptive response to airway obstruction (Purcell, 1976);

Structual features or changes of the respiratory tract (Sasaki, Levine, Laitman, Phil, & Crelin, 1977; Tonkin, 1975); and

Infanticide (Guntheroth, 1977).

Epidemiological studies have identified male sex, low socioeconomic status, feeding techniques other than breast feeding, blood type B, winter or cold climate, ethnicity, maternal age, and passive smoking as possible predisposing factors (Babson & Clarke, 1983; Bergman *et al.*, 1972; Bergman & Wiesner, 1976; Cunningham, 1976; Fleshman & Peterson, 1977; Naeye, Ladis & Drage, 1976; Peterson & Chinn, 1977; Tonkin, 1975). Infants less than 1 month of age are rarely victims; the syndrome is most common between 1 and 5 months of age, with a peak incidence at 2 – 3 months and a declining incidence thereafter (Bergman *et al.*, 1972). Indeed, the specific and narrow age distribution of SIDS is nearly unique among causes of infant death and suggests a window of developmental vulnerability, although its basis remains a mystery.

It is likely that there are several final common pathways for SIDS and a large number of predisposing factors, both intrinsic and environmental. The multiplicity of possibilities and a complex literature of incomplete replications have led some writers to question the status of SIDS as a "syndrome" (Avery & Frantz, 1983). Nevertheless, the possibility of interactions of specific aspects of infant care with predispositions to SIDS has not received adequate consideration, and that is the concern we raise here. Our thesis does not question the potential validity of previously proposed explanations. It calls attention, rather, to a separate cluster of independent variables that has largely eluded the public notice of investigators; specifically, the proximity of infants to primary caretakers during sleep and waking and the associated frequency of feeding and other stimulation. This cluster is salient to the anthropologist because of its extremely distinctive features in 20th-century urban Western cultures.

Comparative Studies of Infant Sleeping Arrangements

Although useful estimates of SIDS are not available from other cultural settings, the unique features of infant care in the United States and other Western industrial societies bear a provocative relationship to some factors relevant to SIDS. Most striking is the high proportion of infants who sleep in a room separate from their parents. A world-wide, cross-cultural study of 90 nonindustrial societies, chosen for mutual independence as cultural units and representative of the world range, found the mother and infant typically sharing the same bed in 41 groups, in different beds in the same room in 19, and in the same room with the bed unspecified by the original ethnographer in 30 societies (Barry & Paxson, 1971). In no society were infants kept in a separate room during the first year, the time of greatest risk for SIDS.

To place the basic human picture in a phyletic context, direct, continuous mother–infant contact during infant sleep is characteristic of all nonhuman higher primates. Experimental disruption of this pattern can be instructive, despite uncertainties in cross-species generalization. In one study using Rhesus monkeys, for example, a mechanical mother surrogate was cooled during the night, leading the infant to withdraw and sleep alone. This proved to have unexpectedly serious consequences, in view of previous experience with such animal models: one infant died during the night, and a second nearly died before reinstitution of the approachable nightly surrogate. Gross and microscopic necropsy revealed no pathological changes other than dehydration (Harlow, Plubell, & Baysinger, 1973).

Possible Consequences of Sleep Arrangements

The consequences for human infants of sleeping in the same room with a caretaker are many. They may include more frequent night feeding and more responsive vigilance on the part of the adult. The more frequent wak-

ing to feed may alter aspects of the sleep cycle, and it is known that SIDS-re-
lated phemonema are differentially associated with stages of sleep and their
transitions (Steinschneider, 1972; Watanabe, Inokuma, & Negoro, 1983).
Sleeping in the same bed with an adult can be expected, in addition, to alter
an infant's microenvironment, for example, to increase auditory stimulation (particularly entraining rhythms from adult breathing), increase somesthetic and perhaps vestibular stimulation, promote heat exchange and
mutual temperature regulation, and increase the concentration of water
vapor and carbon dioxide in the air breathed by the infant. Taken together,
the effects of cosleeping are relevant to at least three phemonena related to
SIDS: sleep apnea, hypoglycemia, and hyperthermia.

Sleep apneas (temporary breathing halts) have been implicated in the
etiology and onset of SIDS, and "spontaneous, pathologically protracted
central apnea" is currently "the most favored hypothesis for crib death"
(Merritt & Valdes-Dapena, 1984; p. 199). Apnea is also implicated in many
"near-miss" cases (Guilleminault et al., 1976, 1979; Steinschneider, 1972),
though others show no respiratory irregularity and there may in fact be
several developmental patterns of respiratory instability (Thoman, Miano,
& Freese, 1975). Based on a variety of theories, investigators have used
warm, mildly oscillating waterbeds or other gentle rocking devices to reduce
apnea and promote regular respiration (Korner, Kraemer, Haffner, &
Cosper, 1975; Korner, 1979; Peterson & Chinn, 1977). They have even been
used to treat asphyxia in neonates at risk (Blurton Jones, Ferreira, Brown, &
MacDonald, 1978). Some of the studies used the estimated rhythm of maternal breathing as the rhythm of oscillation (Korner, 1979). McKenna
(1984, 1987) has paid particular attention to the role of respiratory rhythms
in his analysis of the literature, and his recent laboratory data appear to
support their importance in stimulating regular infant breathing (J. J.
McKenna, personal communication, 1985). The possibility of increased
carbon dioxide concentration in the infant's microenvironment is of note
because CO_2 concentration in the blood stream is a primary mechanism for
stimulating breathing, and recent evidence suggests that chemoreceptors in
the upper respiratory tract may allow an infant to detect carbon dioxide in
the air with similar stimulating effect (Sullivan & Yu, 1983).

Hypoglycemia resulting from impaired gluconeogenesis (Cornwell, 1979;
Lardy, 1975) or pancreatic islet cell hyperplasia (Polak & Wigglesworth,
1976; Cox et al., 1976) may be a factor in some cases of SIDS. The reduced
feeding frequency associated with separate sleeping arrangements may be
relevant to this risk factor. Observations pointing to possible role for com-
promised blood glucose level include: (1) the greater likelihood of SIDS in
cold weather and cold climates, where greater body heat production is required (Bergman et al., 1972); (2) the greater likelihood of SIDS in poorer
and presumably less well-nourished families (Bergman et al., 1972); (3) the

fact that incidence peaks at the age when infants begin to sleep through the night, thus skipping a feeding (Bergman *et al.*, 1972); and (4) evidence that in some instances the victim had refused or vomited the last feeding before sleep (Lardy, 1975; see also Silverstein *et al.*, 1983). These circumstances led to a blind study of levels of three liver gluconeogenic enzymes in SIDS victims and controls (Lardy, 1975). Two of the enzymes did not differ between the groups, but phosphoenolpyruvate carboxykinase (PEPCK) levels were found to be substantially lower in SIDS victims than in victims of other diseases or of accidents. Lardy (1975) argues that under conditions of serious challenge to blood glucose regulatory dynamics, low PEPCK activity might compromise an appropriate adaptive response, resulting in death. If blood glucose dynamics figure in the syndrome, then attention should be given to the possibility that sleeping through the night may increase risk through reduction in feeding frequency and that the maintenance of night feeding during the age of high incidence may thus reduce risk.

The identification of heatstroke as a cause of death in some heavily wrapped infants (Bacon, Scott, & Jones, 1979) led Stanton, Scott, and Downham (1980) to examine 33 consecutive cases of unexplained infant death in two English cities. Fifteen of the cases were excessively clothed or covered at the time of death, and 8 showed histological changes in the small intestine similar to those found in heatstroke. The authors point out that while infants will cry to lowered temperatures, they remain passive to raised ambient temperature (Rutter & Hull, 1979). Others have demonstrated that higher environmental temperature is associated with increased apneic episodes in premature babies (Daily, Klaus, & Meyer, 1969; Steinschneider & Weinstein, 1983). These observations are consistent with the epidemiological findings of higher rates of SIDS in winter or cold months, when infants are more likely to be overdressed and covered; Stanton *et al.*, (1980) cite as one case an 18-week-old boy who was wearing, at death, "a vest and night-gown, covered by two flannelette sheets each folded into eight, with a blanket wrapped round the sheets and the baby, and two more blankets on top" (p. 1055). The findings, in some victims of SIDS, of delayed disappearance of fetal brown fat cells (Gadson & Emery, 1976; Naeye, 1974), which are thought to be involved in the generation of body heat (Hull, 1966), is also relevant. Even though some of the cases presented by Stanton *et al.*, (1980) were attended by their parents just prior to death, it seems possible that physical separation at night decreases the likelihood of parental detection of infant hyperthermia and intervention to restore normal temperature.

The Management of Infant Sleep

The present speculations aside, we know little about the effects of nightly separation and isolation on infants. Since it has not often been conceptualized as a variable by behavioral scientists, it has not been well studied. However, two problems well known to most American parents, bedtime protest and night waking, may be relevant. One widely read child care manual (Spock, 1976) solves the first problem by letting the infant "cry itself to sleep," even if the enragement results in vomiting. Night waking is identified as a problem by 20–30% of English and American mothers of infants (Bergman & Wiesner, 1976; Bernal, 1973; Jenkins, Owen, Bax, & Hart, 1984; Lozoff, Wolf, & Davis, 1985). Since infants sleep separately, they presumably must cry vigorously to be heard. It seems reasonable to raise the possibility that prolonged or exhausting crying at bedtime or during night waking could compromise respiration in infants already at risk, even though SIDS victims do not seem to die during crying spells. It is also perhaps worth noting in this connection that endogenous endorphin release has been shown to be a consequence of physical stress (at least in adults: Carr *et al.,* 1981; Chung & Dickenson, 1980) and a cause of sleep apnea in infants (Chernick, 1981). The respiratory depressant effects of exogenous opiates may thus have a stress-induced natural counterpart (Kuich & Zimmerman, 1981). In addition, in infants whose glucose reserves are marginal, long crying could conceivably deplete them to dangerously low levels. Finally, if prolonged crying were habitual, chronic hypoxia would be more likely, and pathological changes indicative of hypoxia (e.g., fat-laden cells in the corpus callosum) are seen in SIDS victims (Naeye, 1974). The importance of these observations is magnified by recent findings that night waking is (1) more associated with pre- and perinatal factors than with parental behavior (Blurton Jones *et al.,* 1978), and (2) often associated with family illness and other indices of stress (Lozoff, *et al.,* 1985), thus raising the possibility of heightened (1) physiological and (2) environmental risk for night wakers as well.

Infant Sleep Management in Two Nonindustrial Cultures

Data from two nonindustrial societies illustrate their typical minimization of these behavioral problems. The !Kung San of Botswana (like the Siriono, the Copper Eskimo, and other hunting and gathering groups) employ what may be a fundamental human pattern of infant care (Konner, 1980). Almost all infant sleep during the mother's waking hours occurs in a "sling" at the mother's side, in direct contact with her body. The remainder, and all sleep while the mother is asleep, occurs within a foot of her body, if not touching it. Infant sleep and waking follow the infant's rhythm but cause little inconvenience due to the close proximity. Infants suckle about four times per hour during the day. At night they wake repeatedly and are fed and consoled before crying vigorously. Some ad lib night feedings occur without the mother waking, all without her rising from her bed. Questions from visiting anthropologists about rolling over on the infant meet with amused declaration that this does not happen. Mothers' descriptions of the pattern of mutual postural adjustments during the night are reminiscent of those of a conjugal couple in our culture. Fathers may sleep on the same mats (Konner, 1977; Konner & Worthman, 1980).

Currently, of course, hunting and gathering is rare and disappearing among human life styles. The critical aspects of infant care as described for the !Kung can also be found, however, in some relatively traditional agricultural peoples, who do represent a major current adaptive niche. The worldwide study cited earlier indicates the continued closeness of sleeping arrangements in most nonindustrial societies. More detailed data are available from the Kipsigis of Kenya, a Highland Nilotic group in the Western Highlands of Kenya.

Although Kipsigis mothers do not use a sling, they and their child care assistants (usually an older daughter) often carry the baby on the hip, held secure by one hand, or on the back, tied in with a cloth. In addition, young babies frequently sit or rest in the caretaker's lap while she carries out food preparation or other chores. When awake, therefore, the infants are found to be touching the caretakers (through two layers of cloth) over 80% of the time during the first 5 months (Super, 1980). When asleep during the day, this figure drops to about 30%, but the caretaker usually remains within eyesight. At night, the baby sleeps with the mother on a skin or mat on the mud floor, covered with a blanket. Other young children sleep in another bed in the same room, while the father typically sleeps in a separate hut.

The sleep–wake pattern is altered by this proximity of the mother and the associated ease of feeding, as in the !Kung case. Twenty-four-hour sleep records on 10 infants indicate several similarities between the development of sleep patterns in Kipsigis and middle class American infants (Super & Harkness, 1982), but they indicate a divergence in one important aspect: while American babies increase their longest sleep episode from 4 to about 8 h during the first 4 months (satisfying their parents' desire to sleep through the night themselves), the Kipsigis babies do not show this change. Their longest sleep episode increases very little for at least the first 8 months.

During both day and night, nursing is ad lib for the Kipsigis infant, although the mother may be away briefly, in the garden or collecting wild vegetables, as the child grows beyond 3 months of age. In any case, the average number of feeds/24 h remains about 20 during the first 8 months.

In addition to the frequency of feeding and the proximity of caretakers, especially during the night, it is worth mentioning a further aspect of infant care in these and other nonindustrial societies: vastly greater levels of somesthetic and vestibular stimulation that result from body contact. Among both the Kipsigis and the !Kung, infants in the first year are touching their caretaker 2–3 times as often as same-aged Americans, while both awake and asleep (Super, 1980, Fig. 8–1; Konner, 1976, Fig. 10.2). The consequences of high levels of somesthetic and vestibular stimulation are substantial. Experimental studies (Clark, Kreutzberg, & Chee, 1977; Porter, 1972) demonstrate that moderate physical stimulation beyond typical American levels can effect a significant advance in reflexive and gross motor behavior. One study increased the gains in reflex and motor skills, during a 1-month intervention, at a rate four times that found in a matched control group. However, the intervention (80 min of rotation at moderate speed in the lap of the experimenter in an office swivel chair, distributed over the course of a month) appears substantially less than the stimulation resulting from being carried on the hip or back for most of every day while the caretaker forages for food, winnows grain, herds cows to the river, and so on. It is conceivable that the typically subdued American pattern of early vestibular stimulation is inadequate for optimal CNS maturation in some infants, putting them at increased risk or extending the period of risk, for centrally mediated disorders such as sleep apnea and some portion of SIDS.

Intervention

The evidence cited thus far is circumstantial. One intervention study, however, suggests SIDS rates may be open to substantial environmental manipulation, specifically, in this case, through promotion of breast feeding. An association of SIDS rate with bottle feeding (as opposed to breast feeding) has been found in some studies (e.g., Cunningham, 1976), although others, from different countries, have failed to replicate this finding (e.g., Biering-Sorensen, Jorgensen, & Hilden, 1978). Indirect mechanisms such as a varying association with sleep patterns could lead to a variety of relationships in different populations. For example, Elias et al. (1986) have found a substantially higher frequency of night waking in American La Leche League infants whose mothers practice intensive breast feeding, including night feeding, with close mother–infant sleeping proximity. Studies like these call into question the assumption that sleeping through the night in the first six months of life is normal.

In any, event, the Sheffield Intervention Programme (Carpenter et al., 1983) reports a reduction of "possibly preventable" infant deaths from 5.2 to 1.9/1000, where 79% of the "possibly preventable" preintervention cases were SIDS (that is, not attributable to any specific cause; the remainder included death from infectious disease, accidents, and violence). Twelve percent of the decline was attributed to demographic changes during the period of surveillance, 9% to a reduction in precipitate deliveries, and 36% to such factors as increased case conferences, home assessments, and general vigilance promoted by the program. Two specific interventions accounted for the remainder of the decline: 18% by a home visiting program for infants identified as being at high risk, the initial and primary effort; and 24% by the promotion of breast feeding, an intervention prompted by the observation of frequent use of overly concentrated formula. Thus, the increase in breast feeding was the most powerful single identifiable factor in reducing infant deaths from SIDS (and other "preventable" causes) by nearly two-thirds. A number of statistical assumptions are employed to arrive at this estimate, and the authors are appropriately cautious about the attributions of cause. Nevertheless, the results are striking not only for their demonstration of a reduction in SIDS but also for the fact that this reduction was effected through a relatively simple change in infant care strategy, one well within the range of normal societal variation, that somehow altered the environmental risk for, presumably, some portion of biologically vulnerable infants.

It is not possible to know in the absence of other information why breast feeding reduced mortality in the Sheffield study. One possibility is that it altered the pattern of night feeding and thus night sleeping. The inconsistent epidemiological reports suggesting some factor closely but not invariably associated with breast feeding are compatible with this interpretation. It has been noted that regional and national estimates of SIDS incidence range widely (see Valdez-Dapena, 1980). The Sheffield results raise the possibility that differences in infant care may contribute significantly to this variation, although no appropriate cross-national analysis has been carried out, and differential reporting is likely to be the major determinant of the variation.

New Research Questions and a Caution

Our purpose in drawing attention to child care variables in relation to SIDS is not to lessen the importance of other factors such as prematurity, dysmaturity, or upper respiratory infection nor is it to add to the potential burden of undeserved guilt SIDS parents often bear, nor necessarily to suggest a major change in American infant care. It is to point to a new paradigm for research on infants at risk, namely, to examine disorders such as SIDS in light of preurban, preindustrial techniques of rearing, particularly those that are likely to have existed as our general species characteristics were established. The contrast between current practices and those more typical of our species can be especially illuminating.

Evolutionary or anthropological studies, however, can only raise questions; they cannot point to solutions. If observations suggest we have departed in some sense from a "natural" infant care adaptation, the solution may also be novel, such as apnea monitors, oscillating waterbeds, and other mechanical devices for infants found to be at risk. Further, in view of a tendency in some quarters to identify "natural" modes of child care with exclusively maternal ones, we note that fathers too have warm, mildly oscillating bodies and are capable of stimulating infants during apnea episodes, consoling them before whimpering becomes crying, and feeding them often enough to prevent declines in blood glucose.

The modern, urban, middle-class method of infant care is clearly superior in several respects to that of hunter–gatherers and subsistence farmers, for instance, in the prevention of infection and nutritional deficit. In addition, adoption of nonindustrial patterns may have different consequences for urban middle-class families than they have in other cultural contexts. The chance of suffocation during cosleeping, for example, however small it is, may be greater on a soft mattress with many blankets than on a skin mat on the ground. More generally, patterns of infant care are intimately related to many aspects of family life, mothers' chores and responsibilities, and the child's later development, in ways which the social and behavioral sciences are only now beginning to investigate (Super, 1980), and it is a universal observation of anthropologists that artificial introduction of culture change has many unforseen effects, sometimes unfortunate ones.

Nevertheless, carefully monitored behavioral interventions, such as the Sheffield Intervention Programme, have been shown profoundly to affect environmentally related, "possibly preventable" deaths. In addition, if one carefully considers the known risks of cosleeping in urban Western cultures, the problem of fatality from suffocation or "overlaying," rarely reported in the medical literature, must be weighed against fatalities from alternatives such as unsafe cribs (Smialek, Smialek, & Spitz, 1977; Bass, Kravath, & Glass, 1986).

While the circumstantial evidence presented here does not recommend any single course of prevention or treatment, it does indicate possible infant care variables worth investigating concerning infants found to be at risk. Infant care practices long accepted by our culture, and endorsed by parents as well as professionals, may provide a background of risk for the incidence of SIDS or for related deaths not included in the SIDS category such as those associated with suffocation. For some portion of cases of the syndrome perhaps we should return to the earlier diagnosis of "crib death," if the crib, by isolating the infant, in fact plays a role in the etiology.

Acknowledgments

The preparation of this paper was supported in part by grants to Konner from the Social Science Research Council, the National Institute of Mental Health (grant number MH-33685), the National Science Foundation, the John Simon Guggenheim Foundation, and the Center for Advanced Study in Behavior Sciences, and to Super from the William T. Grant Foundation, the Carnegie Corporation of New York, and the National Institute of Mental Health (grant number 33281). We thank Marjorie Elias, Sarah Harkness, Lawrence Konner, and James McKenna for helpful discussions. All statements made and opinions expressed are the sole responsibility of the authors.

References

Anderson-Huntington, R. B., & Rosenblith, J. F. (1976). Central nervous system damage as a possible component of unexpected deaths in infancy. *Developmental Medicine and Child Neurology, 18,* 480–492.

Avery, M. E., & Frantz, I. D. (1983). To breathe or not to breathe. What have we learned about apneic spells and sudden infant death? *New England Journal of Medicine, 309,* 107–108.

Babson, S. G., & Clarke, N. G. (1983). Relationship between infant death and maternal age. *Journal of Pediatrics, 103*(3), 391–393.

Bacon, C., Scott, D., & Jones, P. (1979). Heatstroke in well-wrapped infants. *Lancet, 1,* 422–425.

Baker, T. L., & McGinty, D. J. (1977). Reversal of cardiopulmonary failure during active sleep in hypoxic kittens: Implications for sudden infant death. *Science, 198,* 419–421.

Barry, H. III, & Paxson L. M. (1971). Infancy and early childhood: Cross-cultural codes 2. *Ethnology, 10,* 446–508.

Bass, M. Kravath. R. E., and Glass, L. (1986). Death-scene investigation in sudden infant death. *New England Journal of Medicine, 315,* 100–105.

Bergman, A. B., Ray, C. G., Pomeroy, M. A., Wahl, P. W., & Beckwith, J. B. (1972). Studies of the sudden infant death syndrome in King County, Washington. III Epidemiology. *Pediatrics, 49,* 860–870.

Bergman, A. B., & Wiesner, L. A. (1976). Relationship of passive cigarette-smoking to sudden infant death syndrome. *Pediatrics, 58,* 665–668.

Bernal, J. (1973). Night waking in infants during the first fourteen months. *Developmental Medicine and Child Neurology, 15,* 760–769.

Biering-Sorensen, F., Jorgensen, T., & Hilden, J. (1978). Sudden infant death in Copenhagen 1956–1971. I. Infant feeding. *Acta Paediatrica Scandanavia, 67,* 129–137.

Blurton Jones N., Ferreira M. C. R., Brown, M. F., & MacDonald B. L. (1978). The association between perinatal factors and later night waking. *Developmental Medicine and Child Neurology, 20,* 427–434.

Carpenter, R. G., Gardner, A., Jepson, M., Taylor, E. M., Salvin, A., Sunderland, R., Emery, J. L., Pursall, E., Roe, J., & The Health Visitors of Sheffield. (1983). Prevention of unexpected infant death: Evaluation of the first seven years of the Sheffield Intervention Programme. *Lancet, 1,* 723–727.

Carpenter, R. G., Gardner, A., Pursall, E., McWeeny, P. M., & Emery, J. L. (1979). Identification of some infants at immediate risk of dying unexpectedly and justifying intensive study. *Lancet, 2,* 343–346.

Carr, D. B., Bullen, B. A., Sbriner, G. S., Arnold, M. A., Rosenblatt, M., Beitins, I. Z., Martin, J. B., & McArthur, J. W., (1981). Physical conditioning facilitates the exercise-induced secreton of β-endorphin and β-lipotropin in women. *New England Journal of Medicine, 305,* 560–563.

Chavez, C. J., Ostrea, E. M., Stryker, J. C., & Smialek, Z. (1979). Sudden infant death syndrome among infants of drug-dependent mothers. *Pediatrics, 95,* 407–409.

Chernick, V. (1981). Endorphines and ventilatory control. *New England Journal of Medicine, 304,* 1277–1278.

Chung, S-H., & Dickenson, A. (1980). Pain, enkephalin and acupuncture. *Nature (London)*, *283*, 243–244.

Clark, D. L., Kreutzberg, J. R., & Chee, F. K. W. (1977). Vestibular stimulation influence on motor development in infants. *Science, 196,* 1228–1229.

Cornwell, A. C. (1979). Sudden infant death syndrome: A testable hypothesis and mechanism. *International Journal of Neuroscience, 10,* 31–44.

Cox, J. M., Guelpa, G., & Terrapon, M. (1976). Islet-cell hyperplasia and sudden infant death. *Lancet, 2,* 739–740.

Cunningham, A. S. (1976). Infant feeding and SIDS. *Pediatrics, 58,* 467–468.

Daily, W. J. R., Klaus, M., & Meyer, H. B. P. (1969). Apnea in premature infants: Monitoring, incidence, heart rate changes, and an effect on environmental temperature. *Pediatrics, 43,* 510–518.

Elias, M. F., Nicolson, N. A., Bora, C., & Johnston, J. (1986). Sleep/wake patterns of breast-fed infants in the first two years of life. *Pediatrics, 77,* 322–329.

Fleshman, J. K., & Peterson, D. R. (1977). The sudden infant death syndrome among Alaskan natives. *American Journal of Epidemiology, 105,* 555–558.

Gadson, D. R., & Emery, J. L. (1976). Fatty change in the brain in perimatal and unexpected death. *Archives of Disease in Childhood, 51,* 42–48.

Gilles, F. H., Bina, M., & Sotrel, A. (1979). Infantile atlanto-occipital instability. *American Journal of Diseases of Children, 133,* 30–37.

Guilleminault, C., Ariagno, R., & Korobkin, R. (1979). Mixed and obstructive sleep apnea and near miss for sudden infant death syndrome: 2. Comparison of near miss and normal control infants by age. *Pediatrics, 64,* 882–891.

Guilleminault, C., Ariagno, R., Souquet, M., & Dement, W. C. (1976). Abnormal polygraphic findings in near-miss sudden infant death. *Lancet, 1,* 1326–1327.

Guilleminault, C., Peraita, R., Souquet, M., & Dement, W. C. (1975). Apneas during sleep in infants: Possible relationship with sudden infant death syndrome. *Science, 190,* 677–679.

Guntheroth, W. G. (1977). Sudden infant death syndrome (crib death). *American Heart Journal, 93,* 784–793.

Harlow, H. F., Plubell, P. E. & Baysinger, C. M. (1973). Induction of psychological death in rhesus monkeys. *Journal of Autism and Childhood Schizophrenia, 3,* 299–307.

Hull, D. (1966). The structure and function of brown adipose tissue. *British Medical Bulletin, 22,* 92–96.

Jeffery, H. E., Raphilly, P., & Read, D. J. C. (1983). Multiple causes of asphyxia in infants at high risk for sudden infant death. *Archives of Disease in Childhood, 58,* 92–100.

Jenkins, S., Owen, C., Bax, M., & Hart, H. (1984). Continuities of common behavior problems in preschool children. *Journal of Child Psychology and Psychiatry, 25*(1), 75–89.

Kelley, D. H., & Shannon, D. C. (1982). Sudden infant death syndrome and near sudden infant death syndrome: A review of the literature, 1964 to 1982. *Pediatric Clinics of North America, 29*(5), 1241–1261.

Konner, M. J. (1976). Maternal care, infant behavior and development among the !Kung. In R. B. Lee & I. DeVore (Eds.), *Kalahari hunter-gatherers: Studies of the !Kung and their neighbors* (pp. 218–245). Cambridge, MA: Harvard Univ. Press.

Konner, M. J. (1977). Infancy among the Kalahari Desert San. In P. H. Liederman, S. Tulkin, & A. Rosenfeld (Eds.), *Culture and infancy: Variations in the human experience* (pp. 287–328). New York: Academic Press.

Konner, M. J. (1980). Evolution of human behavioral development: An interpretive review. In R. L. Munroe, R. H. Munroe & B. B. Whiting (Eds.), *Handbook of cross-cultural human development* (pp. 3–51). New York: Garland Press.

Konner, M. J., & Worthman, C. (1980). Nursing frequency, gonadal function and birth spacing among !Kung hunter-gatherers. *Science, 207,* 788–791.

Korner, A. F. (1979). Maternal rhythms and waterbeds: A form of intervention with premature infants. In E. B. Thoman (Ed.), *Origins of the infant's social responsiveness* (pp. 95–124). Hillsdale, NJ: Lawrence Erlbaum Associates.

Korner, A. F., Kraemer, H. C., Haffner, M. E., & Cosper, L. M. (1975). Effects of waterbed flotation on premature infants: A pilot study. *Pediatrics, 56,* 361–367.

Korobkin, R., & Guilleminault, C. (1979). Neurologic abnormalities in near miss for sudden infant death syndrome infants. *Pediatrics, 64,* 369–374.

Kuich, T. E., & Zimmerman, D. (1981). Endorphins, ventilatory control, and sudden infant death syndrome—a review and synthesis. *Medical Hypotheses, 7*(10), 1231–1240.

Lardy, H. A. (1975, July). *Defective phosphoenolpyruvate carboxykinase in victims of sudden infant death syndrome.* Paper presented at the first annual conference on sudden infant death syndrome, National Institutes of Health, Bethesda, MD.

Lozoff, B., Wolf, A. W., & Davis, N. S. (1985). Sleep problems seen in pediatric practice. *Pediatrics, 75*(3), 477–483.

MacFadyen, U. M., Hendry, G. M. A., & Simpson, H. (1983). Gastro-oesophageal reflux in near-miss sudden infant death syndrome or suspected recurrent aspiration. *Archives of Disease in Childhood, 58,* 87–91.

Marx, J. L. (1978). Botulism in infants: A cause of sudden death? *Science, 201,* 799–801.

McKenna, J. J. (1987). An anthropological perspective on Sudden Infant Death Syndrome (SIDS): The role of parental breathing cues and speech breathing adaptations. *Medical Anthropology* (in press).

Merritt, T. A., & Valdes-Dapena, M. (1984). SIDS Research Update. *Pediatric Annals, 13*(3), 193–207.

Murphy, J. F., Newcombe, R. G., & Sibert, J. R. (1982). The epidemiology of sudden infant death syndrome. *Journal of Epidemiology and Community Health, 36,* 17–21.

Naeye, R. L. (1974). Hypoxemia and the sudden infant death syndrome. *Science, 186,* 837–838.

Naeye, R. L. (1976). Brain stem and adrenal abnormalities in the sudden infant death syndrome. *American Journal of Clinical Pathology, 66,* 526–530.

Naeye, R. L. (1977). The sudden death syndrome. *Archives of Pathological Laboratory Medicine, 101,* 165–167.

Naeye, R. L., Fisher, R., Ryser, M., & Whalen, P. (1976). Carotid body in the sudden infant death syndrome. *Science, 191,*567–569.

Naeye, R. L., Ladis, B., & Drage, J. S. (1976). Sudden infant death syndrome. *American Journal of the Diseases of Children, 130,* 1207–1210.

Naeye, R. L., Messmer, J. III, Specht, T., & Merrit, T. A. (1976). Sudden infant death syndrome temperament before death. *Journal of Pediatrics, 88,* 511–515.

Peterson, D. R., & Chinn, N. M. (1977). Sudden infant death trends in six metropolitan communities, 1965–1974, *Pediatrics, 60,* 75–79.

Polak, J. M., & Wigglesworth, J. S. (1976). Islet-cell hyperplasia and sudden infant death. *Lancet, 2*(798), 570–571.

Porter, L. S. (1972). The impact of physical-physiological activity on infants' growth and development. *Nursing Research, 21,* 210–219.

Pottgen, P., & Hillegass, L. (1977). Botulism and sudden infant death. *Lancet, 1,* 147–148.

Purcell, M. (1976). Response in the newborn to raised upper airway resistance. *Archives of Disabilities in Children, 51,*(8), 602–607.

Quattrochi, J. J., Baba, N., Liss, L., & Adrion, W. (1980). Sudden infant death syndrome (SIDS): A preliminary study of reticular dendritic spines in infants with SIDS. *Brain Research, 181,* 245–249.

Rutter, N., & Hull, D. (1979). Response of term babies to a warm environment. *Archives of Disease in Childhood, 54,* 178–183.

Sasaki, C. T., Levine, P. A., Laitman, J. T., Phil, M., & Crelin, E. S. (1977). Postnatal descent of the epiglottis in man. *Archives of Otolaryngology, 103,* 169–171.

Shannon, D. C., Kelly, D. H., & O'Connell, K. (1977). Abnormal regulation of ventilation in infants at risk for sudden-infant-death syndrome. *The New England Journal of Medicine, 297,* 747–750.

Silverstein, R., Nelson, C. L., Lin C., *et al.* (1983). Enzyme stability and SIDS: Studies with phosphoenolpyruvate carboxykinase. In J. T. Tildon, L. M. Roeder, & A. Steinschneider (Eds.), *Sudden infant death syndrome* (pp. 233–242). New York: Academic Press.

Smialek, J. E., Smialek, P. Z., & Spitz, W. U. (1977). Accidental bed deaths in infants due to unsafe sleeping situations. *Clinical Pediatrics, 16,* 1031–1036.

Spock, B. (1976). *Baby and Child Care.* New York: Simon and Schuster.

Stanton, A. N., Scott, D. J., & Downham, M. A. P. (1980). Is overheating a factor in some unexpected infant deaths? *Lancet, 1,* 1054–1057.

Steinschneider, A. (1972). Prolonged apnea and the sudden infant death syndrome: Clinical and laboratory observations. *Pediatrics, 50,* 646–654.

Steinschneider, A., & Weinstein, S. (1983). Sleep respiratory instability in term nenates under hyperthermic conditions: Age, sex, type of feeding, and rapid eye movements. *Pediatric Research, 17*(1), 35–41.

Sullivan, T. Y., & Yu, P. C. (1983). Airway anesthesia effects on hypercapnic breathing pattern in humans. *Journal of Applied Physiology, 55,* 368–376.

Super, C. M. (1980). Behavioral development in infancy. In Munroe, R. H., Munroe, R. L., & Whiting, B. B. (Eds.), *Handbook of cross-cultural human development* (pp. 181–270). New York: Garland Press.

Super, C. M. & Harkness, S. (1982). The infant's niche in rural Kenya and metropolitan America. In Adler, L. L. (Ed.), *Cross-cultural research at issue* (pp. 47–56). New York: Academic Press.

Thoman, E. B., Miano, V. N., & Freese, M. P. (1975). *The role of respiratory instability in SIDS.* Paper presented at the International Society for Developmental Psychobiology, New York.

Tonkin, S. (1975). Sudden infant death syndrome: Hypothesis of causation. *Pediatrics, 55,* 650–661.

Valdes-Dapena, M. A. (1980). Sudden infant death syndrome: A review of the medical literature 1974–1979. *Pediatrics, 66,* 597–614.

Watanabe, K., Inokuma, K., & Negoro, T. (1983). REM sleep prevents sudden infant death syndrome. *European Journal of Pediatrics, 140,* 289–292.

Zebal, B. H., & Friedman, S. B. (1984). *Pediatic Annals, 13*(3), 188–190.

5

Alternatives to Mother – Infant Attachment in the Neonatal Period

MARTEN W. DEVRIES

Mothers and babies have been of scholarly interest at least since Hippocrates wrote the *Third Book of Epidemics* in the fourth century B.C. (Adams, 1886). In the 19th century, Esquirol (1838) and Marcé (1858) focused attention on the range of adverse maternal reactions observed during the "postpartum" period. Today, while developmental psychologists, with intensive studies of early mother – infant interaction, have uncovered the neonate's capacity and readiness for interaction (Lewis & Rosenblum, 1974; Hofer, 1975), maternal behavior during the postpartum period remains less understood. Following the work of Bowlby (1952) and Ainsworth (1973) on infant attachment, Klaus and Kennell (1975) postulated a reciprocal readiness for attachment on the part of the mother soon after birth. Relying on clinical observations and animal behavior studies, they offered the provocative hypothesis that there is a "sensitive period" for maternal attachment during the postpartum period. In Klaus and Kennell's formulation, maternal activities with the newborn after delivery were likened to behavior patterns observed across many mammalian species. Accordingly, they advocated recognition of a postpartum maternal – infant bonding period, with the goal that clinical practice might facilitate rather than hinder mother – infant interaction.

Their clinically useful and influential idea fit with the Western ideal of the instant attachment and joy of motherhood and the need to reform rigid hospital practices. This romantic view of motherhood was generally ac-

The Role of Culture
in Developmental Disorder

cepted. Almost as a crusade, "bonding" became a primary orientation in obstetric and pediatric practice, as well as in the culture at large.

The variety of maternal responses to the newborn have been obscured by this sole focus on mother–infant attachment. Observations in other cultures, in the Western delivery room, as well as maternal reports after delivery present a more perplexing picture. Consider this clinical vignette by Leboyer:

> Many mothers do not know how to touch their babies. Or, to be more exact, do not dare. They are paralyzed. Many will not admit it. Or are even conscious of it. But it is true never the less, if you can recognize the signs. There is something that restrains these mothers. Some profound in inhibition . . . Seized by a profound confusion she no longer knows what she feels for this "thing" that is there, on her belly. An immense disgust? A passionate interest?" (Leboyer, 1975, p. 72).

Films of delivery room behavior show women turning away from their babies, occasionally with facial expressions of disgust (MacFarlane, 1977). In other studies women describe feelings of unfamiliarity, indifference, and strangeness toward their infant immediately after delivery that persist through the first few days of life (Robson & Moss, 1970; Robson & Kumar, 1980). In one large study, 65% of the mothers after normal delivery evaluated their infants negatively or worse than the average infant (Broussard & Hartman, 1971). These feelings were absent at 1- and 4-month follow-ups, leading the authors to conclude that during the first and second days postpartum, maternal perception of the newborn is in a fluid state. Obstetrical texts often briefly state that it is very common for women to feel apathetic, detached, and uninterested in the newborn for the first few days (Beescher & Mackey, 1979). Moreover, the most updated publications of Klaus and Kennell (1983, p. 37) suggest that feelings of love "are not instantaneous" with the initial contact. Great individual variation in maternal response actually exists and most women describe a peak of positive emotions toward the infant at the end of the first week. The timing of these emotion is greatly influenced by newborn behavior and other factors (Levy, 1958; MacFarlane, 1977).

These observations draw attention to an univestigated aspect of maternal behavior in the normal mother, characterized by distance, negative feelings, and strangeness toward the infant after delivery. In pondering these findings MacFarlane (1977) states that until this century, childbirth often ended in death. Under these conditions, it is unlikely that an immediate tie between mother and infant would have evolved. She views the behaviors in the postpartum period as illustrating that the special relationship between mother and infant develops over a period of time. The gradual growth of attachment, however, has greater implications for understanding maternal behavior than the managing of neonatal death. It suggests that a variety of alternative maternal responses are possible, including the rejection of the offspring and even infanticide. Consider this example, recorded by a hidden camera. In an New Guinea tribe, a woman sits fatigued in a forest clearing after a long labor, staring with indifference at her normal female infant. Listlessly, she reaches for nearby leaves and shrubs and covers the naked, struggling form before her. First the face and then the torso are covered. Just the arms and feet remain as the mother passes her placenta and walks away (Schiffelbein, 1975). This remarkable film shows that women do not just blissfully surrender to reproductive orientations. Women, over time and across cultures, have had to regulate their fertility and endure the inadvertent death of their neonates (Dumond, 1977; Spencer, 1949). Furthermore, mothers with already living children to whom they are devoted and mothers who will go on to bear other children may choose to rear or not rear a given infant. The stereotypical view of the hormonally driven postpartum female coerced by internal forces to exhibit bonding behavior seems improbable given these realities. In actuality a range of maternal behavior is observed, including loving feelings, detachment, ambivalence, as well as calm rejection. The postpartum period rather than a time for programed attachment is best thought of as a decision-making time during which exploration of the infants as well as reckoning with psychological, social, and economic resources take place. Most commonly this culminates in acceptance of the offspring, "attachment," but in certain cases, in rejection. The evidence for maternal attachment and other perspectives on the postpartum period then need to be explored.

Maternal Attachment Research

Klaus and Kennell (1975, 1983) consider the immediate postpartum period a crucial time for the development of maternal attachment to the newborn and submit evidence for a pattern of maternal behavior which "lock" mother and infant together. This behavior pattern includes a high-pitched maternal voice to which the infant orients and a sequence in which the mother first touches the infant only with her fingers and then gradually progresses to grasping the infant fully with her palms and hands. In this manner, the mother explores the infant's body: first the extremities, then the trunk, and ending with the eyes, eye-to-eye contact ("enface"). Klaus and Kennell reported that mothers who had $\frac{1}{2}$ h of contact with their infants during the first 12 h were more attached later in the postpartum period than mothers who had no contact. They further held that early contact resulted in more mother – infant interaction in the first year (Carlsson, 1978) and produced evidence that these infants had higher IQs (deChateau & Wielberg,

1977b). Klaus and Kennell thus concluded that the finger-to-palm exploration of the newborn and "enface" behavior during the first hours consolidated attachment, which in turn was beneficial for the infant's development. Accordingly, they viewed the postpartum period as a crucial "sensitive period" for maternal attachment and advised against hospital policies that separated mother and infant after delivery.

Many studies followed that questioned the critical nature of the immediate postpartum period for maternal attachment and infant development. Some suggested that the effects of early contact were unimportant or short-lived (Sosa, 1978; Hales, Trause, & Kennel, 1976) and that long-term effects were either not significant (Egeland & Vaughn, 1981) or complexly interrelated with other factors (Lynch, 1975). Critics of the sensitive period notion often based their arguments on sampling problems (Liederman, 1978), lack of generalizibility across samples (Svejda, Campos, & Emde, 1980), and lack of attention to cultural issues (Lozoff, Brittenham, Trause, Kennell, & Klaus, 1977). Other researches stressed the important role played by maternal experience (Lynch, 1975; Liederman, 1978) and current personal relationships (Minde *et al.,* 1978). Yet others pointed to the influence of the actual process and quality of the birth experience for the woman and family (Peterson & Mehl, 1978). These studies document the multiple factors that influence mothers after delivery. They suggest that maternal behavior is not directly released or consolidated at childbirth as Klaus and Kennell had predicted. Instead the development of affection for the newborn seems to appear gradually, the result of a flexible system of maternal perceptions that evolve throughout pregnancy and delivery, in concert with environmental and personal variables.

It appears that Klaus and Kennell, while correcting an error in pediatric and obstetrical care, overemphasized the developmental importance of their maternal bonding theory. Their work, however, underscores an important aspect of the postpartum period by assigning the mother's feelings and reactions a more central and, most important, active role after delivery. If we then emphasize more the evaluative and investigative nature of early contact for the mother and less its more traditionally assumed receptive aspects, as well as taking the social and personal factors impinging on maternal behavior into account, an alternative perspective on the postpartum period becomes possible.

Postpartum Reactions

While pregnancy and delivery may be a rewarding and life-fulfilling experience, a woman's acceptance of motherhood is also a complex and often conflicted process. In some societies pregnancy and childbirth provide women with higher social status, and in most other, ego gratification through mastering a difficult period (Bibring, 1959). But motherhood also results in the relinquishing of previous interests, relationships, and work functions, changes which are often accompanied by anger and sadness (Douglas, 1963; Yalom *et al.*, 1968). The pregnancy may also make a woman uncomfortable, and its physical manifestations may expose her to stereotypic tales of danger, praise, and at times ridicule. Mixed feelings naturally accompany this process. The psychological experience of pregnancy is often described as accompanied by regressive and vulnerable feelings (Shereshkefsky & Yarrow, 1973). These culminate in the abrupt transition of labor and delivery, during which some disequilibrium of the personality is often experienced (Bibring, 1959). For example, a study of 98 new mothers with normal infants and deliveries showed that 30% had marked emotional reactions during the first days postpartum that impaired cognitive functions as measured by a number of psychometric tests (Gorden, Kupestens, & Gorden, 1963; Jarrah-Zadeh *et al.*, 1964). While neuroendocrine changes are often cited as causing these postpartum feelings, these data remain controversial and mixed, and no tested neurological (Slotnick, 1975) or hormonal (Zarrow, Rosenberg, & Sock, 1972) explanations are available (Brockington & Kumar, 1982). The impairments may also be viewed as reactions to the crisis of delivery (Chertok, 1969), and indeed the typical crisis reaction (Lindemann, 1944; Hirschowitz, 1973) depicts rather well the indifference, ambivalence, negative feelings, uncertainties, and gradual resolution of feelings described during the postpartum period.

Psychological studies, however, differentiate the type of reactions and exacerbating factors that occur after delivery from problems experienced in pregnancy and at other times of stress in a woman's life (Nilsson & Almgren, 1970; Harder, 1967; Hamilton, 1962). These studies point to the unique quality and etiology of postpartum symptoms. The female pioneers in psychoanalysis, Deutsch (1945) and Bibring (1959), had discussed these symptoms in detail. Although views differ, a typical psychodynamic formulation likens postpartum symptoms and feelings to reactions to the loss of any part of the body, frequently seen in surgical patients postoperatively, which goes as follows. Normal women experience the fetus as a part of their own body, in particular as part of their body image. Then during childbirth this part of the self is removed and lost; many women react to this loss with a very brief spell of mild depression — the "postpartum blues" (Yalom *et al.*, 1968). In normal women this is a self-limiting reaction and is quickly followed by the establishment of an affectionate and loving relationship with the newborn baby. Some women, however, are unable to accept the loss of the baby, a part of themselves, in the process of delivery and to relate to it in a mature and loving way. Yet other women may develop an urge to destroy something they feel is a bad part of themselves. This bad part is only too easily identified with the baby, especially if the baby is experienced as a foreign body and not a thing to be loved (Asch, 1968).

These formulations suggest that postpartum reactions and depressive states develop in women who have never been able to deal adequately with the problems of loss and separation in the course of their own childhood and maturation. The expression of unloving feelings by the mother are essentially viewed as abnormal and linked to idiosyncratic life history and developmental variables (Carloni & Nobeli, 1976). Rheingold (1964, 1967) challenges this view and offers the provocative hypothesis that negative and hostile thoughts are not only normal but extremely widespread maternal reactions after delivery. After extensive maternal interviews he describes the prevalence of maternal death wishes toward the infant and postulates a powerful urge to "undo" motherhood. He traces the origin of both infanticidal wishes and postpartum depressive states not to hostility toward the child itself but, rather, to a woman's need to sacrifice the child to propitiate her own mother. He adds that infanticidal impulses were described by some women as problematic and frightening, while others treated them quite normally and casually. Psychoanalysts, then, whether they consider infanticidal feelings normal or abnormal tend to interpret them in terms of unconscious processes generated in individuals through the internalization of earlier relationships, such as those with their mothers. Bloch (1978), arguing from a different perspective, states that infanticidal feelings are widespread and that children seem to have an almost "built-in" fear of infanticide and that fairy tales as well as life styles may be designed to expunge these fears.

The anthropologist, Cowlishaw (1978), counters these psychological formulations with a study among Australian aboriginals. He states that infanticidal wishes are not the result of identification with the mother but originate in the conscious resentment toward the father, brother, and husband generated by the day-to-day reality of social life. In this formulation infanticidal wishes are not viewed as unconscious processes but as experienced emotions that result in consciously planned social and relational adjustments of which infanticide may be a part.

The above descriptions disagree on the processes but not on the existence of hostile or infanticidal emotions toward the newborn after delivery. The psychological literature further presents a picture of the uniqueness of the postpartum period. It offers the crisis paradigm, reactions to loss, the cognitive disruption created by transition, and the influence of previous experience as possible explanations for the timing and the variety of behaviors observed. Epidemiological studies of the postpartum period have not clarified these issues (Bluglass, 1978, Brockington & Kumar, 1982), and most theories remain incomplete or only partially supportable. The idea that not only negative feelings but also infanticidal wishes are a normal part of the birth domain offers a provocative counterpart to current maternal attachment formulations. Examining the historical and cross-cultural incidence of infanticide should then prove instructive.

Infanticide

Along with postwar inquiries into alternatives to mother-centered infant care (Rich, 1976) and social (Spiro, 1965), as well as paternal (Parke, 1979), responsibility for child care, a literature emerged that questioned basic ideas about motherhood (Badinter, 1981). These writings stressed the complexity of a woman's social role, highlighted the notion of offspring rejection, and offered rather unpopular news about infanticide. This perspective illuminates the nature and timing of maternal bonding in another light and suggests that infanticide may not be an abnormal human event and that in certain psychological and cultural contexts it may be understood as a sensible maternal strategy.

While at first infanticide may seems a repugant, rare, and remote varient of maternal behavior, these accounts suggest that it is deeply rooted in the history of both Western and non-Western cultures (Trexler, 1974). Available information on infanticide shows that it may entail the intentional destruction of the infant soon after birth through abandonment, exposure, or violent means or may involve less direct forms of parental behavior which decrease the likelihood of infant survival, such as neglect, nutritional discrimination, and other forms of inadequate infant care. Because infanticide is rarely advertized and may or may not be socially sanctioned, we must often rely on indirect inferences from historical accounts and demographic data, but surprisingly, much information is available.

Infanticide in Historical Perspective

Infanticide may have been systematically used to control family size, accounting for the fertility shifts described in human populations during the paleolithic period (Bakan, 1971; Carr-Saunders, 1972). In antiquity the killing or abandonment of legitimate and illegitimate offspring was regularly practiced. All the infants with inappropriate behavior, shape, or size were exposed to the environment or killed directly (deMauss, 1974). Literary sources mentioning infanticide during the middel ages are numerous (Kellum, 1974; Pier, 1978). Later in 18th-century France, infanticide seems to have been used as a prevalent form of birth control (Shorter, 1974). The incidence of abandonment and infanticide were related to increased grain prices, which stressed the domestic capabilities of the family. Foundling homes apparently further stimulated the desertion of offspring, most of whom perished in the overcrowded institutions. One home in France received 164,319 infants in 1830 alone (Langer, 1979). The value of infants, little enough to start with, rose and fell with economic fluctuations.

In the 19th century, birth control and safer abortion alternatives released living infants from large-scale reproductive control measures, and a decrease in infant mortality and marital fertility was recorded (deMauss, 1974). In spite of these changes infanticide still occurs. In 1966, 1 out of every 21 murders in the United States was of a child murdered by his parents (Resnick, 1972). Even in highly regulated societies such as West Germany, between 1968 and 1974, 899 child murders were recorded (Dorman, 1975); 25% of these were newborns, and 47% were carried out by the mothers. In Japan, infanticide has occurred across social class and geographic areas at rates of up to 25% of live births until 1940 (Dickeman, 1975). The breakdown of the family (Yamagami, Nakata, Rukushima, & Sanra, 1975), maternal stress in the demanding dependency fostered by Japanese childrearing practices (Sasaki, 1973), and the persistance of traditional infanticidal practices have been cited as reasons.

The ramifications of changes in abortion laws on infanticide provide an example of the role of social forces. Following the repeal of liberal Japanese abortion laws in 1970, an epidemic of infanticide occurred in which newborns were reportedly found daily in coin lockers of Tokyo subways (Kumasaka & Smith, 1973). The reverse effect was noticeable in New York City: After the passage of laws allowing medical abortions in 1960, illegitimate births dropped 12–16%, and infant mortality dropped. In one large hospital, adoption and abandonment declined by 56% during this period (Garcia, 1977). More recently, in China, an epidemic of female infanticide is linked to governmental rules aimed at reducing family size (China and girl babies, 1983). The availability of alternative methods of reproductive control and social rules governing family size are related to the prevalence of infanticide. Social factors, therefore, strongly influence the women's and families' reproductive decisions.

Ethnographic Reports

Ethnographic reports document the incidence of infanticidal practice. Whiting (1977), in a sample of 99 societies drawn from the Human Relation Area Files, found that 84 reported infanticide. A common explanation offered was the removal of defective offspring, and, indeed, where this practice is reported, a lower incidence of particular malformations than would be suspected is found in the adult population (Dickeman, 1975).

Infanticide as a means of family planning is often found in economies with an unpredictable subsistence base. The hunter – gatherers provide a good example (Carr-Saunders, 1972; Hassan, 1973). Infanticide among the hunter – gatherers dates back to the paleolithic period. They have lived under conditions that characterized the social and environmental context of human adaptation during 99% of the genus *Homo's* evolutionary history. Hunter – gatherer women are strongly motivated to space out births, since they spend considerable energy carrying their infants around during food gathering (Howell, 1976; Lee, 1970, 1978). Birth spacing and food gathering requirements make it necessary to at times kill or abandon an infant born too soon after an older sibling. Thirty-six percent of the total Whiting sample reported this custom, and 52% of societies depending primarily on hunting fishing or gathering practiced this. In contrast, only 8% of the pastoral and agricultural societies documented killing an infant if it was born too soon after an older sib. Incidence reports of infanticide for the hunter – gatherers range from substantial occurrence, 15 – 50% of births for the Australian Aboriginals (Nag, 1962; Birdsell, 1975), to common occurrence in early reports for the Kalahari !Kung, followed by reports of barely 1% or suspect in modern reports for the same group (Howell, 1976; Shostak, 1982). Rather than suggesting error, it is likely that the different rates for infanticide reported for the !Kung result from data collected at differing points during a century of social change created by increasing contact with the West (Dickeman, 1975).

Agricultural societies such as China and the Tikopia have reportedly used infanticide as a means of family planning, dictated or sanctioned by the village council among the Tikopia (Firth, 1927) but unlawful in modern China. Infanticide may then act as a strategy to limit family size, but other social forces may also play an important role. Apetkar (1931), for instance, documents varied examples drawn from the ethnographic literature at the beginning of this century. He describes that the Todas viewed infanticide as important in maintaining its polyandrous social organization. The people of the Torres Straits apparently allowed young women to kill their infants in order to spare them the burden of child rearing. The Apache killed "half-breed" infants to save them from their low social status as adults. A similar fate has often been described for slaves and illegitimate offspring from the time of the Vikings till the present (Whiting, 1977). Social pressures impinging on families or women's reproductive decisions are also indicated by the sex ratios for infanticide. A social preference for the elimination of female infants has been inferred from the unexpectedly skewed sex ratios in the adult population (Birdsell, 1968; Freeman, 1973; Harris, 1976). Although evidence exists that sexual customs and illness play a role (Landauer & Whiting, 1977; Guerrero, 1979; James, 1971; Beckerman, 1976; Drew *et al.*, 1978), most researchers hold that a preponderance of female infanticide occurs as a conscious and socially influenced reproductive check.

In sum, infanticide for social, moral, economic, and health reasons is recorded across time and culture. Throughout history, infants—who as a group offer no resistance, incur little parental cost, and with whom emotional ties are easier to cut—were the easy targets for limiting reproduction. The common occurrence of infanticide as a means of birth control strongly suggest that alternatives to attachment exist in the immediate postpartum period.

Neonaticide

Does infanticide commonly occur during the postpartum period, and is there evidence that mothers do it? Although infanticide is reported as widespread, the actual timing of the event is less often recorded. For our purpose infanticide should be separatable into two categories: neonaticide and filiacide. Neonaticide is defined as the killing of offspring in the first 24–72 h; and filiacide is the killing of an offspring after 24–72 h (Resnick, 1972). Most discussions, however, do not limit their analysis or distinguish the destruction of offspring during the first 24 h from a later period, confusing the immediate period with the increasingly complex 6-month to first-year period that follows. Factors that may contribute to the understanding of infanticidal behavior are thereby obscured. In the Whiting sample, for societies where timing was reported, all of the infants were killed before naming and immediately postpartum. In 56% of the total sample of 84 societies, infants were killed by the mother alone (Whiting, 1977).

After examining 168 cases of child murder occurring from 1751 to the present in the United States, Resnick (1972) found that neonaticides comprised 25% of the sample. These mothers were psychologically a much healthier population than filiacidal mothers. They manifested only moderate characteristics of passivity and impulsivity, when compared to mothers normally seeking abortion. No suicide or psychotic behavior was reported in the neonaticidal mothers. In general, these woman were young, unmarried, and primiparous with no criminal or psychiatric history. They did not reveal their pregnancies to their mothers. Their motivation was based on the illegitimacy (81%) and unwantedness (83%) of the infants. Their infanticides were clandestine affairs accomplished alone in a cool, detached manner. Long-term psychological sequelae and clinical recidivism after discovery of the incident were low. Neonaticidal behavior in these woman was consistent with antireproductive feelings. As a group they denied pregnancy, maintained their previous shapes with corsettes, and assumed that the child would be stillborn, and, accordingly, made few plans for delivery, for nurturing, or for murdering the infant.

In contrast, filiacidal acts were shared more equally by both parents, who further demonstrated an extremely high incidence of psychological disorder, a finding also reported by Kaplan and Riech (1976). Seventy-one percent were depressed, 66% had psychotic symptoms, and 33% made suicide attempts (Herzog & Detre, 1976). Filicide is also most likely to occur when the infant is 6-months-old, generally the peak time for postpartum depressive reactions. In the populations studied, filicide had a variety of motivational characteristics, generally associated with psychopathology. The varied and abnormal circumstances surrounding filicide contrasts sharply with the cool, detached destruction of offspring possible during the first 24 h by neonaticidal mothers.

d'Orban (1979) in a clinical study of mothers charged with the murder of their infants also found the neonaticidal group to be distinctively different. They killed their infants aggressively by drowning, suffocation, or battering and then concealed the body. Few were in psychiatric care, and only one had a current or previous history of mental disorder. As in the Resnick study, these women were the youngest group, were single or separated from their mate, had concealed their pregnancy, did not seek medical help, and, in retrospect, usually gave altruistic reasons for their actions. Although postpartum depression is often implicated as contributing to infanticidal behavior, depression does not seem to be a critical ingredient of neonaticide. Numerous international studies reiterate this point (Harder, 1967; Hirschmann & Schmitz, 1958; Gerchow, 1957; Lukianowicz, 1971; Scott, 1973): The killing of a newborn is rarely associated with psychosis and psychopathology and should be distinguished from the killing of older infants and children. Most of these studies suggest that neonaticide deserves a special place in the penal code. Indeed, there is evidence that it already has such a place, since neonaticide rarely leads to conviction; when it does, only short sentences or probation are imposed. Filicides are aggressively prosecuted. Laws which provide a waiting period before birth registration and consider death prior to registration as a stillbirth are common (Arbolida-Flerez, 1975; Knight, 1975). This and the late naming (delay of personhood) of infants common in preindustrial societies may be viewed as providing legal tolerance of infant mortality regardless of cause.

The legal tolerance of neonaticide in the West and the solitary deliveries described by the Resnick and d'Orban studies find an interesting counterpart in ethnographic reports. The solitary and confidential setting provided by

Bushman birth practices (Birdsell, 1975; Lee, 1970), which excludes males and generally includes only older females, could provide the private opportunity to carry out infanticide. Sargeant (1977) also describes a preference for solitary delivery among the Bariba of Benin. Bariba women state that they must evaluate their infants and kill them if signs of witchcraft are found that could endanger the mothers and their already living offspring. A wish for autonomy in reproductive matters is postulated allowing for covert solutions to social and familial problems (Cowlishaw, 1978). In these cases where birthing has been examined closely, a female preference to deliver alone under certain conditions seems to emerge. These customs may be interpreted as limiting the culpability of the mother and as accepting female reproductive control during the postpartum period. Neonaticide then appears socially, legally, and psychologically different from the killing of older infants. A most striking and interesting factor is the absence of psychopathological sequelae or concomitant disorder in the neonaticidal group.

It is likely that a delay in full maternal involvement with the infant accounts for the lack of psychological and mourning reactions observed at the time of neonaticide. It is also unlikely that neonaticide could be so common in certain cultures and historical contexts if there were really a biological drive for immediate attachment.

Evolutionary Rationale and Animal Models

Evolutionary theory and animal studies have been used extensively to support maternal attachment concepts (Klaus & Kennell, 1975, 1983). The evolutionary rationale, although generally not clearly stated, goes as follows: We belong to a group of animals which evolved in tropical environments, where populations existed at the carrying capacity of the environment and competition for resources between and within species was keen. Under these conditions our evolutionary forebears developed a propensity for single births, intense parental care, long life span, late maturation, and complex level of social organization. Although the ultimate evolutionary strategy under any condition is to maximize the number of offspring produced, limited environmental resources in these environments require parental strategies that channel available energy into a few extremely fit offspring. The delayed development of these offspring claims a high proportion of parental resources (deBeer, 1958; Gould, 1977; Wilson, 1975). Maternal bonding then was viewed as vital for infant survival, and immediate maternal attachment was thereby viewed as a consequence of natural selection.

Under these conditions, however, both the limitation of offspring and the need for maternal attachment may be defended. One could argue equally well that the human mother could not afford to raise all the offspring that she is capable of producing. The high degree of parental investment required of the mother by the offspring necessitated the limiting and selection of offspring. The mother must consider the welfare of potential and already existing progeny (Trivers, 1974), as well as her social function and work contribution. As the Bushman mother illustrates, mothers have heen actively involved in reproductive control. In addition one could argue that when other forms of birth control, such as those provided by social rules, coital abstinence, and abortion, are inadequate, the limiting of family size is most effectively exercised immediately after birth when loss of maternal resources is the lowest. Neonaticide or abandonment may then under certain conditions be the most adaptive choice.

Studies of mammalian maternal behaviors have also been widely used to investigate attachment behavior (Klopfer, 1971). The existence of postpartum maternal behavior in a wide range of mammalian species seems to underscore the evolutionary history of maternal behavior and suggests a probable genetic and physiological basis for maternal bonding. This lends support, as Klaus and Kennell argue, to the idea of a "sensitive period" for maternal attachment. But the variety of parental care behavior in vertebrate orders is astounding, a diversity that undermines generalization about maternal care. Maternal behavior is closely related to the specific physiological and ecological adaptations of a particular species (Slotnick, 1975). For example, some species such as sheep and goats may actually be preready for attachment, while other demonstrate a delay in maternal care. Moreover, maternal care is influenced by numerous situational factors that can produce a wide spectrum of maternal behavior (Rosenblatt, 1970; Rheingold, 1963) such that no single species can act as an adequate model for human behavior. While there is general agreement that from rats to monkeys interest in the neonate is increased in pregnant females (Rosenblum, 1972; Sackett & Ruppenthal, 1974; Bridges, 1977), no clear behavioral evidence for hormonal control of maternal behavior exists. For example, in the well-studied rat, multiple hormonal systems are active during the last weeks of pregnancy and after delivery (Schmidt, 1971; Cowie & Tindal, 1971); these occur in phases and may equally stimulate aggressive as well as nurturing behavior (Rosenblatt, 1970, 1975; Rodriquez-Sierra & Rosenblatt, 1977).

Nonhuman primates are often used in mother–infant studies (Harlow, 1971; Mason, 1978). Maternal behavior in the Rhesus monkey has been cited by Klaus & Kennell (1975) as linking attachment behavior to our evolutionary forebearers. In primates, however, no clear evidence for the biological triggering of maternal behavior exists. In addition, while most primate mothers eventually become capable mothers, the timing of this process is variable and certainly not immediate (Altman, 1980; Nicolson,

1982). Although infanticide of a mother's own infant is not often observed outside of capativity (Hrdy, 1976), intense field studies of baboon mothers and infants have reported neglect and abandonment of apparently healthy neonates resulting in their deaths during the first days and weeks of life (Altman, 1980; Nicolson, 1982).

In species where a delay in attachment is observed, cannibalism and neonaticide by the mother have been more regularly reported. Rats (Bridges, 1977; Rosenblatt, 1970), cats (Schnierla, 1963), lions (Cooper, 1942), and rabbits (Ross, 1963) have been observed to cannibalize or abandon their newborns in nonstressful and wild environments. The deermouse (King, 1963) and hamster (Siegel & Rosenblatt, 1980; Day & Galef, 1977) are a striking example of infanticide as a matter of maternal routine during parturition and not as a consequence of situational influences or experimental endocrine manipulations. Eighty percent of the hamsters studied kill an average of 3 pups in the first 72 h, leading to the conclusion that neonaticidal behavior is an organized and regulated aspect of maternal behavior in this species that allows the parturitional female to adjust the number she must nurture. Furthermore, the destruction of her offspring is carried out as part of the nesting and evaluative behaviors at parturition.

In the animal kingdom then, infanticide, aggressive neglect, and attachment are regularly reported (depending on species) as part of maternal behavior in the postpartum period. Reporting only supportive and selective evidence for bonding behavior primarily gathered from domestic animals out of the vast domain of animal studies and observations as Klaus and Kennell have done provides an incomplete picture of naturally occurring postpartum events.

Conclusion

This paper argues for a view of maternal behavior in the postpartum period that includes negative feelings and destructive acts. The evidence seriously questions the common assumption in Western culture that a mother's response to her newborn is one of instant attachment and inevitable rapture. A more complex and evolutionary important period is proposed than the "sensitive period" for maternal attachment heralded by Klaus and Kennell (1975, 1983) and in clinical use today. The reason for offering an alternative view is to accommodate the following evidence.

Many studies do not support immediate maternal attachment. First, the data overwhelmingly suggest that the timing of bonding depends on a variety of factors. These include maternal life experience and current resources, available social support and cultural sanctions, and psychological and physical state of the mother postpartum and the quality of the delivery. Second, cross-species observations provide good evidence for gradual and delayed maternal attachment and no evidence that bonding has to occur immediately in order for it to exist at all. Third, postpartum behavior reported in the animal kingdom is complex and varied and includes infanticide. This undermines the evolutionary justification for bonding and the logic of applying attachment behaviors found only in some species to humans. Finally, the historical, contemporary, and ethnographic evidence suggest that neonaticide may be an adaptive maternal strategy under certain conditions. Indeed, the fact that women are capable of carrying out neonaticide without evident psychopathology or profound grief directly challenges the immediate postpartum period as a time when only biologically motivated attachment is active.

In light of these data, the postpartum behaviors defined as indicators of attachment need to be reinterpreted (Klaus and Kennell, 1975; deChateau & Wielberg, 1977a). These behaviors described in a variety of species comprise all or part of the following: licking, calls, placental ingestion, touching, and looking. They are best described as maternal assessment behaviors with which she screens, explores, and evaluates her offspring. The human mother's pattern of interacting with her baby by touching, looking, and talking is also best viewed in this light. They are assessment not attachment behaviors.

Shortly after delivery women commonly feel distant from the newborn. This delay in the onset of nurturing feelings allows mothers to evaluate their infants. Evaluation may set the stage for recognition and mothering if the infant is accepted, or lead to abandonment if rejected. Needless-to-say, modern obstetrical contraceptive and abortion practices have minimized the need to make birth control decisions postpartum. The detached, negative, and infanticidal feelings described at deliverly are both remnants and part of the process of maternal appraisal. The delay in bonding feelings then may well act as a reproductive control measure "built in" to the postpartum behavior of women and may thereby allow cultural, personal, and economic forces to shape a flexible maternal response. Infant rejection is therefore an alternative maternal reproductive strategy and not the failure of bonding. A period of uncertainty and ambivalence is a natural sequel to childbirth.

Implications

Many mothers know that instant attachment is far from their personal experience, which may have been highly ambivalent until the development of feelings of love for the infant. Guilty feelings and anxiety about not meeting a cultural prescribed expectation is a common result. The idea that the growth of love for an infant is a gradual process influenced as much by social and experiential forces as biological ones has important clinical implications. This is so particularly in cases of unavoidable mother–infant separation due to infant or maternal illness or prematurity. In these instances, it is extremely important for the mother and family to know that the loss of early contact is not catastrophic for the mother–infant pair. The growth of parental love for adopted children is also a strong example that the development of attachment is not limited to a biologically derived finite period of time. An overzealous application of attachment theory can therefore create iatrogenic anxiety in the mother. Clinical expectations for the early expression of maternal bonding should therefore be deemphasized, and the individualized acquisition of motherhood should be the cornerstone of postpartum care. Furthermore, the expression of mixed, anxious, hostile, or disappointed feelings toward the newborn should be considered natural feelings that may be discussed. They should not be viewed as threats to bonding or feared as leading to child abuse. Child abuse results from different psychological and social factors (Anthony, Koupernick, & Chiland, 1978; Kemp, Silverman, Steele, Dceogenicalla, & Silver, 1962; Grey, 1976). Although suggestive for research, no good current evidence exists in support of a link between hostile postpartum feelings and later abusive behavior (Broussard & Hartman, 1971; Sameroff & Chandler, 1975; Lynch & Roberts, 1977; Egeland & Vaughn, 1981).

The timing of bonding feelings are intricately woven with the role the pregnancy has played in the women's life and family. Women eager to have children in supportive environments may indeed feel attached during the pregnancy (MacFarlane, Smith, & Garrow, 1978), particularly at quickening (Bibring, 1952; Liederman, 1978). In these woman infanticide is rather unlikely. A still-born baby or neonatal death in these families is extremely traumatic (Furman, 1978), and the family requires caring and humane social and clinical interventions as outlined by Klaus and Kennell (1975, 1983). The grief reactions of this group is, in fact, used to illustrate the power of early attachment to the newborn (Klaus & Kennell, 1975, 1983). Mourning in this situation seems peculiar to the group described, however, and stands in sharp contrast with the group of women for whom pregnancy does not make social or personal sense (Resnick, 1972; d'Orban, 1979). These woman deny their pregnancy, do not prepare for birth, and are able to reject their infants in a detached manner without overt evidence of mourning. Mourning, as an indicator of loss, occurs because of the meaning ascribed to the pregnancy and birth, not as a result of thwarted maternal drive.

The management of the postpartum period and the expression of attachment feelings is determined to a large extent by the degree of social involvement of the mother. We may then conclude that the more integrated the pregnancy experience, with the husband, mother, and other members of the group, the more the outcome will be dictated by cultural and family orientations. On the other hand, the more "isolated," or in a positive sense "autonomous," the more the outcome will be dictated by the reproductive strategy of the individual mother alone. In this sense, early maternal attachment is more a measure of fit among the infant, mother, and social group than attachment to the infant.

Early contact between mother and infant, however, may be important, if the woman wishes it, because it gives her control over birthing events and provides her with an active role at birth. For example, when Western women are afforded greater influence in birthing events such as home deliveries (Klaus & Kennell, 1975), when they are well prepared (Liederman, 1978), or when they take an independent approach (Breene, 1975), a more positive inception of the mother – infant relationship is generally recorded. On the other hand, we see that control provided by the private solitary birth practices of the Bariba and hunter – gatherers (Sargeant, 1977; Lee, 1978; Cowlishaw, 1978) allow these women to exercise the reproductive control necessary in their particular social setting. Contact after delivery then offers a woman the opportunity to work out her relationship with the infant and the environment and perhaps allows her to make an active choice potentially beneficial for both mother and infant.

In sum, every infant is not inevitably reared; the mother must choose to do so. The denial of this fact in our theoretical and clinical orientations is not helpful. Clinical approaches should target the mother and her family toward the goal of helping them manage the feelings and transitions of birthing and not just assuring that bonding time has taken place. Research that takes into account more fully the complex nature of the early postpartum decision and its influence on the development of both mother and infant is required. Such research must inevitably focus on the realities of women's lives within their families and social systems and not just on the cultural ideal of maternal attachment.

References

Adams, F. (1886). *The genuine works of Hippocrates* (Vol. 1). New York: William Wood & Co.

Ainsworth, M. D. (1973). The Development of infant-mother attachment. In (Eds.), *Review of child development Research.* B. B. Caldwell & H. W. Recutti Chicago: Univ. of Chicago Press.

Altman, J. (1980). *Baboon mothers and infants.* Cambridge, MA: Harvard Univ. Press.

Anthony, E. J. Koupernick, C., & Chiland, C. (1978). *The child and his family: Vulnerable children.* New York: Wiley.

Aptekar, H. (1931). *Anjea: Infanticide, abortion and contraception in savage society.* New York: Goodwin.

Arbolida-Flerez, J. (1975). Infanticide: Some medico-legal considerations. *Psychiatric Association Journal, 20,* 55 – 60.

Asch, St. S. (1968). Crib Deaths: Their possible relationship to postpartum depression and infanticide. *Journal of Mount Sinai Hospital, 35,* 214 – 220.

Badinter, E. (1981). *Mother love: Myth and reality,* New York: Macmillan.

Bakan, P. (1971). *Slaughter of innocents.* San Fransisco, CA: Jossey-Bass.

Beckerman, S. (1976). An unusual live-birth sex ratio in Ecuador. *Social Biology, 23*(2), 172 – 174.

Beescher, N. A., & F. V. Mackey (1979). *Obstetrics and the newborn.* Antarmore, Australia: Holt-Saunders.

Bibring, G. (1959). Some considerations of the psychological processes in pregnancy. *Psychoanalytic Studies of the Child, 17,* 113 – 121.

Birdsell, J. B. (1968). Some predictions for the Pleistocene based in equilibrium systems among recent hunter-gatherers. In R. B. Lee & I. DeVore (Eds.), *Man the hunter.* Chicago: Aldine.

Birdsell, J. B. (1975). *Human evolution.* Chicago: Rand McNally.

Bloch, D. (1978). *"So the witch won't eat me": Fantasy and the child's fear of infanticide.* Boston, MA: Houghton Mifflin.

Bluglass, R. (1978). Infanticide. *Bulletin of the Royal College of Psychiatrists,* 139 – 41.

Bowlby, J. (1952). *Maternal care and mental health, 1952.* Monograph Series, Vol. 2, WHO, Geneva.

Breene, D. (1975). *The birth of a first child.* London: Tavistock Publication.

Bridges, R. S. (1977). Parturition: The role in long-term retention of maternal behavior in the rat. *Physiology and Behavior, 18,* 487 – 490.

Brockington, F., & Kumar, K. (1982). *Motherhood and mental illness.* New York: Grune & Straton.

Broussard, E. R., & Hartman, M. S. (1971). Further consideration regarding maternal perception of the first born. In J. Helmuth (Ed.), *The exceptional infant studies in abnormality.* New York: Brunner, Mazel.

Carloni, G., & Nobeli, D. (1976). Madri cattive. *Revista Sperimentale di Frewiatria, 100*(5), 1013 – 1049.

Carlsson, S. G. (1978). Effects of amount of contact betwen mother and child on mother's nursing behavior. *Development Psychobiology, 11,* 143 – 150.

Carr-Saunders, P. M. (1972). *The population problem: A study in human evolution.* London and New York: Oxford Univ. Press (Clarendon).

Chertok, L. (1969). *Motherhood and personality.* London: Tavistock Publication.

China and girl babies. (1983, February 20). *Boston-Globe.*

Cooper, J., *Comparative Psychology Monographs,* 1942, 17, 91, 1 – 48.

Cowie, A. T., & Tindal, J. S. (1971). *The physiology of lactation.* Baltimore, MD: Williams & Wilkins.

Cowlishaw, G. (1978). Infanticide in aboriginal Australia. *Ocienia, XLVIII* (9), fum,

Day, C. S. D., & Galef, B. G. (1977). Pup cannibalism one aspect of maternal behavior in the golden hamster. *Journal comp. physiol. Psychol., 91,* 1179 – 1185.

deBeer, G. R. (1958). *Embryos and ancestors.* London and New York: Oxford Univ. Press (Clarendon).

deChateau, P., & Wielberg, B. (1977a). Long-term effect on mother-infant behavior of early contact during the first hour postpartum. *Acta Paediatrica Scandaniva, 66,* 137.

deChateau, P., & Wielberg, B. (1976). Long-term effects on mother-infant behavior of early contact during the first hour postpartum II. A follow up at 3 months. *Acta Paediatrica Scandaniva, 66,* 145 – 151.

deMauss, L. (1974). *The history of children.* New York: Psychohistory Press.

Deutsch, H. (1945). *Psychology of women: Motherhood, II*. New York: Grune & Stratton.

Dickeman, M. (1975). Infanticide and demographic consequences. *Annual Review of Ecology and Supplematics, 6*, 107–137.

Dorman, W. (1975). Sonderstatistic: Vollendete Totungsdilekte an Kindern, 1968–1974. *Kriminalistik, 20*(10),1165.

Douglas, G. (1963). Puerperal depression and excessive compliance with the mother. *Journal of Medical Psychology, 36*, 271–278.

Drew, J. S., London, W. T., & Lustbader, E. D. (1978). Hepatitis B virus and sex ratio of offspring. *Science 201*, 692.

Dumond, D. E. (1977). The limitation of human populations and natural history. In D. Landy (Ed.), *Culture, disease and healing*. New York: Macmillan.

Egeland, B., & Vaughn, B. (1981, January). Failure of "Bond Formation" as a cause of abuse neglect and maltreatment. *American Journal of Orthopsychiatry, 51*(1).

Esquirol, J. E. D. (1838). *Des Maladies mentaler consideree ssous les rapporter medical hygiènique et medio-ligal*. London: Ballière.

Firth, R. (1927). *We, the Tikopia*. London: Allen and Cherwin.

Freeman, M. M. R. (1973). Systematic female infanticide among the Miloith Eskimo. *American Anthropologist, 73*, 1011–1018.

Furman, E. D. (1978). The death of a newborn: Care of the parents, *Journal of Birth and Family, 5*, 214–218.

Garcia, C. (1977). *Human fertility: The regulation of reproduction*. Philadelphia, PA: Davis.

Gerchow, J. (1957). *Die ärtzlich-forensische Beurteilung von Kindesmörderinnen*. Halle.

Gorden, R. E. Kupestens, F. F., & Gorden, K. K. (1963). Factors in postpartum emotional adjustment, *OB + Gyn.*, Vol. *25*(2) 158–166.

Gould, S. J. (1977). *Ontogeny and Phylogeny*. Cambridge MA: Belknap Press.

Grey, J. et al. (1976) *The Denver Predictive Study from the National Center for the Prevention and Treatment of Child Abuse and Neglect*. Unpublished, University of Colorado Audiovisual Center, 1976.

Guerrero, R. (1979). Association of the type and time of insemination within the menstrual cycle with the human sex ratio at birth. *New England Journal of Medicine, 291*, 1059.

Hales, D., Trause, M. A., & Kennel, J. H. (1976). How early is early contact? Defining the limits of the sensitive period. *Pediatric Res., 10*, 448.

Hamilton, A. M. (1962). *Postpartum psychiatric problems*. St. Louis, MO: Mosby.

Harder, T. (1967). The psychopathology of infanticide. *Acta Psychiatrica Scandinavia, 43*(2), 196–245.

Harlow, H. F. (1971). *Learning to love*. New York: Ballantine Books.

Harris, M. (1976). *Cannibals and kins*. New York: Random House.

Hassan, F. A. (1973). Size, density and growth rate of hunter-gathering populations. In S. Polgar (Ed.), *Population, ecology and social evolution*. The Hague: Morton Publisher.

Herzog, A., & Detre, T. (1976). Psychotic reaction associated with childbirth. *Diseases of the Nervous System, 37*, 229–235.

Hirschmann, J., & Schmitz, E. (1958). Strukturanalyse der Kindermöderin, *Z. Psychoter Med. Psychol., 8*, 1–20.

Hirschowitz, R. G. (1973). Crisis-theory: A formulation. *Psychiatric Annals, 3*, 12.

Hofer, M. A. (1975). *Parent-infant interaction*. CIBA Symposium, Amsterdam: Elsevier.

Howell, N. (1976). The population of the Dobe area Kung Bushman. In R. B. Lee & I. DeVore (Eds.), *Kalahari hunters and gathers*. Cambridge, MA: Harvard Univ. Press.

Hrdy, S. W. (1976). Care and exploration of non-human primate infants by conspecifics other than the mother. *Advances in the Study of Behavior, 6*, 101–158.

James, W. H. (1971). Cycle day of insemination, coital rote and separation. *Lancet, 1*, 119.

Jarrah-Zadeh, A. et al. (1964). Emotional and cognitive changes in pregnancy and early pepertum. *British Journal of Psychiatry, 113*, 797–805.

Kaplan, D, & Riech, R. (1976). The murdered child and his killer. *American Journal of Psychiatry, 133*, 809–813.

Kellum, B. A. (1974). Infanticide in England in the later Middle Ages. *History of Childhood Quarterly, 1*, 367–388.

Kemp, C. H., Silverman, F. W., Steele, B. F., Dceogenicalla, W., & Silver, H. K. (1962). The battered child syndrome. *Journal of American Medicine, 181*, 17–24.

King, J. A. (1963). Maternal behavior in the promycius. In H. Rheingold (Ed.), *Maternal behavior in mammals.* New York: Wiley.

Klaus, M. H. & Kennell, J. H. (1975). *Maternal-infant bonding.* St. Louis, MO: Mosby.

Klaus, M. H., & Kennell, J. H. (1983). *Bonding.* St. Louis, MO: Mosby.

Klopfer, P. (1971). Maternal love: What turns it on? *American Scientist, 59*, 404–406.

Knight, B. (1975). Perinatal deaths and the law. *Nursing Mirror and Midwives Journal, 170*, 74–75.

Kumasaka, Y., & Smith, R. J. (1973). Crimes in New York and Tokyo. *Community of Mental Health Journal, 11*, 19–26.

Landauer, J., & Whiting, J. W. M. (1977). *Sex ratios in infanticide.* Paper presented at the Annual Meeting of the Society for Research in Cross-cultural Research, Ann Arbor, MI.

Langer, W. (1979). Infanticide: An historical survey. *History of Childhood Quarterly, 1*, 353, 365.

Leboyer, F. (1975). *Birth without violence.* New York: Alfred A. Knopf.

Lee, R. B. (1970). Population growth and the beginnings of sedentary life among the !Kung Bushmen. In B. Spooner (Ed.), *Population growth* (pp. 329–342). Anthropologic Implications, Cambridge, MA: M.I.T. Press.

Lee, R. B. (1978). *Lactation ovulation, infanticide and women's work: A study of hunter-gatherer population regulation.* Paper presented at the meeting of the Hudson Symposium and Biosocial Mechanism of Population Regulation. Plattsburgh: State Univ. of New York.

Levy, D. (1958) *Behavioral analysis.* Springfield, IL: Thomas.

Lewis, I. M., & Rosenblum, L. A. (1974). *The effect of the infant on its caregiver.* New York: Wiley.

Liederman, P. H. (1978). The critical period hypothesis revisited. In F. O. Horowitz (Ed.), *Early developmental hazards: Predictors and precautions.* Western Univ. Press.

Lindemann, E. (1944). Symptomatology and management of acute grief. *American Journal of Psychiatry, 101*, 141–148.

Lozoff, B., Brittenham, G. M. Trause, M. A., Kennell, J. H., & Klaus, M. H. (1977). The mother-newborn relationships: Limits of adaptability. *Journal of Pediatrics, 91*, 1–12.

Lukianowicz, N. (1971). Infanticide. *Psychiatria Clinica, 4*, 145–58.

Lynch, M. A. (1975). Ill health and child abuse, *Lancet.*

Lynch, M. A., & Roberts, J. (1977). Predicting child abuse: Signs of bonding failure in the maternity hospital, *British Medical Journal, 1*, 624–626.

MacFarlane, A. (1977). *The psychology of childbirth.* Cambridge, MA: Harvard Univ. Press.

MacFarlane, J. A., Smith, D. W., & Garrow, D. H. (1978). The relationship between mother and neonate. In (Ed.) Kitzinger, Sand Davis J. A. *The place of birth.* London and New York: Oxford Univ. Press.

Marcé, L. V. (1858). *Taite de la folie des femmes en ceinter des nouvelles accouchees it des nourrier,* Paris: J. B. Baloorè et Jole.

Mason, W. A. (1978). Social ontogeny. In: *Social Behavior and Communication.* New York: Plenum.

Minde, K., Trehub, S., Corter, C., Boukydis, C., Celhoffer, L., & Marton, P. (1978). Mother–

child relationships in the premature nursery: An observational study. *Pediatrics, 61*, 373 – 377.

Nag, M. (1962). *Factors affecting human fertility in non-industrial society: A cross-cultural study* (Vol. 66). Yale Univ. Publisher in Anthropology, New Haven, CT.

Nicolson, N. A. (1982). *Weaning and the development of independent in Olive Baboons.* Unpublished doctoral dissertation, Harvard University, Cambridge, MA.

Nilsson, A., & Almgren, P. (1970). Paranatal emotional adjustment Part I + II. *Acta Psychiatry Scandinavica 220* (Suppl.).

d'Orban, A. I. (1979). Women who kill their children. *British Journal of Psychiatry, 134*, 560 – 571.

Parke, R. D. (1979). Perspectives on father-infant interaction. In J. D. Osofsy (Ed.), *Handbook of infancy.* New York: Wiley.

Peterson, G. H. & Mehl, R. (1978). Some determinants of maternal attachment. *American Journal of Psychiatry, 133*(10), 1168 – 1173.

Pier, M. W. (1978). *Infanticide,* New York: Norton.

Resnick, P. J. (1972). Infanticide in psycho-obstetrics. In J. G. Howells (Ed.). *Psycho-obstetrics.* New York: Brunner-Mzael.

Rheingold, H. (1963). *Maternal behavior in mammals,* New York: Wiley.

Rheingold, J. C. (1964). *The fear of being a woman: A theory of maternal destructiveness.* New York: Grune & Stratton.

Rheingold, J. C. (1967). *The mother, anxiety and death; the catastrophic death complex.* Boston, MA: Little, Brown.

Rich, A. (1976). *Of women born.* New York: Norton.

Robson, K. S., & Moss, H. A. (1970). Patterns and determinants of maternal attachment. *Journal of Pediatrics, 77*, 976 – 985.

Robson, K. S., & Kumar, R. (1980). Delayed onset of maternal affection after childbirth, *British Journal of Psychiatry, 136*, 347 – 353.

Rodriquez-Sierra, J. F., & Rosenblatt, J. S. (1977). Does prolactin play a role in estrogen enclustered maternal behavior in rats. *Hormones and Behavior, 9*, 1 – 7.

Rosenblatt, J. S. (1970). Views on the onset and maintenance of maternal behavior in the rat. In L. R. Aronson et al. (Eds.), *Development and evolution of behavior* (pp. 489 – 513). San Fransisco, CA: Freeman.

Rosenblatt, J. (1975). Maternal behavior in the rat. In M. A. Hofer (Ed.), *Parent-infant interaction.* CIBA Symposium. New York: Elsevier.

Rosenblum, L. A. (1972). Sex and age differences in response to infant Squirrel Monkey, *Brain and Behavior and Evolution, 5*, 30 – 40.

Ross, S. (1963). Maternal behavior in the rabbit. In H. Rheingold (Ed.), *Maternal Behavior in Mammals,* New York: Wiley.

Sackett, G. O., & Ruppenthal, G. C. (1974). Some factors influencing the atraction of adult female macaque to the neonate. In I. M. Lewis, & L. A. Rosenblum (Eds.), *The effect of the infant on the caregiver.* New York: Wiley.

Sameroff, A. J., & Chandler, M. J. (1975). Reproductive risk and the continuum of caretaking casualty. In F. D. Horowitz et al. (Ed.), *Review of child development research* (Vol. 4). Chicago: Univ. of Chicago Press.

Sargeant, C. (1977). *The integration of the traditional midwife in a national health delivery system.* Paper presented at Ford Foundation Regional Family Health Management Workshop, Catonou, Benin.

Sasaki, Y. (1973). Psychological study of infanticide. *Child Study, 29*(8), 1494 – 1500.

Schiffelbein, D. (1975). Cross-cultural research. What makes the difference? *Menninger Perspective, 6*, 10 – 11. (Film Max Plank Archive, Parche, WG.)

Schneirla, T. C. (1963). Maternal behavior in the cat. In H. Rheingold (Ed.), *Maternal behavior in mammals,* New York: Wiley.

Schmidt, G. H. (1971). *Biology of lactation.* San Francisco, CA: Freeman.

Scott, P. D. (1973). Parents who kill their children. *Medicine, Science and the Law, 13,* 120–6.

Shereshkefsky, P. M., & Yarrow, L. J. (1973). *Psychological aspects of the first pregnancy and early post-natal adaptations.* New York: Raven.

Shorter, E. (1974). Infanticide in the past. *History of Childhood Quarterly, 1,* 1978–181.

Shostak, M. (1982). *Nisa.* Cambridge, MA: Harvard Univ.

Siegel, H., & Rosenblatt, J. S. (1980). Hormonal and behavioral aspects of maternal care in the hamster: A review. *Neuroscience and Biobehavioral Review, 4*(00), 17–26.

Slotnick, B. M. (1975). Neural and homronal basis of maternal behavior in the rat. In G. Eleftheriou & R. L. Synott (Eds.), *Hormonal contributions to behavior: Vol. 2: An organismic view.* New York: Plenum.

Sosa, R. (1978). Maternal-infant interaction during the immediate postpartum period. *Advances in Pediatrics, 25,* 451–465.

Spencer, R. F. (1949). *Primitive Obstetrics.* CIBA Symposia. *11,* 1158–1188.

Spiro, M. (1965). *Children of the Kibbutz,* Cambridge, MA: Harvard Univ. Press.

Svejda, M. J., Campos, D. D., & Emde, R. (1980). Mother-infant "bonding": Failure to generalize. *Child Development, 3*(1), 775–779.

Trexler, R. C. (1974). Infanticide in Florence. *History of Childhood Quarterly.* 98–116.

Trivers, R. L. (1974). Parent-offspring conflict. *American Zoologist, 14,* 244–264.

Whiting, J. W. M. (1977). *Infanticide.* Paper presented at the Society for Research in Cross-cultural Research, Ann Arbor, MI.

Wilson, E. O. (1975). *Sociobiology: The New synthesis.* Cambridge, MA: Belknap Press.

Yalom, T. D. et al. (1968). Postpartum blues Syndrome. *Archives of General Psychiatry, 18.*

Yamagami, A., Nakata, C., Rukushima, S., & Sanra, M. (1975). A discussion of filicide and suicide by mothers. *Acta Criminological et Medicinai Legalis Japenia, 41,* 278–284.

Zarrow, M. X., Rosenberg, V. M., & Sack, B. D. (1972). Hormones and maternal behavior in Mammals. In S. LeVine (Ed.), *Hormones and behavior* (pp. 106–134). New York: Academic Press.

6

"Basic Strangeness": Maternal Estrangement and Infant Death — A Critique of Bonding Theory

NANCY SCHEPER-HUGHES

Bonding: The Biological Basis of Mothering

In recent years there has been considerable interest in exploring the biological components of mother – infant attachment. Beginning with the pioneering inquiries of Lorenz on "imprinting" in birds (1935), followed by comparable research on mammals and nonhuman primates, a number of ethologists, human biologists, anthropologists, pediatricians, and developmental psychologists have posited the parallel existence of a sequence of *innate* behaviors in human mothers' responses to their newborn. Such maternal behaviors as smiling, gazing, cooing, nuzzling, sniffing, fondling, and enfolding the infant have been observed, recorded, and quantified in an attempt to demonstrate that, unless interrupted or separated, mothers and their infants would simply do what comes naturally according to a preordained biological script referred to as maternal – infant "bonding" (Klaus & Kennell, 1976).

Support for the evolutionary genetic basis of human bonding has come from recent studies of hunter – gatherer populations. Research by Draper, Howell, and Konner (see Lee & DeVore, 1976) indicates that the relationship between mother and infant in such small, mobile social groups is characterized by a high degree of physical skin-on-skin contact (for 70% of the day and night in the early months of life); continuous and prolonged nursing

The Role of Culture
in Developmental Disorder

131

(up to 4 or 5 years); and close, attentive, and seemingly "indulgent" maternal behavior. These behaviors "typical of most primate species living in large groups [and of most] hunter – gatherers known today . . . probably represents the usual social environment for development in our species going back millions of years" (Social Science Research Council Committee on Biosocial Science, 1987, p. 2). Bonding, therefore, is thought to be part of our human evolutionary inheritance.

Rossi (1977) suggests that whereas "biologically males have only one innate orientation, a sexual one that draws them to women, women have two such orientations, a sexual one toward men, and a reproductive one toward the young" (p. 5). Human mothering has a strong unlearned component, argues Rossi, because of the precarious timing of human birth. The extremely immature and dependent human neonate requires particularly close attention and care in order to assure its survival. Therefore, it was particularly advantageous for a "maternal instinct" to become genetically encoded in women's evolutionary psychology.

Maternal bonding is activated or triggered in the mother in response to various infant behaviors, especially crying, smiling, sucking, and clinging. The automatic "milk let-down" reflex in nursing mothers' responses to hungry infant cries is often cited as evidence of the unlearned and innate components of maternal behavior. In his mammoth three-volume study of maternal – infant attachment, Bowlby (1969, 1973, 1980) argues from an ethological perspective similar to Rossi's that attachment is a *primary* instinct (rather than a secondary instinct as Freud had suggested) which developed within "man's environment of evolutionary adaptiveness" (Bowlby, 1980, p. 40). Bowlby's focus is on the innate attachment behaviors of the *infant* and the negative consequences for the child (later the adult) if these primary affectional bonds are disrupted during the first year of life. The attachment of the human infant to his mother, writes Bowlby, "is a class of social behavior of an importance equivalent to that of mating behavior" with "a biological function specific to itself." (Bowlby 1969, p. 179)

Bowlby's research led him to conclude that in human infants the "attachment instinct" is activated around the age of 6 months (when "stranger anxiety" becomes apparent), and it remains intense until about the age of 3 after which it gradually declines as the child matures into adulthood and relative autonomy.

An interesting concept is that maternal attachment to the infant appears to follow a slightly different trajectory. Klaus and Kennell and their associates and followers have identified a "critical" or "sensitive"[1] period for maternal bonding that occurs *immediately* postpartum:

---

[1]As defined by Lamb (1982a), critical periods are "discrete phases of development during which specific events must occur if development is to proceed normally" (p. 3). By contrast, sensitive periods are "phases of development during which aspects of development are more

> There is a sensitive period in the first *minutes* and hours of life during which it is *necessary* that the mother and father have close contact with the neonate for later development to be optimal. (Klaus and Kennell, 1976, p. 14)

If the mother and infant are separated[2] during this time (as is customary in the traditional biomedical management of labor and delivery in hospital), maternal bonding may be inhibited with consequences as serious as maternal indifference toward, or even rejection of, the infant when the two are reunited. Unlike other mammals, however, rarely are these consequences irreversible in *human* mothers:

> The process that takes place during the maternal sensitive period differs from imprinting in that there is not a point beyond which the formation of an attachment is precluded. This is the *optimal* but not the sole period for an attachment to develop. Although the process can occur at a later time, it will be more difficult and take longer to achieve. (Kennell, Trause, & Klaus, 1975, p. 88)

The by now extensive maternal–infant bonding literature[3] has had, among other effects, a profound influence on changes in the obstetrical management of pregnancy, labor, and delivery in this country and elsewhere. Many hospitals now have "birthing rooms" and rooming-in wards in order to enhance early mother–infant interaction. Sousa, Kennell, and Klaus (1980) demonstrated among a large sample of relatively poor Guatemalan women the salutary effects on perinatal problems, length of labor, and mother–infant interaction of including a "doula" (a supportive lay woman companion for the laboring woman) on the obstetrical team. The immediate benefits of so humane a gesture were readily observable.

Unfortunately, however, some of the "disciples" of Klaus and Kennell enlarged the claims made for the significance of early bonding. This led to the naive belief among some health professionals that if early contact was *necessary* to ensure *optimal* parenting, perhaps this was *all* that was needed to ensure *competent* parenting. A number of hospital-based intervention programs, based on this shaky assumption, were launched during the 1970s when belief in the critical importance of early bonding was at its height (see

---

readily influenced than at other stages" (p. 3). Unfortunately, the terms are often confused and used interchangeably in the bonding literature. In their introduction to the revised edition of *Maternal–Infant Bonding* (*Parent–Infant Bonding,* 1982), Klaus and Kennell interpret the postpartum experience as a *sensitive,* rather than a critical, period for mother–infant attachment.

[2]It is curious that Klaus and Kennel mean to include the father in the early bonding experience immediately postpartum. In much of the bonding literature it is rather explicitly stated that only females have an *innate* biological orientation to parenting. "By comparison to the female attachment to an infant," states Rossi (1977, p. 5), "The male attachment is a socially learned role."

[3]See Klaus and Kennell (1976, 1982); Klaus, *et al.* (1972); Lozoff, Brittenham, and Trause (1977); Sluckin, Herbert, and Sluckin (1983); Klaus and Robertson (1982).

Lamb, 1982b, p. 356). Some programs identified high-risk populations for "inadequate" parenting (usually this meant the poor, nonwhite teenage or single mothers, mothers of low birth-weight infants, and previous child abusers) and manipulated the hospital environment in order to "promote" bonding in the high-risk mothers who were sometimes observed against a matched control group. Rarely was there any attention paid to providing a supportive environment for the mother and child once they left the hospital. Similarly, the child abuse literature is replete with references to abuse and neglect as the outcomes of failure in early bonding.

Such reductionist interpretations and naive applications of the bonding hypothesis in medical and social work practice have led to a recent critical examination and reevaluation of the scientific basis of bonding (see Svejda, Campos & Emede, 1980; Lamb, 1982a, b, c; Korsch 1983; Chess & Thomas, 1982). Lamb, the most prolific of the bonding critics, dismissed the highly "equivocal" and inconclusive nature of the evidence and the "methodological impoverishment" characteristic of research in this area (1982b, p. 763). Meanwhile, longitudinal studies have tended to discredit the belief in any long-term positive or negative effects of early mother–infant interaction (see Curry, 1979; deChateau, 1980; Ali & Lowry, 1981; deChateau & Wiberg, 1977; Chess & Thomas, 1982).

This paper will take a slightly different path in exploring the limitations of the bonding hypothesis and the biological determinants of maternal behavior. Based on preliminary research (see also Scheper-Hughes, 1984, 1985) on the sociocultural context of infant mortality and selective neglect among a sample of poor *favela* (hillside shanty-town) women living in a market town in the state of Pernambuco in Northeast Brazil, I will suggest that there are, of course, no simple or unmediated biological effects with respect to maternal behavior. Rather, maternal bonding and attachment (or their absence) are always mediated by the mother's evaluations of her social and economic circumstances and, more important, by culturally derived meanings of maternity, fertility, nurturance, love, care, loss, infant death, etc. In other words, rather than a universal biological script for largely innate behaviors that can be artifically "triggered" in unsuspecting and passive women, I suggest that "bonding" is always complex, culturally constructed, and individually negotiated depending on the kinds of choices and options available to the mother and her evaluation of the costs, risks, and benefits of emotional investment in her offspring. Among the impoverished and economically exploited rural migrants and wage laborers inhabiting the hillside shanty-town called *Alto do Cruzeiro* (Crucifix Hill), the accumulated experience of frequent loss of infants and young children has led to a very different expression and experience of maternal bonding surrounding birth, infancy, and early childhood.

The Construction of Childhood Mortality
as a Sociomedical Problem

The dialectic between fertility and mortality, reproduction and death, and survival and loss, is a powerful one in the lives of most people living outside or on the periphery of the "modern," industrialized world where disease epidemics and famines consign millions to an early grave and where the "life of the species" is only marginally under human control. In the world in which most of us live, however, the tension between fertility and mortality has lost its edge, become buried in the consciousness of most North Americans and Europeans, for whom each birth signifies new life rather than the threat of premature death and for whom some control over fertility is assumed. Yet it was not long ago in our own Western world (barely more than a hundred years) when reproduction was as unpredictable and death as random and chaotic as in the contemporary Third World. In many pockets of the Western world up through the mid- to late 19th century, childhood mortality tended to be viewed as an unfortunate but altogether predictable *natural* occurrence, and a 15–20% mortality rate during the first year of life was not regarded as intolerable or unacceptable. For one, child mortality had a clear social class reference which allowed it to remain masked. The pernicious living and working conditions of the urban proletariat during the first half of the 19th century corresponded to the lack of social concern for the mortality of working- and underclass children.

The mundaneness and ubiquitousness of child death—a fairly permanent feature of the history of childhood until very recently—contributed to the plethora of individual and collective defenses, among these the failure to recognize it as a significant personal or social–medical problem.

For example, childhood malnutrition (still one of the greatest "pathogens" affecting childhood survival throughout the world today) was *first* identified as a pediatric disorder in 1933, while the more specific diagnoses of marasmus, kwashiorkor, and protein energy or protein calorie malnutrition have come into clinical usage only since the 1950s. In a provocative series of articles, Cassidy (1980, 1982, 1987) has argued that toddler malnutrition is so rarely noted by Third World mothers as a childhood problem or an illness or a deficiency that it might just as well be thought of as a "culture bound syndrome," specific to Western biomedical practitioners.

Given the relatively recent perception of child survival in advanced industrial nations as a socio-medical problem in which the state has a clear and vested interest, it should not be surprising that this public consciousness is absent in many societies undergoing an early and rapid phase of industrialization or mired in a relatively crude form of industrial capitalism. In these Third World contexts, so often characterized by a high pressure demography of high fertility and high mortality, the frequent experience of child death remains a powerful shaper of maternal thinking and practice. In those areas of the world today where chronic hunger and food shortages, unchecked infectious disease, poor sanitation, and unclean water contribute to a high incidence of childhood mortality, it should not be surprising that individuals might approach reproduction and parenting with a range of sentiments and practices very different from our own. These may serve as individual and collective defenses against experiencing each loss as a tragedy, rather than as a minor misfortune, an unalterable fact of life and one to be accepted with resignation and equanimity.

Following from a high expectancy of loss, reproductive logic may be based on an assumption of the interchangeability and replaceability of offspring, which can contribute to the spiral of high fertility, high childhood mortality, in a kind of macabre lock-step dance of death which I will illustrate at some length later in this paper.

Mother Love and Child Death

Of all the many pathogens that endanger the lives of young children, by far the most difficult to examine with any degree of dispassionate objectivity is the quality of parenting. Historians and social scientists, no less than the public at large, are influenced by old cultural myths about childhood innocence and mother love as well as their opposites. The terrible power and significance attributed to *maternal* behavior (in particular) is a commonsense perception based on the observation that the human infant (specialized as it is for prematurity and prolonged dependency) simply cannot survive for very long without considerable maternal love and care. The infant's life depends, to a very great extent, on the goodwill of others but, most especially, that of the mother. Consequently, it has been the fate of mothers throughout history to appear in strange and distorted forms. They may appear as larger than life or as invisible, as all powerful, or as helpless and angelic. Theories of a maternal instinct compete with theories of a near-universal infanticidal impulse (see, for example, Piers, 1978; Badinter, 1981; Rich, 1976). Some of these contradictions and psychological projections can be found in the medical and social science literature so that a healthy dose of skepticism should accompany all cross-cultural and historical examinations of the quality and the consequences of mothering for child survival.

For example, Langer (1974), among others, concluded that infant death by "over-laying" occurred widely from the Middle Ages through the 19th century in Europe, sometimes reaching epidemic proportions. Langer suggests that many poor and working class mothers of the 19th century were reduced to such survival strategies as enrolling their babies in burial societies and then killing them by smothering during the dark and quiet hours of the night in order to collect the burial benefits (1974, pp. 360–365). Hence, even the common practice among the poorer classes of nursing mothers sleeping with their infants becomes suspect of an infanticidal motive. A species of this pernicious belief has persisted up through the 20th century in clinical discussions of "sudden" and otherwise unexplained death where the term "crib death" often served as a euphemism in the medical (especially psychiatric literature) for suspected infanticide until the 1960s when an alternative biomedical explanation—sleep apnea—challanged the earlier view.

We do not know, and can scarcely imagine, what the loss of children meant to women living on the edge of the great epidemiologic transition of modern Europe. Their histories are minor histories, left for the most part unrecorded, undocumented. In trying to understand the meaning of lives very different from our own, we are sometimes tempted to attribute our own ways of thinking and feeling to them. Hence, even the barest suggestion of infanticide, so abhorrent to our modern sensibilities, is rejected out of hand. Or, conversely, we may distance ourselves from our female subjects, suggesting that certain classes of poor women hardened their hearts against the threat of loss so that they scarcely knew how to love or cherish their children. The truth, as they say, is sure to lie somewhere between. Motherhood—as a cluster of practices, sentiments, and ideas regarding sexuality, fertility, child-bearing, and child-caring—needs to be thoroughly deconstructed. And caution is advised with respect to second guessing the motives of mothers living either long ago or far away from the experiences of contemporary middle class people.

As a cultural anthropologist I do not have the tools with which to probe the past, but I can study the lives of women and children today living in those parts of the peripheral or Third World where economic and demographic conditions are similar to those which obtained in Europe and North America at an earlier phase of industrialization and "modernization." This I shall proceed to do with reference to the cultural constructions of motherhood and childhood in contemporary Northeast Brazil, the heart of the Third World in that otherwise advanced industrial nation. My research is concerned with exploring the meanings of mother love and child death in a shantytown (Alto do Cruzeiro) attached to a rural market town where my sample of households indicates that approximately 420/1000 infants die during the first 5 years of life. What was once celebrated as the "Economic Miracle of Brazil" has bypassed the marginalized residents of the Alto do Cruzeiro.

The cluster of problems that I am addressing—the effects of economic deprivation, scarcity, and loss on maternal sentiments and practices—was one that first concerned me in 1964 when I witnessed the wholesale die-out of shantytown babies in the first months and years of their lives and the seeming indifference of their mothers, who appeared to hasten the deaths caused by malnutrition, dehydration, fevers, and parasites with their own selective inattention to their child's obvious needs for water, food, and medical attention. Working then as a *visitadora* (a door-to-door health worker), I found that while it was possible to rescue babies and toddlers from death by malnutrition and dehydration, it was more difficult to encourage their mothers to attach themselves to babies from whom they had already distanced themselves, convinced that the child was only a "visitor," only "passing through" the household on his way to a certain death.

Case Studies

When I returned to the Alto do Cruzeiro in 1982 almost 20 years had elapsed since I had first lived and worked in the community. I returned this time as a medical and psychological anthropologist, in order to understand events which had puzzled me then and which continue to elude easy interpretation even now. The following case studies are intended to be illustrative of the paradoxes in maternal sentiments and practices in this one small threatened human community. They should serve as a check against generating any grandiose or universalizing discourse on motherhood.

Within the first week of my arrival to the Alto in the fall of 1964, a mother came to me with a very sick and wasted baby. Seeing that the infant's condition was precarious, indeed, I rushed the baby off the the local hospital where he died within the hour. I was devastated. I had come from a society in which babies do not die. How could I ever break the news to the mother? Would she hold me accountable for the death? Would I be forced to leave Brazil within a week of my arrival? To my great wonder and perplexity, however, the young woman took the news placidly, almost seemingly indifferently. And, noting my distraught state, she commented to the neighbor women standing by, "engraçada, nao e?" (Amusing, isn't it?), referring to my inappropriate expression of concern.

The mundaneness and therefore high expectancy and defensive conformity to infant death were not just an aberration of desperately poor mothers in Alto do Cruzeiro, it was a point of view shared by the politicians, doctors, and priests of the community. After I tried to sensitize the very amiable and "leftist" mayor of Timbauba to the extraordinarily high childhood mortality of the community, the mayor responded by opening an infant coffin factory behind his office. He promised a "free" baby coffin to all registered voters according to their needs. (Of course, this was not quite the kind of response I had had in mind.)

Mothers of the Alto understand a baby's life to be a provisional and undependable thing—a candle whose flame is as likely to flicker or go out as to burn brightly and continuously. Hence, child death is interpreted less as a major tragedy than as a misfortune, one to be accepted with grace, calm, and resignation. Anything else would be unseemly and could test fate even further. Worse, unrestrained weeping is believed to lead to madness. Babies are said to be *dificil de criar* (a real struggle to raise-up). Threats to the very young baby lurk everywhere—in the water, under fingernails, on the baby's nipple, in the cough of a neighbor's child. Death is to be expected. One could almost say that it was normative. Yet, this is *not* to imply that maternal affection and grief are absent, as the following vignette illustrates.

During my first stay in the Alto, I lived in a *taipa* (mud-wall) hut with a 30-year-old woman, Nailza, and her common-law husband, Ze Antonio. Nailza had suffered several miscarriages and the death of two babies, one a healthy toddler of 2 ½ years, who was "taken" suddenly by a fever. Nailza's prayers to the Virgin often included the angry, challenging question, "Is this what you expect of me? To leave this life without ever raising up a single living child?" When, during the year of my stay in her hut, she once again miscarried, Nailza fell into a deep depression which she, nonetheless, managed to hide from her neighbors. When they remarked on her flat stomach, she would banter back, "Yes, free and unburdened, thanks be to God!" I told Nailza of an infant that had been abandoned a few days before at the local hospital where I worked part time. We went immediately to the back door of the hospital and adopted "Marcelino," a scrawny, wasted infant whose pathetic cries stimulated Nailza's own milk to come in. Nailza was delighted to be able to nurse her *"filho de criação,"* her adopted child (literally, her child by *rearing,* by socialization), and as he grew in strength, so did her affection for him.

Here we see that maternal attachment can be quite strong in the *absence* of biological motherhood. Informal adoptions, like this one, are, in fact, very common among the women of Alto do Cruzeiro, and a third of the 72 women I interviewed (see below) had *filhos de criação* that they were raising permanently or temporarily, in addition to the children born to them. What was even more striking was the fact that some of the older women in my interview sample were raising the abandoned or severely neglected babies of younger, poorer women of the Alto, while many of their own natural children (now grown) had likewise been rescued and reared by older women. Families in the Alto are very consensual units, made up of shifting and voluntary alliances, based neither necessarily on blood nor on marriage. Kinship—especially "motherhood" and maternal sentiments—is not about blood, not about biology.

Finally, I will recount the story of Ze (told more fully in Scheper-Hughes,

1985). Ze was a severely malnourished toddler on whom his 16-year-old mother, Lourdes, had given up, while she lavished a doting attentiveness on her second child, a newborn who was understood as a better risk: a lusty, robust, fair-headed little tyke. I intervened on behalf of Ze and carried him up to the cooperative day nursery that I ran with some of the more activist women of the Alto. They mocked my efforts to save Ze, cautioning me that it was playing with danger, that a child who "wanted" to die as much as this Ze did, should be left alone. One should not fight with death, and one could already see the film of blue in this child's eye that meant he was already on his way to the next life. I managed (through extraordinary effort—for Ze himself resisted my attempts and had to be force fed) to salvage Ze, but then worried about the ethics of returning him to poor Lourdes in her little scrap material lean-to where she was barely able to care for herself and the new baby. Was this fair to her? Or to Ze? Would he face a longer, more painfully gradual death at a later date?

Lourdes did agree to take Ze back now that he looked more human than a spider monkey, and I left them to their own miserable resources. Better socialized into shantytown values, never again would I put so much effort into a situation where the odds were so poor.

When I returned to the Alto in 1982, there among the women who formed my research sample, was Lourdes, still battling to put together some semblance of a life for herself and her five living children, the oldest of whom was Ze, now a man of 21 and functioning as "head of household." He struck me as a slight, reserved young man, with a droll sense of humor. Much was made of my reunion with Ze, and the story was told again and again, amid gales of laughter, how I had force fed Ze like a fiesta turkey, how he had been given up for dead but managed to live and fool everyone. Ze would laugh the longest and hardest of all at these survivor tales and of his near miss with death. Ze and his mother had an intimate and affectionate relationship. In fact, when I asked Ze (in private) who was the best friend he ever had in life, the one person he could count on, he gave me the answer that most of my respondents gave to the same question, "Why, my mother, of course."

The point is that both severe selective neglect *and* strong sentiments of maternal attachment coexist, dialectically, in this highly charged and physically threatening environment. Mother love is a richly elaborated theme in Brazilian *Nordestino* culture and society, celebrated in folk art, in music, in folkore, and in an intense devotion to the Virgin Mother. Nonetheless, the gradual and selective neglect of certain ill-fated children is also very common and is not considered socially inappropriate or "deviant." Part of learning how to mother in the Alto do Cruzeiro includes learning when to "let go" of a child who shows that it "wants to die." The above vignettes also indicate that it is essential to look at the mother–child relationship over time, to follow the life history and the enfolding drama of attachment, separation, and loss that shapes the expression of maternal psychology and child rearing practices. In all, these vignettes are meant to illustrate that maternal practice and thinking are extremely complex and very sensitive to context.

The Setting

Ladeiras, once a sleepy little market town where rural sugar cane workers would come each Saturday to buy or sell their fruits and vegetables in open stalls and to be milked of their petty cash in the bars, cafes, and the *zona* (the red light district), has doubled in size in the past two decades to a population of 34,000. The mechanization of the sugar industry resulted in the proletarianization of the rural laborer, who today migrates from sugar mill to sugar mill in search of seasonal employment. Ladeiras, centrally located in the *zona da mata* (sugar plantation district) has become a home base for many displaced sugar workers and their families. The majority live on the hillside shantytown of Alto do Cruzeiro. Over the years the Alto has been transformed from a highly stigmatized rural slum grafted onto the edges of the market town into an almost respectable and almost working-class neighborhood. Like its residents, Alto do Cruzeiro has been proletarianized. Where two decades ago all homes were lit by kerosene lamps, today virtually all homes have electricity, either properly paid for or pirated from steet lamps. However, the water supply (from two public faucets), sewage, and sanitation remain precarious and life-threatening to residents of the Alto, especially to babies and young children, who virtually from birth are afflicted with parasitic and infectious diseases.

The Sample

The 72 mothers who formed the research sample (representing the first to volunteer after a general meeting called at the top of the hill) ranged in age from 19 to 71. With a median age of 39 years, most women in the sample were still potentially fertile, and hence their reproductive histories are incomplete.

The "average" woman in the sample was born in a rural community on the lands belonging to a *dono do engenho* (a sugar mill owner). She grew up working alongside her father and brothers "at the foot of the cane." She attended school briefly, and while she can do her sums with great facility, she cannot read or write and can barely (although proudly) sign her name. As a teenager she left home for the city of Recife where she worked in a "rich man's house" as a maid, cook, or nursemaid for the children. Disillusioned with city life and the conditions of her servitude [including, not infrequently, sexual servitude to the *dono da casa* (the head of the house) or his adult sons], she returned home, sometimes pregnant. The men in her life (often there were several) are described as "good" but "fraco" (weak) — poor, unskilled, sick, often alcoholic. She will put up with a lot from men, but if and when her "husband" lays a finger on her or one of the children, that is when she is most likely to put him out. The house is more often hers, rented from a neighbor or bought, for a very small mortgage, from the *prefeitura* (the mayor's office). She works sporadically and part time, as do all adult female members of the household and in some marginal or menial work for the *gente fina* (the fine or rich people of the town). Together they manage to *fazer feira* (to buy food for the week) on an income that puts the tiny household somewhere on the border between poverty and absolute grinding misery.

Reproductive Histories

The 72 women reported 686 pregnancies among them and a staggering 251 childhood deaths. The average woman had experienced, at the time of the research, 9.5 pregnancies; 1.4 miscarriages, abortions, or stillbirths (probably underreported); and 3.5 deaths of children. Alto children are at greatest risk in the first year of life; 70% (175) of the deaths had occurred in the first 6 months of life, and 82% (205) deaths had occurred by the end of the first year. The majority of Alto infants (those that survive as well as those that die) generally suffer their first "crisis" of vomiting and diarrhea by the time they are a month old. The average infant suffers four or more such virulent "attacks," lasting from a few days to several weeks during the first year of life. Neither sex nor birth order biased the deaths in favor of males, females, or earlier or latter born children, but deaths did often occur in "runs," so that a woman might experience a period of 5 or more years where births and deaths followed hard on each other.

Causes of Death: Mothers' Explanatory Models

The majority of births to women of the Alto are unregistered, as are the majority of infant deaths. Unlike poor people in the United States and in other advanced industrial capitalist or socialist societies, the people of the Alto are not subject to a high degree of public surveillance. Their domestic lives are, at the very least, private and autonomous. They tend to avoid civil marriages and only register their children if, and when, they decide to send them to school. However, given the scarcity and deprivations that define their day-to-day existence, this privacy and autonomy might be interpreted as public abandonment, and their lives, as ones lived in private and quiet *desperation*. With extremely limited access to a wholly inadequate system of public medical care — one State health post and a municipal "free clinic" — most people of the Alto diagnose and treat themselves and their children according to a blend of folk and biomedical concepts and principles. They rely on "popular medicines" — mainly herbal teas and washes — and the ability to purchase restricted medicines over the counter at local pharmacies. Most women in my sample had a vast knowledge of patent medicines, their effects and their side effects. In the absence of medical records or death certificates, there was no way to compare the mothers' explanations of their children's deaths with biomedical diagnoses.

Although illiterate and without formal education, the mothers interviewed were all too keenly aware that the primary cause of infant mortality was gastroenteric and other infectious diseases interacting with chronic undernutrition. When asked *the general question,* why do so many babies and young children of the Alto do Cruzeiro die, the women were quick to reply with a *general condemnation* of the *porcaria* (pig sty) in which they and their children were forced to live. They replied, among the following: "Our children die because we are poor, because we are hungry"; "They die because the water we drink is filthy with germs"; "They die because we cannot keep them in shoes or away from this human garbage dump we live in"; "They die because the milk from our breasts is as contaminated and diseased as the water from the public faucets"; "They die because we get worthless medical care, 'street medicine'"; "They die because we have no safe place to leave them when we go off to work."

When asked what it is that infants need most in order to survive the first and most precarious year of life, Alto mothers invariably answered, "good food, fresh milk, meat, vitamins." They were quick to denounce the value of their own breastmilk and just as quick to denounce powdered milk as a "baby killer" in the Alto. As one mother commented, referring to the widespread practice of overdiluting powdered milk with contaminated water, "Babies fed on water, turn to water" (referring to the watery diarrheas that carry off so many Alto babies). While these highly politically charged answers were given to my general questions, it was ironic that not a single Alto mother stated that poverty or malnutrition was a primary or even a contributing cause of death for any of her *own* children. Perhaps they must exercise a certain amount of denial because the alternative — the recognition that a child is slowly starving to death — is too painful.

Turning to the mothers' explanations of the causes of death for each of her *own* children, Table I offers a very condensed rendering of these women's

Table I.

Causes of Infant/Childhood Deaths (Mothers' Explanations)[a]

I.	The Natural Realm (locus of responsibility: natural pathogens)		
	A. Gastroenteric (various types of diarrhea)		71
	B. Other infectious, communicable diseases		41
	C. Teething (*denticão*)		13
	D. Skin, liver, blood diseases		13
		Total	138
II.	Supernatural realm (locus of responsibility: God, the saints)		
	A. *De repente* (taken suddenly by God, saints)		9
	B. *Castigo* (punishment for sin of the parent)		3
		Total	12
III.	The social realm (locus of responsibility: human agency is directly or indirectly implied)		
	A. Malignant emotions (envy, shock, fear)		14
	B. *Reguardo quebrado* (postpartum or illness precautions broken)		5
	C. *Mal trato* (poor care, including poor medical care)		6
	D. *Doenca de crianca* ("ugly diseases" involving benign neglect)		39
	E. *Fraqueza* (perceived constitutional weakness that involves maternal underinvestment)		37
		Total	101

[a] $N = 251$ deaths (birth – 5 years)

perceptions of the major pathogens affecting the lives of their children. Certainly, naturalistic explanations predominated in which biomedical conceptions of contagion through germs and microbes competed with aspects of humoral pathology and with folk conceptions regarding, for example, the etiological significance of teething. Although God and the saints were seen as the final arbiters of human destiny, in very few instances did mothers attribute a child's death to the direct intervention of a diety or supernatural. Most childhood deaths, then, were explained as plain events, bad things that just happen and for which there is no *jeito* (no solution). But fully 101 of the 251 deaths were attributed to human agency of some kind, including the gradual "letting go" of those babies seen as wanting to die or as having an aversion for the *luta* (the struggle) that is life. These include the 37 deaths attributed to *fraqueza* (a perceived innate weakness in the child) and the 39 deaths attributed to *doença de crianca* (any "ugly" childhood illness with a high likelihood of leaving a mother with a permanently damaged child). The latter, *doença de crianca,* is a flexible ethnomedical diagnostic category that allows mothers a great deal of latitude in deciding which among her children she may, in a sense, surrender to God's care so that her extremely limited domestic and personal resources might go to a child more likely to survive the rigors and demands of life on the Alto. The symptoms that alert a mother to a possible *doença de crianca* include: wasting, deleriums, convulsions, extreme passivity, loss of hair, and loss of body fat so that the baby appears old, spirit-like, nonhuman. Such a child may be called a *sabido* (a wise one), but in the negative sense of one who already has too much knowledge of this world and, hence, chooses not to remain in it. Such children, in particular, are labeled *dificil de criar* (difficult to raise-up), and no one blames a mother for turning her attentions to her less fated and less fragile offspring. Such infants and babies are neither physically abused nor maltreated. Rather, they are pitied and are allowed to gradually slip away. No heroic efforts are made to force food or water or healing herbal teas on them. Like their healthier brothers and sisters they are fed and responded to "on demand," the problem is, in their case, the demand is so weak, so highly underdeveloped. One hopes, for the child's sake and for one's own, that such children die quickly, without putting up much of a fight. As one mother said of her tiny, premature twin infants, "It wasn't very bad. They just rolled their eyes to the back of their heads and were still."

The mother does not hold herself responsible or feel terribly guilty about the deaths that are caused from diarrheas, slow starvation, and dehydration. The cause of the death is seen as a deficiency *in the child,* not a deficiency in the mother. And, of course, in this context, they are correct. One mother explained:

> They die with this disease because they have to die. If they were meant to live, then it would happen that way as well. I think that if a child was always weak, he wouldn't be able to defend himself.

Another one offered:

> These illnesses [*doenças de crianca*] we don't like to talk about. With these sicknesses it takes them a long time to die. It makes you sad. But if you treat the child he will never be right.

What was sadly apparent, however, was that the symptoms of *doença de crianca* or of a baby otherwise difficult to raise were often those produced by chronic hunger and dehydration interacting with parasites. What mothers understood as an innate predisposition in the child toward passivity, sickness, and death were altogether treatable and transitory symptoms. Because the principal underlying maternal care and nurturance was that of "demand," hungry and dehydrated babies are relatively neglected. Such babies are passive, shy away from human contact, and are mournful and perpetually fussy. They are difficult to satisfy. Although slowly starving to death they rarely cry for food, so that they appear to be *unnatural,* spirit-like beings. Because they are so passive, such babies are left alone for long periods of time, dangling in their hammocks while their mother is away or busy at some task, and sometimes not even a sibling or nextdoor neighbor (asked to look after the baby) may hear, amid the loud, crashing din of Alto life, the feeble cries that signal a final crisis, so that some babies even manage to die alone and unattended, something we are far more likely to associate with life in a large anonymous postindustrialized city. The baby's body is washed and dressed in white lace or satin and covered with tiny, sweet-smelling white flowers befitting a tiny angel. The simple coffin is selected from the wall of the local shop where they are hanging arranged in order by size, many more of the tiny ones than of the larger ones. Children form the funeral procession. In this way children are socialized to accept as natural the death of babies, as later they will have to accept, perhaps, the deaths of their own children.

Implications for Bonding Theory

When social and behavioral scientists involve themselves in the study of women's lives—reproduction, sexuality, fertility, and infant care—across the borders of comfortable, middle-class life, they often find their theories inadequate to describe or to explain the radically different ways in which such people experience and make sense of their lives. All too often theories of human nature or, in this case, of maternal nature have been generated from assumptions uncritically derived from the study of the modern, bourgeois family. The bonding model of maternal behavior, for example, strikes me as both culture and history bound, rooted in a reproductive logic that is adaptive to the modern, bourgeois nuclear family but not to the high-pressure demography of high childhood mortality and high (compensatory) fertility found in early modern Europe and in many pockets of the so-called Third World today. Intense maternal "bonding" makes sense in a context in which both childhood mortality and fertility have been somewhat tamed and where, consequently, reproduction is governed by the following strategy: to give birth to few babies and to invest heavily in each one. This is a strategy that was alien to most of our European history, and it certainly does not reflect the reproductive logic and behavior of the women of the Alto do Cruzeiro nor, one might imagine, of a great many women living under similar conditions of poverty, scarcity, and death. The alternative fertility strategy in operation throughout much of the poor and non-Western world is more along the lines of: Produce as many offspring as possible, invest selectively, and trust that a few will survive. Obviously, this strategy and logic requires a very different conception of maternal sentiments and a very different conception of the value and meaning of the child. Since this alternative strategy is characteristic of a large proportion of the world's population, it would seem that some revision of the bonding model as a universal psychobiological script might be in order.

Women whose cumulative experiences lead them to a high expectancy of child mortality will respond somewhat differently to their newborn than women who expect each of their children to live. Infant life and death will carry very different meanings, determined by the experience and anticipation of death and the cultural script that tells women how to respond to birth and to death. One of the ways that Alto women prepare themselves for disappointment and for loss is through a much more delayed and gradual process of bonding and attachment. Rather than allowing themselves the kind of unrestrained and passionate love of their newborn that we have become accustomed to (and so take for granted that it appears to us altogether "natural"), poor women of the Alto respond to their infants with a somewhat emotionally distanced and guarded stance of watchful waiting. This stance does not, however, preclude a great deal of physical contact and affection. Alto infants are generally born at home, are breastfed at least initially, and sleep in the same bed, cot, or hammock as their mothers. There is plenty of that magical skin-on-skin contact that Klaus and Kennell (1976) see as the foreplay of maternal bonding.

Alto mothers protect themselves from close attachment to their infants through a form of nurturance that is, from the start, less individualized and personalized than that which occurs in the typical middle-class Brazilian home. Many poorer infants remain unchristened and unnamed until they begin to walk and talk or until a crisis (and a fear of immediate death) prompts an emergency baptism. In this case the name given to the child may be purely coincidental, any name that an observer spontaneously volunteers will serve. Sometimes an infant is given the name of the last infant to have died in the family. Those babies without a name are simply called *ne-ne* (baby) by everyone in the household. The affection for the baby is often diffuse, not focused on any particularly cherished characteristics or traits of the infant as a little person.

In all, what is constructed is an environment in which loss is anticipated and where maternal bonding is attenuated or at least delayed during the first year of life. What makes this possible is a different cultural construction of the infant and small baby. The infant is viewed as human but as significantly less human than older children and adults. Perhaps this is close to the estrangement from, and almost reification of, the infant that Piers (1978, p. 37) wished to convey in her conception of a psychologically "primitive" state of maternal unconnectedness, of "basic strangeness." She writes that basic strangeness represents the opposite of empathy, a condition of "turning off" toward others, an inability to see them as fellow humans, and a tendency to view them as inanimate objects. In conditions of "abject poverty," continues Piers, even one's own children can be viewed as competitors (p. 39).

While worthy of further refinement, Piers' notion of maternal estrangement may be somewhat exaggerated or useful only in certain situations in which an underlying psychological pathology is in evidence. Rather than a *reification* of the infant as an object, what I have seen in a context of abject poverty could be better described, following the lead of James (1980) and of O'Neill (1985, p. 26), as a failure to anthropormorphize the infant. By this I mean that there is a failure to attribute to the infant and small baby such human characteristics as conscious will and intention, self-awareness, and memory. As one mother said of her severely malnourished toddler with evident pity, *"Coitado, mas bichinos não sentem nada"* (Poor thing, but little critters (or "kids") have no feelings). The baby is seen as incapable of real human feelings and, consequently, incapable of real human suffering.

Similarly, the impoverished mothers of the Alto are slow to personalize the infant by attributing specific meanings to their cries, facial expressions, flailings of arms and legs, kicks, and screams. Nor are they likely to recognize in the face of the infant or small baby a resemblance to other family members. The infant, in short, is not attributed with an individualized "self" that would make its death unbearably painful. Rather, each infant's humanness, its person, and its claim on the mother's attention and affections grow with time and with the child's proven ability to survive the risks of life on the Alto. As the child gradually proves its intention to stay, rather than just to pass through as a visitor, mother love and maternal attachment grows slowly, fearfully.

Nonetheless, I do not mean to suggest in the foregoing that Alto mothers never suffer the loss of their children. Indeed, amid the generally controlled and emotionally muted rendering of their lives as women and as mothers, the memory of a particularly painful and poignant loss would sometimes break through and shatter the stoicism and "conformity" to death that is so highly valued. There would be cases of older toddlers who had been expected to live, who "fooled" everyone with their "willingness" to die and hence who took the mother unprepared. And, there were cases of particularly loved and beautiful (although frail) infants, in whom a mother's hopes for the future *had* been entrusted, and she would weep in the telling of that particular death of all the many deaths she had endured. Other women present would calm the woman, and I, too, would help to console her with the words I heard used in so many similar contexts, "You are strong, Dona Maria. You will conform. It is useless to grieve. Your life must go on. You *will* endure." And as I repeated the ritual and the woman would gradually regain her composure I would wonder for how many generations women had been telling each other the same message, shaping their experiences of loss, controlling their reactions to that which is unbearable, unmanageable. If there is, in fact, a universal sisterhood of women, no doubt it has its basis in the collective comforting of those afflicted woman "whose children are no more."

The reproductive and life histories of these women of the Alto do Cruzeiro lead me to question the usefulness of such ill-defined and culturally decontextualized terms such as "bonding," "attachment," "critical period," and so forth. The terms seem inadequate to describe and to contain the experiences of mothering and nurturing under conditions of extreme scarcity and high risk of child death. The psychophysiological maternal bonding model focuses too much attention on too few critical variables and on too brief a period in the maternal life cycle: birth and the hours or days following it. The model underestimates the power and significance of other variables that shape mother–child relations over time: cultural meanings of fertility, sexuality, motherhood, and childhood; mother's prior experience of child loss or of abandonment by her own mother or by the men in her life; mother's social support system and her available resources; family size and composition; characteristics of the particular infant and young child.

The more reductionist versions of maternal bonding are insensitive to the life history of maternal attachments, to the evolution and fluctuations in attachment and intimacy over time and throughout the life of a woman and her children. An early "failure" to bond does not preclude the possibility of an enfolding drama of mother–child attachments later on in the life cycle. One of the benefits of longitudinal research is that by returning to the Alto many years later I was able to observe the eventual outcomes of several memorable cases of "benign neglect," children who had been rescued from their indifferent mothers and nursed back to life by older women, less often rescued by health workers. Restored to health and today grown to maturity these same seriously neglected children were often still (like Ze) devotedly "attached" to their now middle-aged and even, in some cases, elderly mothers. Despite its often rocky start, the relations between a mother and her children on the Alto do Cruzeiro remain among the most intimate an individual will ever have in his or her life.

Finally, the experiences of these women and children suggest that the prevailing psychobiological models of maternal bonding and attachment are class and culture bound and overly mechanistic. The early analogies between human attachment and animal "imprinting" are reductionist and do not help to enlighten our understanding of human sentiments. The existence of a "critical" or a "sensitive" period for maternal bonding is inadequate to explain the behaviors and maternal emotions of women for whom the life history of attachment to others (parents, siblings, lovers, and spouses, as well as children) follows a tortured path, fraught with many separations, losses, reversals, and deaths, reflecting the altogether desperate, vulnerable, and precarious nature of their existence. That there must be a biological basis or foundation to maternal emotions and behavior is not disputed. In fact, one could read the *persistence* of mother–child attachments over time and through terrible adversity in this small community in Northeast Brazil as demonstrating the tug of biology on ever so fragilely constituted human social relations. What is being argued is that human attachments are extremely complex and grounded as well in specific social, historical, and demographic contexts. A more richly contextualized and flexible model of mother-infant attachment is needed.

References

Ali, Z, & Lowry, M. (1981). Early maternal-child contact: Effect on later behavior. *Developmental Medicine and Child Neurology, 23,* 337–345.
Badinter, E. (1981). *The Myth of Motherhood.* London: Souvenir Press.
Bowlby, J. (1969). *Attachment.* New York: Basic Books.
Bowlby, J. (1973). *Separation: Anxiety and anger.* New York: Basic Books.
Bowlby, J. (1980). *Loss, sadness, and depression.* London: Hogarth.
Cassidy, C. (1980). Benign neglect and toddler malnutrition. In L. S. Greene & F. Johnson (Eds.), *Social and biological predictors of nutritional status, physical growth and neurological development.* New York: Academic Press.
Cassidy, C. (1982). Protein-energy malnutrition as a culture-bound syndrome. *Culture, Medicine, and Psychiatry, 6,* 325–345.
Cassidy, C. (1987). World-view conflict and toddler malnutrition: Change agent dilemmas. In N. Scheper-Hughes (Ed.), *Child survival: Anthropological approaches to the treatment and maltreatment of children.* Dordrecht, The Netherlands: D. Reidel Publishing Company.
Chess, S. & Thomas, A. (1982). Infant bonding: Mystique and reality. *American Journal of Orthopsychiatry, 52*(2), 213–222.
Curry, M. A. H. (1979). Contact during the first hour with the wrapped or naked newborn: Effects on maternal attachment behaviors at 36 hours and at three months. *Birth and Family Journal, 6,* 227–235.
DeChateau, P. (1980). Parent-neonate interaction and its long-term effects. In E. G. Simmel (Ed.), *Early experience and early behavior.* New York: Academic Press.
DeChateau, P., & Wiberg, B. (1977). Long-term effects on mother-infant behaviors of extra contact in the first hour post partum. *Acta Paedietrica Scandinavica, 66,* 145–151.
James O. W. (1980, June). *Diminished maternal anthropormorphization of infant behaviors in a society with a high infant mortality rate: patterns of mother-infant interaction in Northwest Ecuador.* Unpublished manuscript.
Kennell, J. H., Trause, M. A., & Klaus, M. H. (1975). Parent-infant interaction, CIBA Foundation Symposium 33. Amsterdam: Elsevier.
Klaus, M. H., Jerauld, R., & Kreger, N. C. (1972). Maternal attachment: Importance of the first post-partum days. *New England Journal of Medicne, 286,* 460–463.
Klaus, M. H., & Kennell, J. (Eds.). (1976). *Maternal-infant bonding.* St. Louis, MO: Mosby.
Klaus, M. H., & Kennell, J. (Eds.). (1982). *Parent-infant bonding.* (rev. ed.). St Louis, MO: Mosby.
Klaus, M. H., & Robertson, M. O. (Eds.). (1982). *Birth, interaction, and attachment.* New Brunswick, NJ: Johnson and Johnson Company.
Korsch, B. (1983, February). More on parent-infant bonding. *Journal of Pediatrics,* 249–250.
Lamb, M. (1982a). Maternal attachment and mother-neonate bonding: A critical review. In M. E. Lamb & A. L. Brown (Eds.), *Advances in developmental psychology* (Vol. 2, pp. 1–39). Hillsdale, NJ: Lawrence Erlbaum Associates.

Lamb, M. (1982b). Early contacts and mother-infant bonding: One decade later. *Pediatrics, 70*(5), 763–768.

Lamb, M. (1982c). The bonding phenomenon: Misinterpretations and implications. *Journal of Pediatrics, 10*(4), 555–557.

Langer, W. (1974). Infanticide: A historical survey. *History of Childhood Quarterly, 1,* 353–365.

Lee, R. B., & DeVore, I. (Eds.). (1976). *Kalahari hunter-gatherers.* Cambridge, MA: Harvard Univ. Press.

Lorenz, K. (1935). Der Kunpan in der Umwelt des Vogels. *Journal of Ornithology, 83,* 137–149.

Lozoff, B., Brittenham, G. M., & Trause, M. A. (1977). The mother-infant relationship: Limits of adaptability. *Journal of Pediatrics, 91,* 1–12.

O'Neill, J. (1985). *Five bodies: The human shape of modern society.* Ithaca, NY: Cornell Univ. Press.

Piers, M. (1978). *Infanticide.* New York: Norton.

Rich, A. (1976). *Of woman born: Motherhood as experience and institution.* New York: Norton.

Rossi, A. (1977). A biosocial perspective on parenting. *Daedalus, 106*(2), 1–32.

Scheper-Hughes, N. (1984). Infant mortality and infant care: Cultural and economic constraints on nurturing in Northeast Brazil. *Social Science and Medicine, 19*(5), 535–546.

Scheper-Hughes, N. (1985). Culture, scarcity and maternal thinking: Maternal detachment and infant survival in a Brazilian shantytown. *Ethos, 13*(4), 291–317.

Sluckin, W., Herbert, M., & Sluckin, A. (1983). *Maternal bonding.* Oxford: Blackwell. Social Science Research Council Committee on Biosocial Science (1987). *Biosocial Foundations of Parenting and Offspring Development.* Unpublished manuscript. New York: Social Science Research Council.

Sousa, R., Kennell, J. H., & Klauss, M. H. (1980). The effect of a supportive companion on perinatal problems, length of labor, and mother-infant interaction. *New England Journal of Medicine, 303,* 597–600.

Svejda, M. J., Campos, J. J., & Emede, R. N. (1980). Mother-infant 'bonding': Failure to generalize. *Child Development, 51,* 775–779.

7

Poor Readers in Three Cultures[1]

HAROLD W. STEVENSON, G. WILLIAM LUCKER,
SHIN-YING LEE, and JAMES W. STIGLER

In cooperation with

SEIRO KITAMURA and C. C. HSU

School failure is a provocative issue wherever it is encountered. When it occurs in elementary school—sometimes as early as the first grade—an examination of its bases becomes urgent. One approach to increasing our understanding of why certain children do so poorly in school is through cross-cultural comparison. Unfortunately, it is a topic about which we have no systematic information. Available reports describe casual observations of classrooms and informal conversations with parents and teachers in different cultures, but comparative data are lacking. Cross-national studies of school achievement have been published, but emphasis in these studies is on national trends, and little attention has been paid to children who receive exceptionally high or very low scores. As a consequence, many questions are unanswered. What are the responses of teachers and parents in different cultures to children who are not doing well in school? Are factors that differentiate low-achieving children from their average peers similar across cultures, or do they differ according to the culture in which the children live? Data related to these and other questions would provide useful cues about techniques for improving the performance of low-achieving children, cues that otherwise might escape the consideration of persons working in only a single culture.

The involvement of our research group with such questions arose from an

[1]The data discussed in this chapter come from a cross-cultural study of reading disabilities we have conducted over the past several years at the University of Michigan.

The Role of Culture
in Developmental Disorder

interest in theoretical analyses of the role of orthography in reading. Arguments have been advanced (e.g., Gleitman & Rozin, 1977) to support distinctions between the processes involved in reading a logographic writing system, such as Chinese, a syllabary, such as Japanese, and an alphabetic writing system, such as English. To evaluate these arguments a great deal of information was obtained about a large number of Chinese, Japanese, and American elementary school children (Stevenson *et al.*, 1982). It is to these data that we turn in investigating the correlates of low achievement in reading.

Comparison of Chinese, Japanese, and American children is especially interesting, for all are from cultures that place a high premium on schooling and academic achievement. At the same time, the cultures differ greatly in their languages, writing systems, and everyday practices at home and at school. Commonalities and differences that occur in characteristics of the children who perform poorly in the schools of these three cultures should be useful in improving our understanding of the genesis and treatment of school failure.

An Overview of the Project

We have chosen one area of school failure for discussion in this paper. Our measure is the score obtained on a test of reading achievement, and our criterion for "failure" is that the child obtained a score on the test in the lowest fifth percentile at the child's grade level. One advantage of this criterion is that it provides a standard that is comparable across cultures. In addition to cross-cultural comparison of groups of children, within-culture comparisons also can be made on this basis between groups of "poor" readers and groups of children who are average in their reading skills. In this case, the average readers were from the same classrooms as the poor readers, were of the same sex and age, and were within one standard deviation from the mean for each culture in their scores on the reading test.

We studied children in the first and fifth grades. In addition to giving them an individually administered reading test, they also were given a test of achievement in mathematics and a set of 10 cognitive tasks. They were asked to rate their reactions to school. The mothers of all the children were interviewed, and observations were made in the children's classrooms. These extensive data make it possible to undertake very comprehensive analyses of the characteristics of poor and average readers in each culture.

Constructing the Reading Test

No reading tests with English, Chinese, and Japanese versions were available. It was necessary, therefore, to construct a reading test that could be used in all three cultures and that was culturally fair, comparable in content, reliable, interesting, and easily administered and scored. Nearly a year was required to construct a test that met all these goals. We rejected the possibility of translating American tests into Chinese and Japanese. Translating tests developed in one culture for use in other cultures would not ensure that our goals would be met, especially those related to the appropriateness of the material for all three cultures.

We started our task by compiling lists of each vocabulary word introduced in Chinese, Japanese, and American elementary school textbooks. For this purpose we selected the current editions of two of the most popular text series in the United States and in Japan and the single series used in Taiwan. Lists were created by entering words in English and romanized transliterations of the Chinese and Japanese words. Accompanying each word were the grade and semester of its first appearance, the number of characters in Chinese, the construction of the word in Japanese *(kanji, hiragana, katakana),* and the English translation.

This information enabled us to include words in the reading test that were comparable across the three languages according to reading level. Preparation also included summarizing the stories in the texts and identifying the grades at which various grammatical structures were introduced. With this information available, we were able to construct relevant items of comparable grammatical complexity in each language. Items were developed simultaneously in all three languages, and decisions about the acceptability of items were made through group discussions in which persons from each culture participated.

Items at the kindergarten level included matching, naming, and identifying letters, *hiragana* (the cursive Japanese syllabary), or *zhuyin fuhao* (the Chinese phonetic spelling symbols). Items constructed for each grade level from 1 through 6 included (1) vocabulary items designed to assess the child's ability to sight-read single isolated words; (2) meaningful text presented in clauses, sentences, and paragraphs; and (3) true – false and multiple-choice questions designed to assess comprehension of the text. Comprehension items included: (1) phrases or sentences describing one of three pictures; (2) sentences in which certain key words were omitted but for which three alternatives were available; and (3) paragraphs about which questions were asked. A total reading score was obtained for each child from a weighted linear combination of the three scores (vocabulary, reading of text, and comprehension) derived from a principal component analysis of the three scores. Examples of the various types of items in the reading test appear in Fig. 1.

The scores for vocabulary, reading of text, and comprehension were highly interrelated. Intercorrelations ranged from .83 to .96. The coefficients of

ENGLISH

q w t m o i u j z

CHINESE

ㄅ ㄨ ㄖ ㄏ ㄍ ㄩ ㄌ ㄣ ㄈ

JAPANESE

む ん の ゆ り ま そ み せ

(b)

ENGLISH

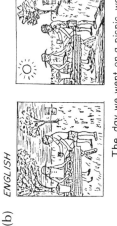

The day we went on a picnic was a cloudy day.

CHINESE

我們去遠足那天是個陰天。

JAPANESE

みんなが遠足に行った日は、くもりでした。

156

(c)

ENGLISH

tobacco

couple

fiery

CHINESE	JAPANESE
家畜 燦爛 試驗	希望 必要 試験

(d) ENGLISH

Ages ago, people depended on hunting to survive. In the autumn of each year they went out to hunt game. When they returned with their catch they smoked the meat and used the fur and skins to make clothing. In this fashion, they provided themselves with food and clothing for the winter.

CHINESE

從前的人，單靠打獵來維持生活，每到秋天他們就出去打獵，打到了野獸就把肉燻成肉乾，把獸皮製成衣裳。到了冬天，就不愁吃的和穿的了。

JAPANESE

むかし、ひとびとはえものをとって生活していました。毎年秋にはりょうにでかけました。とった動物をころしたあと、肉はかんそうしてとっておき、毛がわで着る物をつくりました。このようにして、ひとびとは冬にそなえて、食べ物と着る物を用意することができたのです。

Fig. 1. Examples of items from the reading test. (a) Letter identification; (b) sentence reading and comprehension (item from second grade level); (c) vocabulary items from fourth grade; (d) paragraph reading and comprehension (item from third grade level).

concordance for the Chinese, Japanese, and American groups, respectively, were .91, .93, and .94. The test is obviously highly reliable.

The Sample

A second major task was to select the samples of children to be tested. Funds were sufficient to work in only one city in each culture. To represent the United States, we selected children in Minneapolis. Several reasons were behind this choice, but the most important was that the residents of Minneapolis tend to come from native-born, English-speaking, economically sound families. Few children are from a minority background. These factors, we assumed, would provide an advantageous cultural, economic, and linguistic environment for learning to read English.

The Japanese city we chose as most comparable to Minneapolis was Sendai, which is located in the Tohoku region several hundred miles northeast of Tokyo. It, too, is a large, economically successful city, with little heavy industry and with a status within Japanese culture similar to that of Minneapolis in the United States. Taipei was the Chinese city in which it was most feasible for us to conduct our research, in terms of language, size, colleagues, and other factors. The economy of Taipei is growing rapidly, but the economic status of families is not as high as it is in either Sendai or Minneapolis.

Having chosen the cities, we had to be sure that we tested a representative sample of children. To accomplish this, ten schools in each city were selected to provide a representative sample of the city's school children. We wanted to test children shortly after they entered school and also near the end of their elementary school education. Thus, we chose, at random, two first-grade and two fifth-grade classrooms in each school. No mentally retarded children were included in our samples.

In all three countries the age of school entrance is the same and there is universal attendance in elementary school. Since the children were tested at comparable times within their school year, children in our samples from each city should be comparable in chronological age. This proved to be true for five of the six pairs of groups formed by grade and country. The mean ages for the poor and average readers at the first grade were 82 months in Minneapolis, 81 and 80 months in Taipei, and 82 and 84 months in Sendai. At the fifth grade, the mean ages for the poor and average readers were 134 and 132 months in Minneapolis, 129 months in Taipei, and 130 months in Sendai.

All children in these 120 classrooms—a total of nearly 5000 children— were administered the reading test. The cutoff score for the lowest fifth percentile was found for the distributions of total reading scores for each grade in each city. Children whose score fell below this cutoff point were assigned to our group of poor readers. A group of average readers was constituted at each grade by selecting children whose reading scores were within one standard deviation above or below the mean for all of the children given the test at that grade. These "average" readers were from the same classrooms as the poor readers and were of the same sex and chronological age. If it proved to be impossible to find an average reader of exactly the same chronological age as a poor reader, an average reader of the same sex and of the closest chronological age was selected from the classroom.

Because the size of classes differs in the elementary schools in the three cities, the number of children included in the lowest 5% necessarily differs. In the first grade samples of poor readers there were 24 children in Minneapolis, 38 children in Taipei, and 35 children in Sendai. The corresponding numbers at fifth grade were 22, 37, and 26. A higher percentage of boys than of girls was found among the poor readers, except for fifth graders in Minneapolis. The ratio of boys to girls in the first grade samples were 15/9 (Minneapolis), 24/14 (Taipei), and 25/10 (Sendai). In the fifth grade, the corresponding ratios were 10/12, 21/16, and 16/10. Across cultures, 66% of the poor readers at first grade were boys, and at the fifth grade, 55%. These ratios are in the direction typically found in studies of reading problems in the United States, but the proportion of boys is somewhat lower than the ratio of 3 or 4 boys to 1 girl that is sometimes cited (e.g., Owen, 1978).

The poor readers came from many different classrooms. In the first grade, they were from 14 of the 20 classrooms in Sendai, 15 classrooms in Taipei, and 11 classrooms in Minneapolis. In the fifth grade the corresponding numbers were 14, 15, and 13 different classrooms.

Achievement Scores

Reading Levels

The average reading level of the poor readers in fifth grade was below that of an average third grader in all three cultures. Thus, being in the lowest fifth percentile of reading scores meant that a child was at least 2 years retarded in reading ability. The degree of retardation in reading of first-graders cannot be ascertained; we can only say that among the poor readers in the first grade none was reading at the first-grade level.

The difference between the scores of first and fifth graders was equivalent across the three cultures; thus data for first and fifth graders were combined in Fig. 2. As can be seen in Fig. 2, our definition of being a poor reader meant much the same thing in each culture in terms of the absolute level of reading skill. The difference between the reading levels of the poor and average readers was no greater in one city than in another. Such a finding is in sharp

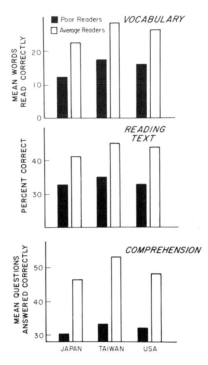

Fig. 2. Scores of the poor and average readers on the three parts of the reading test.

contrast with the observations of Makita (1974), Kuo (1978), and others that severely retarded readers are not found in the Japanese and Chinese cultures. Had the learning of Chinese characters and the Japanese syllabary facilitated the acquisition of reading skill one would have expected that the "poor" readers in Sendai and Taipei would have had higher scores than their counterparts in Minneapolis.

Mathematics Scores

Scores also were available from an individually administered mathematics test that had been constructed in the same careful manner as the reading test. As can be seen from Fig. 3, the poor readers consistently received lower average scores on the mathematics test than did the average readers. This difference was highly significant, $p < .001$. (Low scores could not be attributed directly to poor reading ability, for all of the items on the mathematics test were read aloud by the examiner as they were presented to the child.)

Such a finding is not especially surprising, for positive correlations generally are found between scores on reading and mathematics tests. In our complete samples, for example, the correlations for groups defined by grade and culture ranged from .40 to .61.

The difference between the mathematics scores for the poor and average readers did differ according to culture, $p < .05$. Poor readers obtained very similar scores in each culture on the mathematics test. Average readers did not. Rather, their scores followed a pattern we found in earlier analyses of the mathematics scores for the complete samples of children tested in each culture (Stigler, Lee, Lucker, & Stevenson, 1982). Among the average readers, Chinese and Japanese children obtained significantly higher scores on the mathematics test than did the American children at both grade 1, $p < .05$, and grade 5, $p < .001$.

Is the severity of the children's problems in mathematics as great as it is in reading? To answer this question we determined the percentage of our poor readers who also were in the lowest fifth percentile in mathematics scores. The percentages were small among both the first- (21%) and fifth-grade (14%) American children. These percentages were much higher for Chinese children. The percentage of Chinese children who were in the lowest fifth percentile in both reading and mathematics was high in the first (50%) and fifth (46%) grades. Relatively high percentages also occurred among the Japanese children at first (29%) and fifth (38%) grades. In other words, American children who were very poor readers were less likely also to be very poor in mathematics than was the case for Chinese and Japanese children. This is the first of several bits of evidence we will discuss which indicate that severe reading problems may be a more distinctive or isolated attribute among children reading English than among children reading Chinese or

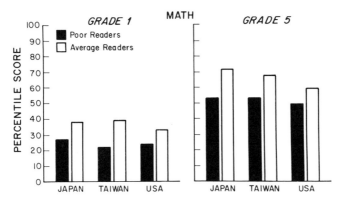

Fig. 3.   Percentile scores of the poor and average readers on the mathematics test.

Japanese. (For comparative purposes, it should be noted that only 5 of the 182 children from all three samples of average readers were in the lowest fifth percentile in their mathematics scores.)

Defining the Reading Problem

The interview conducted with the children's mothers contained questions we thought might be related to their children's academic performance in elementary school. Among the questions were ones dealing with the mother's attitudes toward school and learning, the mother's ratings of her child's academic characteristics, and the mother's perceptions of the type, seriousness, and cause of her child's reading problem.

Mothers' Attitudes

"How about reading problems?" the mothers were asked in the interview, "Has _____ had any problems in reading?" Chinese and Japanese mothers of poor readers were much less likely to acknowledge that their child had a "problem" than were the American mothers of poor readers. Among American mothers of poor readers, 71% gave a positive answer to this question, but only 45% of the Japanese mothers and 41% of the Chinese mothers did so. However, more mothers of poor readers believed their children had problems in reading than did mothers of the average readers. Among mothers of average readers, 27% of the American, 27% of the Japanese, and 32% of the Chinese mothers answered the above question positively. Greater awareness might have been expected from the mothers of fifth graders than of first graders in view of the longer time the mothers of fifth graders have for observing their children's reading skills, but the replies of the mothers of children at the two grade levels did not differ significantly.

The mothers of poor readers who acknowledged that they believed their child had a reading problem were then asked to rate the seriousness of the problem. There were three alternative answers: very serious, moderately serious, not serious. Few (4%) American mothers considered their child's problem to be very serious. More Chinese (42%) and Japanese (26%) mothers chose this answer.

We see, therefore, that mothers of children in the lowest fifth percentile in reading scores were not equally likely in these three cultures to acknowledge that their children had problems in reading. We are confident that the question was asked with equal clarity in all three languages. It seems that either American mothers are more likely to regard their child's poor reading skills as a problem or they simply are more aware that their children are poor readers, whether by means of teacher reports, their children's reports, or their own observations.

Ratings made of their children's reading ability help us in choosing between these two alternative interpretations. Nine-point scales, ranging from "much below average" (1), through "average" (5), to "much above average" (9) were used. As can be seen in Fig. 4, there were large (and highly significant) differences between the ratings made by the mothers of poor and average readers. The difference between the ratings was as great in one culture as in another; Chinese and Japanese mothers of poor and average readers differed just as much in their ratings of their children's reading skill as did the American mothers. What seems to be the case, therefore, is that mothers in the three cultures have different attitudes toward poor reading skills. For American mothers, poor reading is not often regarded as a serious problem. This is not so true for the Chinese and Japanese mothers. Of the mothers who are aware that their child has a problem, more Chinese and Japanese mothers regard it as a serious one.

The sensitivity of the mothers to their children's scholastic problems can be assessed further by looking at their answers to a companion question about their children's problems in arithmetic. About the same percentage of mothers of poor readers in each culture believed their children had problems

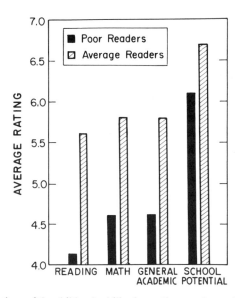

Fig. 4. Mothers' ratings of the children's ability in reading, mathematics, general academic ability, and potential for success in school.

in arithmetic: American, 40%; Chinese, 45%; Japanese, 44%. Among mothers of average readers, the percentages differed according to culture: American, 30%; Chinese, 58%; Japanese, 16%. These perceptions were not in close accord with the children's actual performance, for it will be recalled that very few of the average readers received low scores in mathematics.

Children's Attitudes

The children were asked how much they liked reading. They were to respond by selecting one of five line drawings of faces that varied from a deep scowl to a broad smile. Poor readers were likely to select the neutral face; average readers, a smiling face. This was true not only for reading but also for their responses for mathematics (see Fig. 5). Poor and average readers differed in their choices to a similar degree for both reading and mathematics in all three cultures.

The poor readers did not have more generalized negative attitudes about their lives at school than the average readers. The poor and average readers did not give significantly different ratings either to their evaluations of school or of homework. Even though the first graders had barely completed 4 months of instruction when they were asked to make the ratings, the choices did not change between the first and fifth grades. Children's attitudes toward reading appear to be established early in all three cultures.

Types of Reading Problems

After the mothers were asked whether their children had any problems in reading, they were asked to describe the problem. Despite the apparent

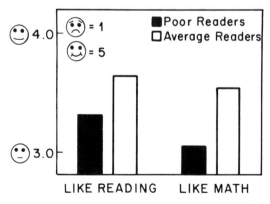

Fig. 5. Children's ratings of how well they like reading and mathematics.

clarity of the question, mothers often talked about possible causes of the problem rather than describing the problem itself. This was especially true for the American and Chinese mothers. Only a quarter of the American mothers discussed their children's deficient reading skills by citing such difficulties as spelling problems, poor reading vocabularies, or problems with phonics. Half of the American mothers of poor readers answered the question by saying that their children had a personality or psychological problem, such as poor intelligence, low motivation, poor attention, or were slow in working. Few Chinese mothers (33%) described problems that could be placed in such categories. Rather, they tended to give idiosyncratic and sometimes tangential answers, such as saying their children had a bad accent, did not receive adequate supervision, or had to repeat a grade. Japanese mothers were most likely to describe an actual reading problem (63%), such as indicating that their children did not know enough *kanji,* misread *kanji,* did not know enough idioms, or were choppy readers. The remaining Japanese mothers discussed psychological or personality problems.

For the most part, then, we found that Chinese and American mothers did not seem to have a clear understanding of what it was about their child's reading that made them believe their child had a reading problem. One wonders how frequently they may have listened to their children read or attempted to assist their children with their reading. Chinese mothers often abdicate supervision of their children's schoolwork to other members of the family. As will be discussed later, American elementary school children generally spend little time doing school work at home. We know from other sources (e.g., Vogel, 1963) that it is the Japanese "kyoiku mama" (education mom), who is most likely to supervise her child's scholastic work.

Mothers of poor readers in all three cities actually indicated that they believed they were less able to be helpful to their children than did the mothers of average readers. This appeared in the responses to the following question: "Children are helped in their school work by their mothers, fathers, and teachers. How much do you think each one contributes to your child's success in school?" These sources of help were to be ranked and points assigned to each according to their importance, with the condition that the total number of points should equal 10. Mothers of both poor and average readers assigned more points to the teacher than to either the mother or father. However, mothers of poor readers considered themselves to be even less important as a source of help to their children than did the mothers of average readers. Mothers of poor readers assigned 6.4 points to the teacher, while mothers of average readers assigned 5.8, a significant difference, $p < .01$. Points assigned to the teacher were greater in Taipei (6.4) and in Sendai (6.1) than in Minneapolis (5.7), $p < .05$.

A further impediment to the mothers' being of assistance to the poor readers was the mothers' excessively positive evaluation of the children's current skills and future academic potential. Even though the poor readers were among the very worst readers in their classes, their mothers' ratings described the children only slightly below average. The differences in the ratings made by mothers of poor and average readers did not differ across the three cultures. Thus, despite the indications by the Japanese and Chinese mothers that more of their poor readers had a very serious problem, they still rated their children as having nearly average ability in reading. Undue optimism is also evident in the mothers' evaluations of their children as having above average potential for academic performance (see Fig. 4).

Mothers of poor readers thus possessed two characteristics that are particularly unproductive for a child's academic progress: a belief in her own ineffectiveness as a helper to their children and an unrealistically positive evaluation of their children's abilities. Both would tend to reduce the motivation of the mother to assist and guide her child in activities that would advance the child's achievement.

Causes of Reading Problems

The mothers were then asked *why* they thought their child had a reading problem. Answers to this question were relevant and did not differ significantly across the three cultures. Over half of the mothers (51%) attributed their children's problem to experiential factors: the children had not been taught properly, did not get sound training in basic skills, lacked stimulation or was overstimulated at a younger age, needed more practice, or did not read enough. Biological bases were described by 16% of the mothers. These mothers suggested that their children were immature, hyperactive, had visual problems, had hereditary problems, had poor nutrition, or were left-handed. None of the other categories under which answers were coded contained more than 11% of the replies. In order of frequency, the mothers mentioned motivational factors, personality factors, attention, and intelligence. In all three cultures, therefore, mothers of poor readers looked primarily to the children's prior experiences as the basis of the reading problem.

When did the mothers believe their children first had a reading problem? The question is meaningful only for fifth graders. Mothers of fifth graders thought their children's problem began early. The following percentages of mothers thought that their children first displayed the reading problem in kindergarten or first grade: 75% of the American mothers, 66% of the Chinese mothers, and 54% of the Japanese mothers. We can deduce from these answers and from those to the preceding question that the mothers believed the experiential factors contributing to reading problems were ones that occurred relatively early in their children's schooling.

Other members of the children's families were described as having a read-ing problem by only 12% of the mothers. Half mentioned another sibling and half mentioned one of the parents. There are few studies of the families of children with severe reading problems, but in comparison with data that have been reported (e.g., Pavlidis, 1981), the incidence reported by the mothers in our study is low.

The Search for Explanations

Our next task is to attempt to isolate some of the correlates of poor reading ability. Why do some children learn to read so much more slowly than other children? Are factors related to performance in one culture equally impor-tant in determining performance of children in another culture? Informa-tion about such questions is available from the interview with the mothers.

Parental Education and Occupational Level

One explanatory factor in the production of poor reading skills may be the educational status of the children's parents. Poor readers may come from homes in which the educational level of the parents is low. This was the case in Taipei but not in Minneapolis or Sendai. The average educational levels of the parents are presented in Fig. 6. There is less than 6 months' difference in

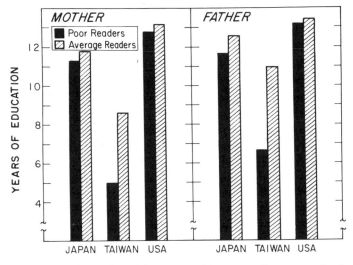

Fig. 6. Mean years of education of the parents of the poor and average readers in the three cultures.

the education of either the mothers or fathers of the poor and average readers in Minneapolis or Sendai. In Taipei, however, mothers and fathers of the poor readers had approximately 4 fewer years of schooling than did the parents of the average readers. In fact, of the Chinese mothers of poor readers, 82% had only an elementary school education, as contrasted with 48% of the mothers of average readers. Parental education was not an important determinant, therefore, of whether the Japanese or American child would become a poor reader but was a significant factor among Chinese families.

Parental education and occupational level are imperfectly correlated. Were the poor readers from families where the father had a low-level occupation? This again was not the case in Sendai or Minneapolis but was true in Taipei, where fathers of poor readers were employed in positions significantly lower in occupational status than were the fathers of average readers.

Birth Order

The only other demographic factor related to the children's level of reading skill was their order of birth. Poor readers tended to be later-born children. This occurred in all three cultures, even though there generally were more children in the American and Chinese than in the Japanese families, $p < .001$. The average birth order of the poor readers was 2.6, while that for the average readers was 2.0, $p < .001$.

Cognitive Abilities

Perhaps poor reading ability is only one index of more general cognitive difficulties. To assess the children's cognitive abilities, a battery of 10 tasks was constructed especially for this study. Some were of the types commonly found in tests of intelligence; others were constructed to tap abilities often hypothesized to be related to reading ability. The following tasks were included: (1) coding, which involved coding simple geometric figures according to numbers; (2) spatial relations, where the child must choose a figure that will complete a partially completed target figure; (3) perceptual speed, where the child must match line drawings; (4) auditory memory for patterns of taps; (5) serial memory for words; (6) serial memory for numbers; (7) verbal–spatial representation, where the child must complete drawings based on verbal descriptions; (8) verbal memory for a short story; (9) vocabulary; and (10) general information.

The poor readers received lower scores than the average readers on all 10 of the cognitive tasks, $p < .001$. Furthermore, the difference tended to be just as great in one culture as in another. This is evident in Figs. 7 and 8, where the

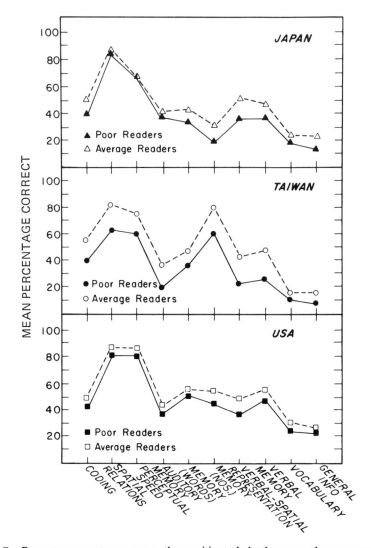

Fig. 7. Percentage correct responses on the cognitive tasks by the poor and average readers in Grade 1.

patterns of scores obtained by the poor and average readers in each culture appear to be comparable. There were two exceptions; differences for the three countries were not comparable for perceptual speed and verbal memory tasks. These do not appear to be important effects, however.

Differences in the cognitive abilities of poor and average readers were

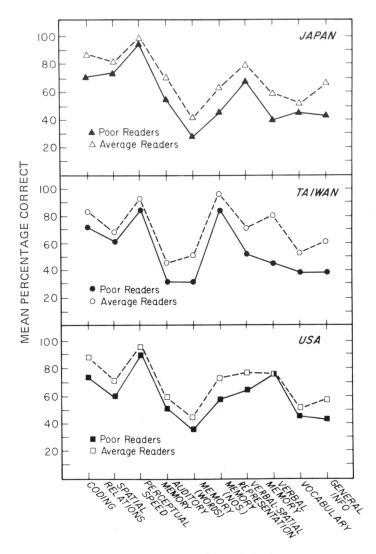

Fig. 8. Percentage correct responses on the cognitive tasks by the poor and average readers in Grade 5.

evident to the children's mothers. During the interview the mothers were asked to rate their children's cognitive abilities on a seven-point scale of the type used in their ratings of reading and mathematics ability. Mothers of poor and average readers made significantly different ratings for memory, learning, verbal expression, intellectual ability, and scholastic motivation, $p < .05 - .001$ (see Fig. 9). Only their ratings of their children's attention and ability to use time effectively failed to differentiate the poor and average readers.

Later in the interview mothers were asked to rate their children's personality and social attributes. In contrast to their ratings of cognitive abilities, these ratings rarely differed according to the children's reading level. Neither group of children was seen by their mothers as being less persistent, anxious, obedient, restless, sociable, shy, communicative, or attentive. Curiosity, self-confidence, and creativity were rated lower by mothers of poor readers than by mothers of average readers, $p < .05 - .001$. The effects found for the personality and social attributes were similar in each culture and at each grade level.

It is on cognitive rather than personality and social characteristics, then, that the mothers of poor readers saw their children as differing from other children. These perceptions were realistic; their children did receive lower scores on cognitive tasks than did the average readers. The accuracy of their perceptions of the children's personality and social skills cannot be readily assessed, for we have no external measures to validate them. We do know, however, that the failure to find differences in the personality and social characteristics was not due to the insensitivity of the scales. The average ratings made by the Chinese, Japanese, and American mothers differed significantly on all of the variables related to personality and social behavior.

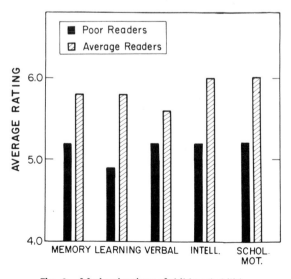

Fig. 9. Mothers' ratings of childrens' abilities.

Verbal and Performance Scores

Poor reading ability has often been associated with deficient verbal, as contrasted with nonverbal, intellectual skills (Vellutino, 1979). Analyses of this type can be made with the data from the cognitive tasks. The cognitive tasks were divided into verbal and performance tasks, depending on whether the child was required to give a verbal response. The percentage of children who performed at or above a normal level on the tasks was determined. For this purpose, "normal" was defined as being above one standard deviation below the mean.

We will look first at the results for the fifth graders. The American children who were poor readers performed no worse on verbal tasks than on nonverbal (performance) tasks. For example, 50% received verbal scores above -1 standard deviation from the mean, and 54% received performance scores above -1 standard deviation from the mean. A different pattern emerged for the Chinese and Japanese children. While 51% of the Chinese and 58% of the Japanese children received performance scores greater than -1 standard deviation from the mean, only 24% and 27%, respectively, performed this effectively on the verbal tasks.

The same pattern was found at first grade. The percentages of American, Chinese, and Japanese children who received scores on the performance tasks above -1 standard deviation below the mean were, respectively, 58%, 45%, and 63%. On the verbal tasks, however, the respective percentages were 71%, 32%, and 37%.

Three of the verbal tasks were especially sensitive to within-group differences in reading scores among the poor readers, but this relation emerged only in Taipei and Sendai. The tasks were general information, verbal memory, and verbal–spatial representation. Results for the fifth-grade analyses are very clear. Correlations between scores on these tasks and the vocabulary portion of the reading test ranged from .31 to .58 for Taipei and Sendai, and from $-.12$ to $-.34$ in Minneapolis. The pattern was similar for reading comprehension. Here, the range of correlations for the groups of poor readers was from .36 to .70 in Taipei and Sendai and from .08 to $-.16$ in Minneapolis. None of these correlations was significant for Minneapolis, but 11 of the 12 correlations in Taipei and Sendai were significant, $p < .05$. (It is not feasible to conduct comparable analyses for the average readers. The constricted range of scores on the reading test precludes obtaining high relationships with other variables.)

These data offer further evidence for a more general disability in learning among the Chinese and Japanese children who were poor readers than among comparable American children. Poor readers among the Chinese and Japanese children were more likely also to be deficient in mathematics and in verbal abilities than were poor readers among the American children.

More information is needed, of course, but these data suggest that severe difficulties in reading may be a more circumscribed or isolated phenomenon among children reading English than among children reading Chinese or Japanese.

Family Correlates of Poor Reading Ability

We might expect that large amounts of information would be available about variables differentiating the everyday experiences of poor and average readers. This is not the case. There have been a few studies (e.g., Owen, Adams, Forrest, Stolz, & Fisher, 1971), but we still have little information about the families of children with poor reading skills.

We did not find widespread differences between the characteristics of families of poor and average readers. When factors did turn out to have a significant relation to reading ability they were ones primarily associated with reading and studying. Children who did not read well also tended not to read often. Mothers estimated that poor readers spent an average of 2.6 h a week reading for pleasure, while the average readers spent 4.5 h, $p < .001$. The percentages of poor readers who were reported to read a newspaper was similar in all three cultures— 15% in Minneapolis, 13% in Taipei, and 16% in Sendai. Among average readers, however, many more children in Taipei (51%) and somewhat more children in Minneapolis (20%) and Sendai (24%) were reported to read newspapers.

The father's reading habits, but not those of the mother, were also related to their children's level of reading ability. Fathers of poor readers were estimated to spend 4.6 h a week reading for pleasure and fathers of average readers, 7.0 $p < 001$. In view of the predominance of boys among the poor readers, the significance of the father as a role model is one possible factor in their lower interest in reading.

Mothers of poor readers estimated that their children spent an average of nearly 20 h a week playing with other children. Average readers were estimated to spend 16 h. The difference is highly significant, $p < .001$. The means for the three cultures differed greatly, however, with the greatest amounts of time being spent on play in Minneapolis and the least in Taipei, $p < .001$. Estimates of the time spent watching television each week differed according to culture but not according to reading level. The estimates for the American, Chinese, and Japanese children were 14.6, 10.8, and 18.0 h per week, respectively.

The time spent working on homework also differed between poor and average readers, but the effects depended on the culture. There was only a slight difference between the two groups of American children. Neither spent much time doing homework: 2.8 h a week for the poor readers and 2.5 h for the average readers. The Japanese children spent more time on homework, but the amount was similar for poor and average readers: 4.5 h for the poor readers and 4.7 h for the average readers. Much greater amounts of time were spent by the Chinese children. The poor readers were estimated to spend an average of 8.2 h a week doing homework, and the average readers, 10.4.

Very little else emerged from our parent interview that differentiated between poor and average readers. In a few areas effects were found when the data were analyzed separately for the fifth graders but disappeared when the responses of mothers of both first and fifth graders were combined. For example, as we have reported elsewhere (Stevenson *et al.,* 1984), ratings made by mothers of poor readers of their own cognitive abilities were often significantly more negative for the fifth-grade sample than were those made by the mothers of average readers. This was not true of the mothers of first graders. In other cases, isolated items turned out to be statistically significant. For example, in an extensive discussion of discipline, no significant differences were found between the mothers of poor and average readers in the discipline techniques used, except for the fact that mothers of poor readers indicated that they used physical punishment more frequently than did the mothers of average readers, $p < .05$. To judge both from the scores of the children on the tests and the mothers' answers to the interviews, level of cognitive abilities appears to be the most pervasive factor in discriminating poor from average readers.

Life at School

A great deal of time was spent in the classrooms observing the behavior of the poor and average readers. This very large study, which involved observing each classroom in each culture from 30 to 40 h, revealed nothing of significance as far as differentiating poor readers from average readers. From what we could observe, these two groups of children did not differ from each other on such variables as attention, volunteering to answer questions, being asked questions, being on-task, displaying inappropriate behaviors, being out of their seats, or receiving feedback for their academic performance or routine classroom procedures. Even though there were large and important differences among classrooms and between cultures on these variables, the groups of poor and average readers did not differ significantly from each other. The interclassroom differences may have obscured differences between poor and average readers. There were insufficient numbers of poor readers in a particular classroom and so many classrooms represented that more detailed analyses of the behavior of poor and average readers was not possible.

Conclusions

From the perspective of theories of reading disability, the most important finding of this study is the similarity in the reading scores of the Chinese, Japanese, and American children who were in the lowest 5% of the distributions of reading scores for each culture. These results are in marked contrast to a prevailing but previously untested belief that children who must learn to read an alphabetic form of writing are disadvantaged, in comparison to children who are learning to read a script based on distinctive whole units, such as Chinese characters, or symbols with high grapheme – phoneme correspondence, such as Japanese *hiragana*. We found, instead, that children's abilities to decode and interpret written symbols were very similar among these three written languages and that some children in each culture found this task extremely difficult.

From the tests of achievement and from interviews with the children's mothers, the most salient characteristic of poor readers in all three cultures was their generally poor cognitive functioning. Poor reading ability was accompanied by poor performance on arithmetic problems and on a broad range of cognitive tasks. The children's difficulties were apparent to their mothers. Although Chinese and Japanese mothers were less likely to describe their children as having a reading "problem" than were the American mothers, their ratings of their children's reading, mathematics, and cognitive abilities differed just as greatly from ratings made by mothers of average readers as did the ratings made by the American mothers.

No specific cognitive deficits of the poor readers were apparent. We cannot conclude that such deficits do not exist, for the tasks used in the study tapped only a limited number of cognitive abilities. It appears likely that if such deficits are found in later studies they will differ according to culture. There were strong indications in our data that the cognitive characteristics of poor readers of English differ from those of children who are poor readers of Chinese and Japanese. Although no particular cognitive task differentiated the poor and average readers of one culture from those in another culture, there were consistently lower scores on verbal as contrasted to performance tasks among the Chinese and Japanese poor readers than among those in the American sample. In addition, the proportion who had severe problems in both mathematics and reading was greater among Chinese and Japanese than among American children. In the case of the Chinese children, it would be easy to attribute these differences to the lower educational and socioeconomic status of the families of poor readers, but such an explanation is unsatisfactory in Sendai, where there was no difference between the educational and socioeconomic status of the families of poor and average readers. Further investigation of the form and organization of cognitive abilities of poor readers in these three cultures would seem to be a productive topic for additional research.

We gain no clues about cognitive functioning from the interviews held with the mothers. Similarities rather than differences characterized the responses of the mothers across the three cultures. By the fifth grade, Chinese children must learn thousands of characters and their combinations. Japanese children must master two syllabaries and learn hundreds of characters. American children must learn to read words composed of parts of an alphabet. Yet, the mothers' reports of characteristics that differentiated groups of poor and average readers of the three writing systems were remarkably similar.

What insights has the cross-cultural study of reading problems provided? First, there is little basis for pessimism in teaching children how to read because of our alphabetic form of writing. Although our orthographic system may provide serious difficulties for some children, other, very different forms of writing produce very serious problems for some of the children learning to read those orthographies. Second, we see that there are common features across cultures in the characteristics of poor readers and their families: The children are not positive about reading and read less often than other children; they spend more time playing and less time at homework; their fathers are less likely to read than are the fathers of average readers; the mothers are more willing to look to the teacher than to themselves or their husbands as important contributors to their child's reading ability; and the mothers appear to be unaware of the severity of their children's reading difficulties. To the degree that a problem is related to environmental factors that occur in more than a single context, we gain confidence that the factors may be ones susceptible to successful intervention. Moreover, when the factors emerge as early as the first few months of attendance at elementary school, efforts at intervention obviously must begin very early.

Acknowledgments

Our research has been supported by the National Institute of Mental Health (Grant MH 30567). The research has involved the close participation of many colleagues and we want to thank especially Ai-lan Tsao, our coordinator in Taipei, Elizabeth Clarke, our coordinator in Minneapolis, and Susumu Kimura and Tadahisa Kato, our coordinator in Sendai. We also want to thank the large number of people who assisted us in the preparation and scoring of the materials and in the administration of the tests and interviews. Finally, it would have been impossible to conduct this project without the assistance of the school authorities, teachers, parents, and children who participated in the project; we thank them for their kind cooperation.

References

Gleitman, L. R., & Rozin, P. (1977). The structure and acquisition of reading I: Relations between orthographies and the structure of language. In A. S. Reber & D. L. Scarborough (Eds.), *Toward a psychology of reading.* Hillsdale, NJ: Erlbaum.

Kuo, W. F. (1978). A preliminary study of reading disability in the Republic of China. *Collected papers.* Taipei: National Taiwan Normal University.

Makita, K. (1974). Reading disability and the writing system. In J. E. Merritt (Ed.), *New horizons in reading.* Newark, DE: IRA Press.

Owen, F. (1978). Dyslexia—genetic aspects. In A. L. Benton & D. Pearl (Eds.), *Dyslexia: An appraisal of current knowledge.* London and New York: Oxford Univ. Press.

Owen, F. W., Adams, P. A., Forrest, T., Stolz, L. M., & Fisher, S. (1971). Learning disorders in children: Sibling studies. *Monographs of the Society for Research in Child Development, 36* (Serial No. 144).

Pavlidis, G. T. (1981). Sequencing, eye movements and the early objective diagnosis of dyslexia. In G. T. Pavlidis & T. R. Miles (Eds.), *Dyslexia: Research and its applications to education.* New York: Wiley.

Stevenson, H. W., Stigler, J. W., Lucker, G. W., Lee, S. Y., Hsu, C. C., & Kitamura, S. (1982). Reading disabilities: The case of Chinese, Japanese, and English. *Child Development, 53,* 1164–1181.

Stevenson, H. W., Lee, S. Y., Stigler, J., Lucker, G. W., Hsu, C. C., & Kitamura, S. (1984). Family variables and reading: A study of mothers of poor and average readers in Japan, Taiwan, and the United States. *Journal of Learning Disabilities, 16,* 150–156.

Stigler, J. W., Lee, S. Y., Lucker, G. W., & Stevenson, H. W. (1982). Curriculum and achievement in mathematics: A study of elementary school children in Japan, Taiwan, and the United States. *Journal of Educational Psychology, 74,* 315–322.

Vellutino, F. R. (1979). *Dyslexia: Theory and research.* Cambridge, MA: MIT Press.

Vogel, E. F. (1963). *Japan's new middle class.* Berkeley, CA: Univ. of California Press.

8

Self-Expression, Interpersonal Relations, and Juvenile Delinquency in Japan

KOSUKE YAMAZAKI, JOHJI INOMATA, and
JOHN ALEX MACKENZIE

In the year 1686, at the age of 43, Matsuo Basho, one of the most renown poets in the history of Japanese literature, sitting near a pond in Fukagawa, at the edge of Edo, present-day Tokyo, composed in one brief moment his most famous verse, one of the most famous in the history of Japanese *Haiku*[1] poetry:

> furuike ya
> kawazu tobikomu
> mizu no oto

or, in translation:

> on rustic pond
> jumps a frog
> plop!

In a sense, modern Japanese youths are this frog that either disturbs or enlivens that which was once more quiet, Japanese society. The frog as an

---

[1]*Haiku* is a major, unrhymed form of Japanese poetry, consisting of 17 syllables in three lines of five, seven, and five syllables, respectively. It has been characterized as "A peculiar form of wit, concentrated to the last degree, too short and rather too stiff to sing" (Miyamori, 1940, p. 3).

effect in *Haiku* poetry expressed a pleasing cry to Japanese people, but the cry of youth today in Japan is in fact grating.

This paper will discuss present-day Japanese youth amid a background of junior high school student mischief, vandalism, and violence; these events are one part of this 20th century which has transformed Japan from the relatively quiet pond of the Tokugawa Era (1603–1868) to the comtemporary torrential movement of people and trends that is modern Japan.

This study is divided into eight parts entitled: (1) this 20th century and the past 100 years as a typhoon of great social change for Japan; (2) differing cultural–semantic nuances of the three key terms of this paper, "self-expression," "interpersonal relations," and "juvenile delinquency"; (3) youth as cult and subculture in modern Japan; (4) self-expression turns to violence; (5) broken families and juvenile delinquency; (6) attachment behaviors: nonverbal communication between mother and child; (7) transition in the father's role in Japan; and (8) discussion and conclusions, in which we seek a twining of the various threads of violence and other antisocial behavior by the young in Japan.

The Twentieth Century and the Past 100 Years as a Typhoon of Great Social Change for Japan

This century has been, particularly for the industrialized countries of the world, what all other centuries have not been: a time of drastically increased food production, improved knowledge of nutrition, improved medical care, and, as a consequence of these, an increased number of elderly and young people. Also, this century has seen the development of long distance and, ultimately, mass media, starting with wire communication and continuing with the wireless radio, the telephone, the motion picture, the television, and, now, the video cassette machine.

This is not all of course. Two world wars and several smaller ones have plagued and continue to plague the increasingly interdependent nations of the world, and total nuclear devastation of the planet as a possibility is no mere fantasy. The world economic system remains unstable, and the past two decades have seen countless expression of difficult change, whether in the form of warning and advice about future shock, or in the form of discontinuity or uncertainty, in the present and beyond. The world does not rest easily.

Even without this world-wide trend for uncertainty and anxiety, Japan would still feel itself in the throes of change, and uncertainty, for indeed the past one hundred years have been a watershed, separating Japan from its Basho past and its high-wave present. Japan was in those years transformed in a dizzying series of changes from a self-isolated, rural, and poor nation with a long cultural past to almost an electronic marvel. Now, many Japanese seek the reaffirmation of vestiges of that cultural past amid the sweep and sound of its rapid trains, its musical wrist watches, and even its semirenegade young people on motorcycles in the early hours of the morning.

The changes in the past 30 years, during which Japan raced from total devastation to almost total prosperity, have been, for the very most part, not only positive but even inspiring, as a source of pride of this country's people. The past 10 years, however, in which youths' violence and related misdeeds and indiscretions have increased and in which the violators are increasingly younger, are less appreciated and most ominously perceived as to this country's future.

School and school-related violence have increased to such a level that the Prime Minister of Japan, Yasuhiro Nakasone, pledged his entire cabinet's efforts to deal with the problem, saying that the Ministry of Education should not have to deal with it alone. National debate centers on the problem.

This is where the Japanese people find themselves now. The answer will be of use, we feel, not only to Japan but to the industrial and industrializing countries facing similar problems in their own societies. The debate turns to the primary question, "What is it in the youths' background and experience that has led to such behavior, that is, why?"

Since Japan has been involved in truly major change in these past years, it is essential to consider not only how such young people are but also how they came to be. As phychic development starts immediately at birth and is affected by social nurturance, we feel it impossible to examine adolescent behavior without crucial reference to some common features and, we feel, results of early child upbringing.

Differing Cultural – Semantic Nuances of the Three Key Terms of This Paper

Self-expression, in the very broadest sense as the child's movement in the womb, begins even prior to birth and proceeds from primitive reflex to socially ordained modes, both verbal and nonverbal; for the infant to grow, self-expression must be received by the primary nurturing individual, the mother. Thus, self-expression for growth implies an interpersonal context, and frustrated self-expression is frustrated interaction, taking such initial forms as headbanging or chronic silence and proceeding to more explicit, often self-damaging forms.

Specifically, therefore, we find three terms of essential use in examining the present question of troubled youths, terms that allow us to consider earlier and present conditions in which the youths have come to be: (1) self-expression, (2) interpersonal relations, and (3) juvenile delinquency. By these terms we mean, respectively, (1) the expression or assertion of one's personality, as in conversation, including nonverbal, almost involuntary communication, as well as written language; (2) the relations between people in an ongoing and mostly hierarchical interaction; and (3) violation of the law by the preadult individual. It is necessary to note some subsidiary, cultural nuances in these terms. In noting such in the Japanese linguistic context, we will be indicating the relevant *kanji* (漢 字), Chinese ideograph or ideographs. These characters were introduced into the Japanese language from the seventh century A.D. on, amid the simultaneous introduction of Buddhism and other features of Chinese civilization. *Kan* (漢) is the old name for China, derived from the Japanese name for the Chinese Han Dynasty (206 B.C.–220 A.D.); *ji* (字) is the Chinese character for "letter, figure," and thus *kan-ji* in essence means "Chinese letter." In speaking of Japanese words, then, we are fundamentally speaking of the appropriate Chinese character or characters.

The English word "self-expression" is rendered into several forms in Japanese, depending on the exact meaning implied. Self-expression, in the sense of literary composition is termed *jiko hyōgen* (自 己 表 現). The phrase is composed of two sets of four ancient Chinese-derived pictorial characters. *Ji* (自) means "oneself" or "itself," and *ko* (己) means "oneself," "myself," "yourself"; *hyō* (表) is derived from the verb expression of the character, *hyō suru* (表 す る) or *arawasu* (表 す), meaning "express, show, manifest"; and *gen* (現) means "present, existing, actual," thus, "one's self expression of what is present in one."

Self-expression in the sense of "self-fulfilment" or "self-realization" is rendered in Japanese by the term *jiko jitsugen,* in which the third character in the previous expression is replaced by the character *jitsu* (実); *jitsu* means "truth, reality, substance, essence."

Whereas a Western person would regard a large portion of his or her actions as expression of one's self, there are a number of actions or manners that a Japanese person would regard as expression not so much of their "one's self" but rather of their "social self." This derives in part from Japan's historical adoption of the Chinese ethical system, **Confucianism,** developed by the fifth to sixth century philosopher of ethics and morality, *Ko-shi* (孔 子) or **Confucius.** The essence of Confucianism in Japanese, traditional Chinese, and even modern Chinese society is polite response to those above due to their superior position and wisdom and respectful response to those in the lower portion of a hierachical relation, indicating the higher individual's possession of a sense of benevolence. In this adopted school of ethics, the correct form of address and behavior to others is essential for the harmony and, to use a modern term, the functioning of society. This is one reason why the Western practice of debate in schools and in society generally is regarded with some diffidence. The reaction is even stronger in immediate interpersonal relations, whether in the home, school, or office (MacKenzie, 1977). There are ways to say essentially anything in Japanese society, but due to Confucian requirements and, particularly, native Japanese stress on interpersonal harmony, these ways may require roundabout, circuitious forms of expression. One's expression in Japan may not always be explicitly one's individual self-expression, and shyness is not looked at with distain, for it is felt to express a common social purpose, mutual restraint, and mutual respect. Thus, the "social self" plays a major role.

There are, however, many situations where an individual's response is derived from "one's self," as in compositions which the elementary student completes for his teacher. Junior or senior high schools, in contrast, have no courses in writing, certainly of the expository kind (although chance for literary composition with poems such as Haiku is possible), nor do the universities have Japanese-language expository writing courses. Thus, for the most part, the first time a Japanese student meets with the practice of self-expression in the written English manner is often in an English-language course of such design.

There are some very definite cultural reasons for such omission. Art in the form of India-ink drawings, calligraphy, or poetry, all very much influenced by the concentrating powers of Zen Buddhism and the Japanese sense of the enlivening power of nature, was often a medium of free self-expression, amid the antagonisms of civil war, as well as the communal requirements for rice farming. What one said to the other villagers or what one set of villagers said to another set could in fact mean life or death, by war or by parched soil, and thus one tended to turn inward for self-expression. There are certainly powers in such forms, and Western individuals are coming to realize this; indeed, Western individuals are taking to Japanese *Haiku* and working at developing an English-language *Haiku* (MacKenzie, 1979). At the same time, Japanese are beginning to look to forms of self-expression which have long been a part of the Western social landscape, including on occasion the expository and even persuasive essay.

Recently, some universities and some employers have included essay questions in their examinations, placing a premium on original thinking, wide reading, and analysis. Some social commentators have urged the remaining large number of institutions which have not included essays to do so (Matsuoka, 1979). The entrance examinations for all levels, however, including those of the companies, still stress mathematical problem solving and memory instead, very much in the manner of the original Chinese bureaucracy-selecting examinations, which inspired the Japanese form. It may be safely said that Japanese education in general stresses the social self, as in quantifiable knowledge explicitly useful for and usable by society, rather than the individual self, in which some knowledge may have a less clear and predictable relation to the general society. This may be one factor in the present junior high school difficulties.

"Interpersonal relations" is rendered in Japanese as *taijin kankei* (対 人 関 係). The double character, *taijin,* means in division "opposite, versus" *(tai),* and "person" *(jin);* The second set of characters, *kankei* (関 係), consists of the characters *kan* and *kei. Kan* by itself means "gateway, barrier," but in the verb form, *kakawaru* (係 わ る), means "concern oneself in, have to do with," and the character *kei,* by itself, as a noun, means "duty, person in charge" and in verb form, *kakawaru,* means "concern oneself in, have to do with." Thus, *taijin kankei* literally means "concerned with or connected with the connection between opposite persons."

Interpersonal relations, as *taijin kankei* (対 人 関 係), is a very recent addition to the Japanese vocabulary, deriving its use in this century from Western psychiatrists and psychologists. In that sense, the terms are more or less similar, but, in fact, while one will sometimes hear "interpersonal relations" in daily conversation in the West, one will almost never hear *taijin kankei* used, outside of a clinical context, to describe relations in daily life in Japan, whether of a higher, lower, or equal relational nature. The term *taijin kankei* is clinically useful due to its relative novelty and its grounding in psychiatry and psychology, but to comprehend the *fact* of interpersonal relations in Japan, in whatever context, it is more useful to know two other facts. The first is that *tai* literally means, as we have noted, "other or versus," and it tends to be used in situations of opposition; *inter-,* derived from a Latin preposition meaning "between, among," does not imply opposition or confrontation. Thus the nuance of *tai* is potentially unpleasant, while that of *inter-* is potentially fruitful, even optimistic, and certainly neutral as to the possibility of abrasive confrontation. *Tai-,* it should be noted as well, is used in the phrase *taijin kyofu,* meaning fear *(kyofu)* of the other person, a neurotic condition particularly but not exclusively to be seen in Japan, where the Confucian-based rules of communication are comparatively stricter than in the West and where offending or even becoming a target of the "opposing" person is not a rare complaint among Japanese neurotics.

Second, in contrast to this objective but somewhat "cold," clinical term is another used by the general populace to describe interpersonal relations in which native Japanese ideas of warmth (or "wetness," in the Japanese parlance, in the sense of a real plant being better than a dry, artificial one), can be expressed without fear of "opposition." This affectively positive phrase is *ningen kankei,* which differs, of course, from the previous in the first double-character word, *ningen,* substituting for *taijin. Ningen* (人 間) consists of the character *nin,* meaning person (a very simple pictograph indeed), and *gen,* meaning "between, among"; thus *ningen kankei* means the relation between people, and "people" is literally the *relation between people.* The relational aspect is deeply stressed in the definition of people or "human beings" (Kondo, 1968). It is accurate that Japanese pointedly translate the whole phrase as "human relations," and this is the popular counterpart to the more neutral "interpersonal relations," which Westerners tend to use synonymously with "human relations." The English term, "human," in fact derives not from an initial meaning of the relation between persons but from "earth," as in the sense of ground; thus, a human is an "earthly being" (Klein, 1971). The very fact that Japanese specialists chose not to render "interpersonal relations" as *ningen kankei* but rather as *taijin kankei* arises from the former term having already being preempted as a long-accepted phrase describing a fundamental orientation in Japanese society regardless of profession or education.

The final term to be reviewed here, "juvenile delinquency," is first of all not a psychiatric term in essence; rather, it is legal and administrative in origin (Mirel & Solomon, 1974). It is also a relatively new term in English, when one considers the longer history of the two terms being used separately, not only in English but also in Latin, from which these terms originally came in separate form. "Juvenile delinquent" in Japanese is rendered as *hikō shōnen* (非 行 少 年), another set of two two-character words. The first set, *hi* and *kō* mean respectively, "mistake, misdeed, wrong, non-, un-, anti-" "party, suite, journey, expedition, line, row." The latter two two-character words, *shō* and *nen,* mean respectively, "small, few, young" and "year." Thus, literally, *hikō shōnen* means "one of young years who is against the row or party of society," whereas the English counterpart to one of these words, "delinquent," means "one who leaves from" [*de* meaning "from" in this case, and *linquere,* meaning "leave," both from the ancient Latin (Lewis & Short, 1879)]. One should note that the Japanese phrase, by use of the *kō* figure, stresses action against the group, that is, society, while the Western, English term only implies this action, which we interpret as evidence of the greater group-oriented conception of society in the Japanese context. Such group emphasis, though, should not be too difficult to grasp for even the more individualistic countries of the West when it is remembered that the ancient Chinese character *kō* was developed from the early pictorial sign in China meaning "traffic intersection," for perhaps if nothing else makes East and West mutually comprehensible, it is the simultaneous presence in both areas of drivers who go over the speed limit and, thus, are regarded as "delinquent" in their driving duties, as determined by those

world-wide, well-known officers of society, the traffic police that both nations understand.

As can be seen, interrelations are particularly emphasized in Japanese
society, and self-expression has greater curbs in Japan than in the West
(although some of these have been lessened in the past three decades). Delinquency is reprehensible to Japanese, not only due to concern over safety but
also because it violates the interpersonal code of Confucian ethics. This is
why current youth behavior is no less than baffling to many Japanese.

Youth as Cult and Subculture in Modern Japan

Japan sought, from the end of the Tokugawa Era on, to catch up with the
West industrially and technologically. This she largely has been able to do.
Though unceasing progress was the view of the 19th century, amid industrial
triumph and technical breakthrough, the 20th century views more wisely the
dual nature of social and technological change. In these days, the dubious
benefits of modernity are making their mark. It is difficult, even at this point,
to brand the emergence of an almost separate subculture, even a cult, of
youth as a plague. It has brought numerous problems, however, in tow. One
of these results is that youth and adulthood cannot clearly make sense of one
another. The development of a youth subculture is so notable, and to some
in Japan so regretable a development, that it can scarcely escape notice, no
matter what the persuasion of the viewer. Since it is so similar to the youth
explosion of the 1960s in the United States, some regard it as mere copying.
Other observers regard it as an inevitable feature of "Americanization." We
regard the latter explanation as essentially correct but would substitute the
terms "urbanization/modernization" as more to the point.

Nonetheless, the United States has had a profound and deep influence,
either directly or indirectly, in supplying the models of industrialization and
change. Thus, in either sense, noting what has happened before in the United
States is useful for comprehending what has and might happen to Japan's
youth. Let us, then, look back to the 1950s in America (MacKenzie, 1982).

The beginning of a so-called youth culture had its roots in the 1950s in the
United States with the emergence of a new form of music, one almost
entirely directed then to teenagers, "rock n' roll," originally only the name
for a particular dance (of sorts, as adults would see it), which became the
symbol and, some would say, "symptom" of a new era. Along with this
music, social commentators in the United States began to notice new attitudes and forms of communication, both verbal and nonverbal, and new
forms of dress.

American parents were at first amused, as one can judge by reading, for instance, *Life Magazine* articles on the emergence of Elvis Presley, but as the years went on and the United States entered the sixties, replacing the mirth and levity were attention and even caution, with the realization that the young had become almost a kind of separate class, distinguished not so much economically as socially, in the manner of behavior.

Japanese youth at that time took to the manner of behavior of youth in the United States to some degree, first in the patronage and even ownership of jazz coffee shops, or in Japanese, *jazu kissa,* and then by the mid-1960s in the slight flowering of hippie-like affectation in dress. Things, though, were still relatively tame among the youth here.

Self-Expression Turns to the Form of Violence

The watershed of change seems to have begun in the very late 1960s when universities both in the Western world and Japan erupted with shrill rockets of almost wholesale revolt, certainly rebellion, in protest over what students felt were domestic and international ills (MacKenzie, 1983). In 1969, officials of the University of Tokyo, in consultation with the faculty, decided to cancel the admissions examination for that year, after the university's main building was under active siege for several months. Western newspaper readers may recall the photograph of this building amid tear gas, masked radical students, and general pandemonium.

With the slow but generally clear winding down of the Vietnam War, the universities in Japan, the U.S., and Europe calmed down. In Japan, the universities became quiet, but the junior and senior high schools perversely took their place. Trouble was then edging more directly into the family. A series of newspaper articles in the early to mid-1970s painted a picture of students who no longer particularly trusted their teachers, some who would exert violence against teachers and principals, and a few who would expend effort at mutilation and destruction by planting homemade bombs immediately near their homes.

Almost uniformly, the source of this violence was grievance over dress standards. Male students increasingly insisted, for the most part unsuccessfully, on wearing long hair, like their university counterparts.

Beyond the mid-1970s is no different, except that the amount of school violence has increased and taken some new twists. Violence has extended beyond the campus. There was, for example, a series of attacks on vagabonds in Yokohama, to the immediate south of Tokyo, perpetrated by junior high school students and their older friends. They all seem to have been quite obedient to authority in school, but their academic performance had been poor since elementary school, and they were hard-to-control youths within the family (*Mainichi Daily News,* 1983). The single motivation for their attack, which led to the death of some of the hobos, was that they found some individuals they could look down on and "lord it over." There are other reports of similar attacks elsewhere in Japan, and psychiatrists and others suggest this tendency to attack the weak may not be so rare among other youths, if recent clinical evidence is indicative.

Broken Families and Juvenile Delinquency

Given this worsening situation, it is not surprising that the number of cases of consultations by psychiatrists and psychologists involving delinquent children has been on the increase (Inomata *et al.,* 1982). Cases are also increasing in severity: In 1975, nearly 8% (1843) of juvenile delinquent cases were sent to child welfare institutions of the Institute for Training and Education of Juvenile Delinquents, and that number is increasing.

In looking at national totals, three basic facts emerge: first, delinquents are now younger than before. The 15-year-old group is now the largest in number, followed by the 14-year-olds (Fig. 1). Second, the female offenders have increased as a proportion of the national totals. Third, what we might call "for kicks only" offenders increased proportionally, their offenses including shoplifting; auto, bicycle, and motorcycle theft; seizure of others' possessions; and the vastly more serious offenses of house theft, arson, and rape. In addition to all of these was violence in the home against parents.

To the south of Tokyo there are eight National Child Guidance Clinics located in Kanagawa Prefecture, and the number of consultations with delinquents and parents at these clinics has definitely increased. There were 848 cases in 1975 and 948 in 1979, a 12% increase. In 1979, 63 children were sent to juvenile delinquent institutions. The number of consultations in the nation was 15,757, and the proportion of delinquent consultations in Kanagawa Prefecture was 6.0% of the national total.

An intensive study of self-image and family background at one juvenile delinquent institution/school, in Kanagawa Prefecture, was conducted in April 1982, involving 44 youngsters. Subjects were examined with standard instruments and the "Parent–Child Test" of the Tanaka Education Institute of Tokyo; this last test was developed in the 1960s to deal with the kind of parent–child difficulties that are the subject of this paper. The questions are in conversational, colloquial form to encourage accurate response. The findings are indicated below:

The delinquent juveniles came primarily from urbanizing or urban districts.

Half of them were 14 or 15 years old; 9 of them were 10 years old.

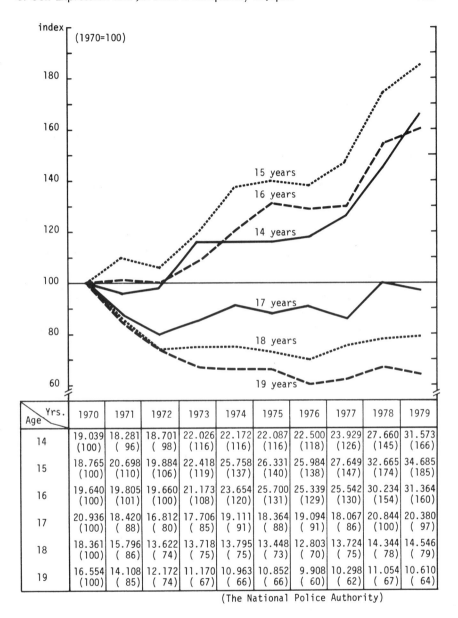

Age \ Yrs.	1970	1971	1972	1973	1974	1975	1976	1977	1978	1979
14	19.039 (100)	18.281 (96)	18.701 (98)	22.026 (116)	22.172 (116)	22.087 (116)	22.500 (118)	23.929 (126)	27.660 (145)	31.573 (166)
15	18.765 (100)	20.698 (110)	19.884 (106)	22.418 (119)	25.758 (137)	26.331 (140)	25.984 (138)	27.649 (147)	32.665 (174)	34.685 (185)
16	19.640 (100)	19.805 (101)	19.660 (100)	21.173 (108)	23.654 (120)	25.700 (131)	25.339 (129)	25.542 (130)	30.234 (154)	31.364 (160)
17	20.936 (100)	18.420 (88)	16.812 (80)	17.706 (85)	19.111 (91)	18.364 (88)	19.094 (91)	18.067 (86)	20.844 (100)	20.380 (97)
18	18.361 (100)	15.796 (86)	13.622 (74)	13.718 (75)	13.795 (75)	13.448 (73)	12.803 (70)	13.724 (75)	14.344 (78)	14.546 (79)
19	16.554 (100)	14.108 (85)	12.172 (74)	11.170 (67)	10.963 (66)	10.852 (66)	9.908 (60)	10.298 (62)	11.054 (67)	10.610 (64)

(The National Police Authority)

Fig. 1. Change in the number of juvenile offenders by age.

Half (48%) were from single-parent families (nearly equal father- and mother-headed households), and 20% had at least one adoptive or step-parent; 9% were in foster homes.

Ten percent of the mothers gave birth while 16–19 years old, 10 times the national rate.

Fifty-six percent of the fathers were temporary, day laborers, and 28% were on welfare.

Only half the parents had graduated from high school, and mothers tended to have more education than fathers.

Nearly 60% of the cases perceived their parents as rejecting, and 25% saw their parents as inconsistent in discipline and without expectations for their children.

Family discord was a background to the majority of cases (59%), with academic underachievement, habitual vagrancy, peer pressure, and other factors being primary in the remainder of cases, as determined by the attending psychiatrist.

Behavior problems were reported to have emerged several years before the child's appearance in the clinics, almost entirely by age 11 (see Fig. 2).

The specific delinquent behaviors nearly always included theft or shoplifting, with interpersonal violence, vagrancy, or truancy also occuring in about

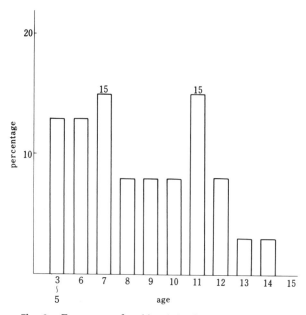

Fig. 2.   Emergence of problem behavior by age ($N = 39$).

one-third of the cases; sexual misconduct, arson, substance abuse, and other vandalism were involved in a few cases each.

Self-concept of the juvenile delinquents was poor; the great majority saw themselves as cruel (100%), selfish (89%), meddling (82%), and irresponsible (73%); they also tended to consider themselves dependent (60%), withdrawn (59%), the object of peer and teacher disapproval (50%), unable to adapt to others (48%), and apathetic (25%).

The majority (61%) had at least normal IQs (90–140), while 34% were borderline (71–90), and 5% had IQs under 70.

Psychiatric examination indicated neurotic symptoms (thumbsucking, tics, etc.) and anxiety in the great majority of cases.

Academic underachievement was common (57%); school personnel rated the majority (59%) of cases as unable to follow directions and said fully half were without a sense of trust.

The students saw their teachers as devoted to their work but did not respect or admire them.

These, then, are the subjects of the Kanagawa study, their family situation, and their subsequent condition; as chronic juvenile delinquents, their expression of self remains deeply limited. The school in which they find themselves has no walls or guards, and the director and instructors seem to be doing the very best they can. The students are, for the most part, able to enter the working world with a determination to further outgrow their difficult beginnings. These youths are not among the most incorrigible of chronic juvenile delinquents.

The school in fact is akin to the "proved school" system in Britain, in that the students, through interview, examination, and ongoing behavior, prove themselves worthy of entrance, continuation, and, at the end, graduation. All of the above does not remove the legacy of their broken family environment. Teachers are severely challenged by the students' poor picture of academic studies. There are periodic staff/faculty conferences on the student problems and problem students. With the parents having had poor education, with the parents' direct and indirect expression to the children of their supposedly hopeless future, with some parents barely, if at all, known by their child now in the institute/school and others divorced, with some of the children having one foster parent along with their other natural one, and with inconsistency in words and deeds by the parent or parents a constantly experienced fact in their upbringing, it is not surprising that these young people find it extremely difficult to trust those in whose charge they find themselves and even for them to trust themselves.

One thing in their favor in a therapeutic context is their honesty, even sincerity, in a one-to-one communication context. Certainly, insight becomes more possible then, but much of what they achieve in understanding and other real efforts for growth is challenged by the force of the group, particularly in the classroom. Once in a group, they revert back to some of their earlier ways, the intensity of which is hardly reduced by their being in the middle of the adolescent rebellion period. But as we have said, most of the students are able to graduate, having shown at least the required minimum academic effort, as well as some perhaps more genuinely self-motivated effort in other aspects of school.

In addition to academic work, general attitude is an area requiring effort. When they enter the school, the students are required to keep medium hair length, but many voluntarily have their hair cut shorter, as a way to signal their efforts to change. In the manner of professional athletes with whom they can identify more easily than those in academic careers, they devote much of their efforts to playing baseball, and the school's students have won a number of pennants in the process. It is very difficult to play life, as it were, in the same spirit that they play baseball, yet the diamond brings them closer to taking life on in the same spirit of good will and effort. Sports, in any event, remains the particular bright spot in an otherwise plodding-through effort.

In the family, these young persons' self-expression, in any sense of the word, was thwarted in the interpersonal relation of child and parent, so thwarted, in fact, as to make it perhaps inevitable that they would be led to choose one of the least developed forms of self-expression, crime. When and how such individuals can be helped is one of the basic questions of the helping professions. Perhaps that effort can begin even before the child has learned to speak, much earlier than is commonly thought.

Attachment Behaviors: Nonverbal Communication between Mother and Child

When did these and other young people begin to receive the various communications from their parents that would in part form them? This is a question relevant to a study by a research group in the Department of Child Psychiatry at the Sapporo City General Hospital (hereafter referred to here as "the Sapporo group") on the question of infant and mother self-expressing communications known as "attachment behaviors," a concept introduced into developmental psychology by Bowlby and developed by Ainsworth, studying mother–child interaction in various cultures including the Ganda people of Uganda. These attachment behaviors are said to be a most important basis for the development of communicative function not only in short but long-range terms.

We should like to note here some features of this theory: The healthy baby usually exhibits behaviors such as spontaneous vocalization, smiling, climbing, movement, and quiet playing, expressed to its mother in the form of "signs" which the mother can correctly interpret and respond to by touching, lifting the baby in her arms, calling, watching, smiling, giving toys, rocking her baby, and so on. Thus, the baby's spontaneous behaviors and the mother's reactive behavior become alternately, in interchanging manner, "initiation" and "response." The interaction between the baby and its mother progresses dynamically, based in part on the biological maturation of the baby's central nervous system.

Considering the question of how the interaction starts, the baby first behaves spontaneously, stimulating the mother, then the mother reacts with timely and adequate responses, thus eliciting more baby behaviors. When these interactions grow continuously and appropriately, the baby's spontaneous behavior will be transformed into social behavior.

Based on the clinical observations of the Sapporo study group, it has been found that the mothers of children with developmental disorders usually report, "He had never cried to me" or "He had been very quiet and never worried about me during the infancy period." In fact, these mothers have had very serious problems already in their interaction with their babies due to this absence, and clinical examination revealed that attachment behaviors expressed by the baby were scarce in quantity and quality and delayed in appearance. These particular problems of attachment behaviors seem to express themselves in various, that is, pathoplastic ways.

It would be clinically useful to classify schematically mental disorders in childhood through the form of manifestation of development of attachment behaviors during the infancy period, and that is what the Sapporo group set out to explore. Although longitudinal investigation of mother–baby interactions would be preferable for some purposes, this preliminary study employed a maternal interview and retrospective checklist, with informal observation of the child, for data collection (Yamazaki, 1982).

The subjects of the investigation were 61 autistic children, 70 children with developmental speech disorders, 61 children with mental retardation, and as normal controls, 100 1-year-old and 70 4-year-old children. All children with developmental disorders were given developmental or intelligence tests with results to suggest no significant variation in degree of retardation. Clinical psychologists investigated attachment behaviors of children with developmental disorders through observation of their actions and by asking their mothers as to the existence of pertinent behaviors, using a check list devised by the group. Then, child psychiatrists examined and observed the children, making the respective diagnoses. Data on normal controls were collected by clinical psychologists, using the same check list. One-year-old children were checked at a public health center, and 4-year-old children, at a kindergarten.

This check list for attachment behaviors during the infancy period, as devised by the group, consisted of 14 items (see Table I). When the group established the items for the check list, they placed emphasis on six kinds of basic behaviors, crying, clinging, sucking, following, smiling, and eye-to-eye contact, and selected concrete behavior patterns related to these interactions from observational reports on retarded children. In addition, the group added finger pointing and modeling which they deemed very important indexes for evaluating levels of mental development.

The results were as follows: 10 of the 14 items were found in similar proportions of the normal 1- and 4-year-old children (Table I). "Crying" and "following" were more common in 1-year-old children, and "active peek-a-boo" (that is from the child to the mother) and "finger pointing" were significantly higher in the 4-year-old children than in the 1-year-olds.

The Sapporo group concluded that there are in fact communication traits demonstrated in the items of the check list that develop from the 1-year-old to the 4-year-old point. Next, the group compared the appearance rates in three groups of children with developmental disorder to the 4-year-old group of normal controls. The appearance rates of all items are lower among

Table I.

Normal Controls

	Percentage children exhibiting behavior	
Behavior	1-year-old	4-year-old
Holding position at feeding	97.0%	100.0%
Anticipatory behavior at feeding	94.0	92.8
Visual attention	96.0	98.6
Eye-to-eye contact	99.0	100.0
Social smiling	—	82.9
Clinging	83.0	64.3
Crying	79.0**	71.4
Response to calling	99.0	100.0
Fear of strangers	79.0	74.3
Following	86.0*	71.4
Passive peek-a-boo	99.0	92.9
Active peek-a-boo	77.0	95.7**
Finger pointing	76.0	98.6***
Modeling	98.0	98.6

*$p < .05$.
**$p < .01$.
***$p < .005$.

Table II.

Comparison with Normal 4-Year-Olds and Developmental Disorders

Behavior	Infantile autism	Developmental disorders[a]	
		Developmental speech disorders	Mental retardation
Holding position at feeding	n.s.	n.s.	***
Anticipatory behavior at feeding	***	n.s.	***
Visual attention	***	n.s.	***
Eye-to-eye contact	**	n.s.	n.s.
Social smiling	***	***	***
Clinging	*	n.s.	n.s.
Crying	***	n.s.	***
Response to calling	***	***	***
Fear of strangers	***	*	n.s.
Following	n.s.	n.s.	n.s.
Passive peak-a-boo	***	n.s.	n.s.
Active peak-a-boo	***	***	***
Finger pointing	***	**	***
Modeling	***	***	*

[a]n.s., not significant.
*$p < .05$.
**$p < .01$.
***$p < .005$.

children with infantile autism, developmental speech disorders, and mental retardation (Table II). The appearance of attachment behaviors is low in those with developmental speech disorders, lower with mental retardation, and lowest with infantile autism. In addition, in mental retardation and developmental speech disorders, attachment behaviors tended to appear late, but in infantile autism they were even later. "Passive and active peak-a-boo" rarely appeared even at the oldest age among the autistic children.

The comparison of attachment–communicative behaviors in infantile autism versus other developmental nonautistic disorders is shown in Table III. The item of "holding position" is higher in the autistic than nonautistic group, but this behavior seems to be very difficult to recall retrospectively at the 3- or 4-year-old stages. The appearance rates of "response to calling," "fear of strangers," following," "passive or active peak-a-boo," "finger pointing," and "modeling" in the autistic group are statistically lower than in the nonautistic group. So, concluded the Sapporo group, these seven

Table III.

Comparison with Autistic and Nonautistic Groups

Behavior	Groups[a]	
	Infantile autism	Nonautistic disorders
Holding position at feeding	*	
Anticipatory behavior at feeding		*
Visual attention	n.s.	n.s.
Eye-to-eye contact	n.s.	n.s.
Social smiling	n.s.	n.s.
Clinging	n.s.	n.s.
Crying	n.s.	n.s.
Response to calling		***
Fear of strangers		**
Following		***
Passive peek-a-boo		***
Active peek-a-boo		***
Finger pointing		***
Modeling		***

[a]n.s., not significant.
$*p < .05$.
$**p < .01$.
$***p < .005$.

behaviors are very important for differentiating infantile autism from mental retardation and developmental speech disorders. Interaction behaviors between the infant and the mother have clinical meaning for developmental pathoplastic processes in infantile autism.

In summary, children with developmental disorders were generally deficient in attachment behaviors, and these behaviors were delayed in appearance compared with the normal controls. Autistic children, especially, were more deficient both in quality and quantity of positive and active behaviors toward their mothers, in comparison with the nonautistic retarded and delayed children.

On the basis of this study of attachment behaviors during infancy and other observations, we distinguish three groups, illustrated in Fig. 3: (1) that in which there is a deficiency in spontaneous attachment behaviors exhibiting infantile autism, mental retardation, and certain kinds of organic behavior disorders; (2) that in which there is no major disturbance of attachment

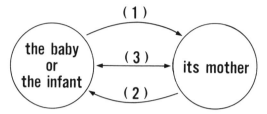

Fig. 3. (1)infantile autism, mental retardation, organic behavior disorders; (2) neurotic manifestations, personality disorders; (3) developmental speech disorders, developmental disorder of congenital visual or auditory disorders.

behaviors in the child but in which the mother shows failure to respond to such behaviors due to insufficient primary maternal involvement, the infants then exhibiting various neurotic disorders; and (3) that in which both the spontaneous attachment behaviors of the children and the primary maternal involvement are lacking, the children exhibiting characteristic developmental disorders of speech, vision, or hearing.

Using this schematic classification in terms of attachment behaviors, we can tentatively locate the Kanagawa youth subjects primarily in category 2, and to a lesser degree, in category 3. But what of those youths who exhibit at most brief juvenile delinquency or, instead, are violent only within the home or, in contrast, show only violence to vagabonds in public parks along with the other preadult members of their group; where do they fit in the context of this nonverbal form of early self-expression? We do not as yet know the answer, indeed (if we can be pardoned for seeming to make a pun), the study of attachment behaviors is yet in its infancy. Its potential for preventive psychiatry is indeed great and it suggests so very much of how little we know as yet. We know even less of the infant's interaction with other members of the family, including the father, and it may very well be in the great interests of Japanese society for research to be able to answer this latter, related question, for even now as we face the future the very likely effects are now in process.

Transition in the Father's Role in Japan

A fundamental change in the father's role in child raising in Japan has occurred in the past 100 years, most pointedly in the past 30, and we speculate that the evidence of this change is now before us in the psychiatric clinic. In looking into the etiology of recent problems of youth—juvenile delinquency, violence at home and school, and others—we can often find clearly marked conflicts between children and their parents, particularly between the children and the fathers. (Yamazaki, 1978/1979).

In studies on child development so far, the mother–child relation has been appropriately, but almost exclusively, emphasized, and until recently it was thought that the preadolescent period was the earliest stage in child development in which the father's influence could be seen. According to newer studies on the effects of paternal absence from the family, however, it has become increasingly evident that the father's role is quite important even in much earlier stages.

Historically, the father's authority in the Japanese family was clear. An ancient Japanese proverb says that one should fear "earthquakes, lightning, fire, and father," in that order. The change in the father's position in Japan began first notably with the entry of Japan into the modern world, with the Meiji Restoration, as this new, modern, and industrializing era was called, but this transformation grew particularly in the aftermath of World War II, in which Japan experienced major political, legal, administrative, and social change. For the most part, Japanese regard these changes favorably, but some of the changes cause nagging doubt and arouse great discussion, although clarity, through nationwide concensus, is lacking on most of such changes at this time. Nonetheless, despite the major changes in the father's role, notably in the education of sons during the Meiji era, the prewar Japanese father had much at his disposal by law, including the system of primogeniture, to ensure and underscore his responsiblity and central authority. Most of these legal features were done away with in the immediate postwar period, to prevent the recurrence of militarism and fascism.

This was in essence the origin of the changes in the father's role as defined in the new constitution of Japan, promulgated over three decades ago. Fascism and militarism have not appeared in Japan, but clearly the father's role has become very weak, so much so that even comic books here have taken to pointing out the limits, if not the miserableness, of the position of father, one example being the comic series entitled *"dame oyaji"* or "Pitiful Pop." This is, as we have suggested, quite a change in the context of Japanese history, and it has been treated seriously by the Japanese historian Kiyoyuki Higuchi in a book entitled *Hoping for Father* (Higuchi, 1977).

Higuchi writes that the Japanese father figure came into prominence in the stone age at a time when Japanese lived in small groups and ate foods gathered by hunting males. From stone implements discovered in shell heaps dating back 9000 years ago, it is quite clear that the art of fishing was highly developed. The stone age father trained his sons in fishing and sailing, an art that contributed to defense from foreign invaders as well.

In the Neolithic Era (or *Jomon* Period, 8000–200 B.C.), however, people grouped into hamlets and started to live in fixed locations. Marriages between the men and women of neighboring hamlets became the accepted pattern. During this age, the parents had their own distinct roles in child education: The father was the transmitter of the art of production, and the mother provided guidance and training in the arts of home life.

In the next age, the *Yayoi* period (200 B.C. – 300 A.D.), people began to engage in rice-based agriculture and to acquire holdings of rice and land. Adult males, with economic control over rice production, came to assume positions of power in society. This was the origin of the Japanese paternal family system. The familiar Japanese word for father, in the sense of the English words, "dad" or "pop," is *"oya-ji"* (お や じ) and is derived from a very early time in Japanese history. Etymologically, "oya" means parent and "ji" means the hand that symbolizes labor. Thus, in ancient times, the father was the person connected with physical labor.

As may have been evident in examining *Kanji* figures earlier in this paper, the ancient Chinese pictograph often tells the story of its meaning, if one examines the figure closely enough. The character representing "father" (父) was formed by a combination of the symbols, "right hand" and "stone ax." Thus, etymologically, the character for "father" is literally "having a stone ax in hand and working" as can be seen in Fig. 4.

Similarly, the character for "mother" (母) tells a social – historical tale and account of role. This character was created at about the same time as the character for "father" and was formed of the subsidiary characters for "woman" and "breast"; the character for "mother" is etymologically in essence "woman nursing a baby," illustrated in Fig. 5.

The periods and eras following that of the Yayoi saw a continuing and progressive strengthening of the father's role at home and in education, increasingly of the written, cerebral type. Looking most briefly at this progression toward recent times, we note that in the *Kofun* Period (4 – 5 century), the Yamato Court succeeded in bringing the country under single rule; in the *Asuka* Era (6 century), in which Buddhism came to Japan, several influential clans moved closer to amalgamation; during the *Heian* period

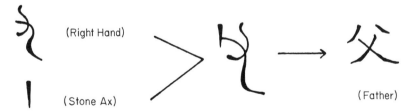

Fig. 4.   Ancient Chinese pictographs. The characters for "right hand" and "stone ax" combine to form the character for "father," meaning "having a stone ax in hand and working."

(Woman)   (Mother)

Fig. 5. Ancient Chinese pictographs. The character for "mother" was formed from a combination of the characters for "woman" and "breast." "Mother" means, in essence, "woman nursing a baby."

(8 – 12 century), known to Westerners through the literary work *Genji Monogatari* by Murasaki Shikibu, husband and wife came to live more together amid the growing power and influence of the imperial court; in the mid-Heian Period, samurai, or warriors arose to oppose and terminate the power of the Heian aristocracy. When not at work on their fields, these warrior–farmers fought for their honor and subsequent authority. When at home they tended to their sons' education and their own in the reading of classic writings. In the *Sengoku* Period, or civil wars period, samurai became indentured to feudal lords, the *daimyo,* and in the *Tokugawa* era (17 – 19 century), rule of the country was resolutely obtained for over two and a half centuries by, first, Tokugawa Ieyasu and then, successively, by appointed rulers of the Tokugawa clan. In this latter era, money lending merchants came to supercede the nominal samurai rulers, themselves forbidden to engage in commerce, and these merchants showed acumen both in finance and in the education of their sons.

It was the *Meiji* Period (1868 – 1912) in which, amid the move to industrialize and modernize in Western terms, a national educational system was created and the right of the father to educate his sons passed to the government. Psychologically, as self-compensation for this loss in privilege and authority and to ward off a sense of alienation, the father grew more affectionate toward his children, replacing the more distant but authoritative relation of several centuries past.

We can see in psychiatric clinics today the effects of this change. Both today's father and child have difficulty delineating their own ego-boundaries, and within these dynamics, both depend on and even psychologically damage one another through unclear and half-hearted authority relations, in which one seeks to guide but have loyalty, through affection, and the other to be guided, at least protected, yet escape the implied controls. Today it is the mother, not the father, who strenuously and, in fact, excessively urges her son on in the almost literal battle to enter a major, elite university. The mother has earned the common sobriquet *kyoiku mama* ("matriculation mom"), for her almost single-minded devotion, if not preoccupation, with her son's entrance to, particularly the elite of elites, Tokyo University, and it is now a yearly ritual for mass-media magazine and newspaper photographers to catch sight of her and son in tow, she unmistakably overjoyed if the university announcement board says her son has made it.

The father plays little role in this except to pay tuition, a mere pecuniary contribution. A gap thus ensues, and to deal with it the father attempts to mold himself into an understanding figure, which in the end fails, the father giving up on his role for the most part, resulting in the attenuation of the father–son tie.

The recent rapid growth of the nuclear family stimulates this attenuation amid the narrowing of what was in prior times authority-related distance. There is now too much "nearness," in various forms, as the Japanese sociologist Matsubara (1968) has pointed out: (1) nearness in interpersonal relations in the family, brought about by the sudden shrinkage in family size; (2) nearness in physical living space in the home, due to the spatial shrinking of Japanese houses and apartments; (3) nearness in access to information and knowledge in this information age; and (4) nearness of others, the wife and the elder children, to the financial support of the home, seen in these individuals also undertaking work, part time or otherwise, to help the family pay its way.

The father in fact wonders what his role is; he has his work in the company, but he plays little role in the home, due to long hours away at work, and neither attempts nor is successful at communicating his work experience to his sons.

Discussion and Conclusions: Twining the Threads

In this paper we have indicated that Japan in so many respects was literally transformed, and the latest feature of this transformation is seemingly permanent estrangement of youths from their elders, increasing in proportion and occurring at decreasing ages. In looking closely at the values of youths in Japan, one finds, from the 1960s on, an increasing consciousness of being young, in fact, of being "young people" in the manner and form of subculture, a cult of youth. Of late, this subculture has increasingly turned to anti-social behavior, as older generations define it, explicit violence, and juvenile delinquency. In the severer expression of this delinquency, broken families with very poorly educated fathers and aspiration-denying parents are the tragic rule. We believe that particularly chronic juvenile delinquency and neurosis may well correlate with the suppression of attachment behavior communication and that what is now being learned of this crucial mother–child link may have its counterpart form between father and child. Recent explicit role confusion by the father and father–son psychological dissonance may be the direct outcomes of primary change in the father's authority and position in the family.

How may one twine these threads of a terribly common hue, and what does one obtain? We feel it is nothing other than the cloak of parental, particularly paternal, authority, increasingly incapable of being worn, such that the father is emerging as the emperor without clothes, except that his modern Japanese counterpart is clearly sensing the bitter and icy wind.

The threads not only can be twined, they are already intertwined in unmistakable junction. One can see both the family in the school and the school in the family, though hardly with a sense of composure. Increasingly, popular television programs seem to call for a "good guy" kind of teacher (MacKenzie, 1982), almost to the point of dissipation, and this parallels the "pal" approach that modern Japanese fathers attempt toward their children, their sons in particular. In universities, many students complain of excessive distance from faculty, but more often the real distance is from study itself. There are undergraduates who chronically fail to graduate, and due to indulgent university regulations, graduation can be prolonged up to 11 years. This graduation phobia seems to have roots in common with preuniversity school refusal (Kasahara, 1974). In both cases, the individual seems healthy, except for a paralyzing desire to avoid competition in life; in most instances the individual is male. One psychiatrist finds the central conflict in such students to be a pervasive unsureness of one's masculinity and notes further that in clinical experience, the father in these families is depicted as weak and vague in performing his role. As the specialist notes, parents fear to exert authority for common fear of stifling their children's freedom, and children themselves resist various controls they regard as "out-of-date."

In marrying, many young people do want freedom, but this "freedom" often translates into leaving troublesome matters to others. There is an increasing number of child abuse cases by young couples who approach their child rearing in the manner of a superficial hobby. A growing number of young fathers seem to be irritated by their children when they are no longer cute and gentle. Mothers too, at an increasingly early age of motherhood, go to work even when family economics do not require it, and the number of Japanese day-care centers (or as they are called here, "baby hotels") has rapidly increased over the past 5 years, despite a somewhat tardy public awareness of their neglectful, even de facto abusive, nature.

These various calls for new freedoms have a similar sound to those issued by youths in the United States during the latter 1960s. The so-called new freedoms, there, have had a chance to jell, and what do U.S. observers see?

Christopher Lasch (1979), in his powerful analytical work, *The Culture of Narcissism,* points to illiteracy and falling standards in secondary and higher education, and Harvard University, in response to a decade of a nationwide smorgasbord approach to liberal education (arising with the cries for "educational relevance" in the 1960s), has brought back a system of required courses within the context of a general plan. Harold Voth in his 1977 warning, *The Castrated Family,* noted a divorce rate among young people of over 50%, 8 $\frac{1}{2}$ million children having only a single parent (usually the mother), a sharply rising number of illegitimate children, day-care centers providing most of the "home life" for the many infants and older children, and increases in child abuse, delinquency, and drug abuse, among many, many other problems. Clearly, then, new freedoms are something to be looked at with caution, even trepidation, but then, where parents' will is lacking, even trepidation is not enough.

Japanese youths seem to be aware of the environment in which they find themselves. One of the present authors included in a literature course at Japan's Waseda University the popular American novel of the 1960s, *I Never Promised You a Rose Garden* (Greenberg, 1964). It held great appeal for the students and over one-third of the final term papers dealt with the social background in that novel, particularly the ineffective father of the young protagonist, who eventually succumbed to schizophrenia. These Japanese students commented in depth on their impressions of the troubled Japanese family of the late 1970s. One student opined, "The lack of the father's authority is caused by 'tender-hearted' fathers who have sham tenderness." Recently, some sons have taken to killing their fathers and some fathers have taken to killing their sons, so at least in some cases the "tenderness" is wearing thin.

The treatment of mental illness does not have as a primary technique the manipulation and reformation of the social structure, but in the manner of a rice farmer's doubts about a village sluice gate as he floats out to sea, some major attention to faulty structure is essential if the cultivation is to be done. That is what this paper has attempted to do.

Acknowledgments

We are indebted to Professor Kiyoshi Makita for his kind advice and counsel in the writing of this report.

References

Greenbert, J. (1964). *I never promised you a rose garden.* New York: Holt.
Higuchi, K. (1977). *Oyaji Taiboron (Hoping for father).* Tokyo: Chikuma Publishing.

Inomata, J., Yamazaki, K., Makita, K., MacKenzie, J. A. (1982, July). *The interrelation between parental attitude and juvenile delinquents in Japan.* Paper presented at the 10th International Conference of the International Association for Child and Adolescent Psychiatry and Allied Professions, Dublin.

Kasahara, Y. (1974). "Graduation phobia" in the Japanese university. In T. S. Lebra & W. P. Lebra (Eds.), *Japanese culture and behavior: Selected readings* (pp. 323–331). Honolulu: Univ. Press of Hawaii.

Klein, E. (1971). *A comprehensive etymological dictionary of the English language: Dealing with the origin of words and their sense development thus illustrating the history of civilization and culture.* Amsterdam: Elsevier.

Kondo, A. (1968). *Noiroze kangeiron: Ningen no kaifuku o motomete (Meeting neurosis: In search of human recovery).* Tokyo: Kōdansha.

Lasch, C. (1979). *The culture of narcissism.* New York: Norton.

Lewis, C. T., & Short, C. (1879). *A Latin dictionary.* London and New York: Oxford Univ. Press (Clarendon).

MacKenzie, J. A. (1977). The psychocultural associations of deliberative assembly. *Bulletin of the Institute of Language Teaching, 16,* 1–24.

MacKenzie, J. A. (1979). In essay of an English language *Haiku,* or: Can a seventeen syllable stranger find happiness in Big Tussle, Texas? *Bulletin of Atomi-Gakuen Women's University, 12,* 5–16.

MacKenzie, J. A. (1982). What various young people are communicating. *Report of the Department of General Education, Tokyo University of Fisheries, 18,* 83–93.

MacKenzie, J. A. (1983). Japan's yearly university entrance exams: Hell or heaven-sent opportunity? Unpublished manuscript.

Mainichi Daily News (Tokyo and Osaka) (1983, February 13). Youth gang eyed in attacks on tramps, p. 12.

Matsubara, H. (1968). The modern family. In *The family* (pp. 29–65). Tokyo Univ. Press.

Matsuoka, H. (1979, July 18). Zooming in: Schools, students need character. *Mainichi Daily News* (Tokyo and Osaka), p. 4.

Mirel, E., & Solomon, P. (1974). Child psychiatry. In P. Solomon & V. D. Patch (Eds.), *Handbook of psychiatry.* Berkeley, CA: Lange Medical Publications.

Miyamori, A. (1940). *An anthology of Japanese Haiku, ancient and modern.* Tokyo: Kodansha.

Voth, H. M. (1977). *The castrated family.* Mission, KS: Sheed and McMeel.

Yamazaki, K. (1978/1979). Transition of the father's role in Japanese family and culture. *Annual Report of the Research and Clinical Center for Child Development,* Hokkaido University, Sapporo, Japan.

Yamazaki, K. (1982, July). *Attachment behaviors of babies and infants with developmental disorders.* Paper presented at the 10th International Conference of the International Association for Child and Adolescent Psychiatry and Allied Professions, Dublin.

Youth gang eyed in attacks on tramps. (1983, February 13). Mainichi *Daily News* (Tokyo and Osaka), p 12.

9

The Straight Path:
A Fijian Perspective on a
Transformational Model
of Development

RICHARD KATZ and LINDA A. KILNER

> *"Mana"* (the spiritual power) is close at hand here in Fiji. Some of us are called to bring that *mana* to the people for healing. That can be frightening, but the hard part is just beginning. To become a healer we must learn to use *mana* properly . . . to use it only for healing. We say that to become a healer we must follow the straight path . . . and also find it. That is a long and difficult process. (R. Katz, 1981, p. 58).

So speaks a highly respected Fijian healer about the process of becoming a healer, which is described, as well as guided, by following the "straight path" (*na gaunisala dodonu*) (R. Katz, 1981). Traveling the straight path means living out certain attributes that characterize the "ideal Fijian." Although it functions throughout Fijian culture, the straight path is often followed most intensely by healers. Because being a healer is an achieved role, one is not prepared by birth to travel the straight path. As one healer put it, "It is hard to walk along this straight path because there are many times when we are tempted to stray, and times when we cannot clearly see where the path goes." The community views healers as approximately the cultural ideal as they struggle to follow that path. The straight path can be seen as a general paradigm for psychological development in Fiji that is distinguished by such concepts as "envisioning" (R. Katz, 1981) and "moral exploration" (Katz, 1982c).

The Role of Culture
in Developmental Disorder

Healers in Fiji do not merely heal the sick; they are involved in seminal tasks of psychological development, constructing a sense of life's meaning and determining what is real. As one villager remarked about the spiritual healer in her village, "He can't get sick, because without him, we would all be lost." The healer's transformation, occurring as the straight path is followed, represents a model of ideal development for the individual, the village and the culture as a whole. The process of following the straight path suggests a transformational model of development (R. Katz, 1982a, 1986, 1987).

The Fijian material presented in this paper suggests an approach to the understanding of individual development that differs from Western approaches. In general, Western developmental theory concerns itself with documenting the consistent patterns of individual activity occurring over time. Theorists such as Piaget (1970) see the individual passing through a series of predetermined, epigenetic stages. However, critiques have been levied against underlying assumptions of hierarchical theories of development (Phillips & Kelly, 1978). The transformational model, in contrast, emphasizes disequilibrium more than equilibrium, transitioning rather than stages achieved. It allows for many developmental trajectories, eschewing both the importance and universality of a teleological framework. The model connects power and vulnerability and integrates individual and sociocultural development, while recognizing the fundamental role of spiritual aspects of development. The transformational model presented here critiques the concept of universal life-span trajectories. Some Western theorists have also pointed to the historical and cultural relativity of Piagetian stages (Demos & Demos, 1969; Kett, 1971; Nesselroade & Baltes, 1974; Ashton, 1978). In proposing the transformational model, however, we hope to go beyond pointing to the relativity of Western stage theories by describing areas of omission in Western theories offering alternative concepts.

Stage theories have been most useful in pointing out the regularities of growth in childhood. Recently, theorists have recognized limitations of these theories in describing adult development (Labouvie-Vief, 1982). Although the transformational model functions for Fijian culture as a whole, the model deals literally with adult development since practicing healers are in fact adults. Therefore, the distinctions between this transformational model of development and Western stage theories may be due in part to the model's relative emphasis on adult development rather than the child-centered focus of stage theories. As Western theories of adult development become clearer, we will be able to clarify the aspects of the model attributable to age differences.

The transformational model is based on and derived from ethnographic data—the model is articulated through a careful description of that data. While the model's description of Fijian development is established, research establishing its applicability to other cultures is just underway (Cheever, 1987; Hahn & Katz, 1985; Hampton, 1985; R. Katz, 1981, 1982b; Menary, 1987; Nûnez-Molina, 1987; Seth, 1987; Simonis, 1984). Nevertheless, because of its alternative dimensions and approach, the model may have much to offer Western theorists constructing new theories of adult development. Before the model is explicated in detail, however, data on the development of Fijian healers must be presented in its ethnographic context. The model's unique qualities will then be highlighted and its cross-cultural applicability considered.

Being and Becoming a Fijian Healer[1]

Data on the process of being and becoming a Fijian healer helps reveal the structure and dynamics of the straight path. Guided by that path, which they help to uncover, the healers' life is one of transitioning. Their development, and the expression of that development in healing practices, is characterized by a constant oscillation between meaning and confusion, power and powerlessness, reality and the unknown. Being and becoming a Fijian healer exemplifies a transformational model of development.

The data discussed in this chapter comes from the field research of the first author in the Fiji Islands for 20 months, from 1977 through 1978. Material was gathered using standard ethnographic methods such as participant observation, spot observations, and interviewing. In addition, psychological tests were given to matched samples of healers and nonhealers to delineate specific healer characteristics, and attitude scales were given to the community to delineate characteristics of healing systems. Finally, more than 1000 client–healer interactions were recorded and analyzed over a 1-year period to document patterns of utilizing healing resources within a village (Katz & Lamb, 1983).

The island nation of Fiji, consisting of 100 inhabited islands and 500,000 people, is situated in the South Pacific, north of New Zealand. Approximately 50% of the population is descended from emigrants from southern India who came as indentured servants more than 100 years ago. The persons who are the focus of this chapter are indigenous Fijians who reside in a chain of rural outer islands. They live in villages of about 100 people, located along the coast, several hours from each other by foot. There is no electricity on those islands nor motorized land vehicles or roads, though outboard engines power the open 20-ft boats used for fishing and transportation.

---

[1]This section is based on R. Katz (1981, 1982c).

These Fijians live primarily by subsistence farming and fishing.[2] A village consists of several groups of closely related kin who jointly own land and choice fishing areas, often working them communally. Sharing of resources is highly valued. When Fijians sit down to eat in the village, their doors always remain open. Whenever anyone passes by, they call out, "Please come in and eat." Fijian social structure is hierarchical, but humility, regardless of status, is valued.

Ceremonial life is essential in Fiji, promoting economic and social exchange and celebrating the religious dimension. Three main elements characterize Fijian ceremonies generally and the healing ceremony in particular: the *Vu* ("ancestors") the *mana* ("spiritual power"); and the *yaqona*[3] ("a plant with sacred use") that brings the *mana* to humans. Dead ancestors are accessible, generally benevolent, and felt to be close at hand. *Mana,* the ultimate power, is an invisible, irreducible force that "makes things happen." As Fijians say, *"Mana is mana,"* and its effects are often described as miraculous. The *yaqona* is called the "nourishment of the gods." When humans offer *yaqona* to the ancestors in the correct ritual manner, the channel of communication to the ancestors is opened, and their *mana* becomes available.

The healing ceremony, centering around the ritual exchange of *yaqona,* typically begins when the patient comes to the healer with a request for help. The patient incorporates the request within a ritual presentation of *yaqona* to the healer. The healer accepts the *yaqona* on behalf of the ancestors from whom he or she draws healing powers. *Yaqona* may be prepared with water and drunk by the healer. In the healer's act of acceptance, the healing is accomplished. In that moment, the *mana* is said to become available, making possible an accurate diagnosis and the selection of an effective treatment plan. The patient returns after 4 days for the conclusion of the treatment or, if necessary, further treatment in the same or some new direction. Herbs and massage are used in about 25% of the instances to carry out the healing. Various types of massage can be employed, and there are numerous herbs in the natural pharmacopia.

Yaqona is the ever-present accompaniment and stimulus of Fijian social life. A Fijian elder voices what is common knowledge, "A Fijian cannot live without the *yaqona.* It is what makes our village live and work together."

---

[2]Valuable ethnographic material on Fiji is provided by Thompson (1940), Nayackalou (1975, 1978), Sahlins (1962), Ravuvu (1976), and M. M. W. Katz (1981). The M. M. W. Katz thesis involves the same district dealt with in this chapter; the Thompson and Sahlins books deal with other rural outer island communities. Spencer (1941) is the most recent work on healing and deals with a group of people on the main island of Fiji.

[3]Yaquona's botanical identification is *Piper methysticum.* It is widely used in the South Pacific and is also called "kava kava."

During day-to-day social occasions, the *mana* lies dormant. The healing ritual turns the *yaqona* into an active channel for the *mana*. Performing the ritual is one of the healer's many technical skills. Healing also requires substantial interpersonal skills and social sensitivity. Helping a patient may require the understanding of belief; resolving a village crisis may also require political negotiation and realignment of groups.

Fijians group sicknesses into two major categories, depending on their etiology. "True" or "real sickness" *(baca dina)* is caused by natural events. For example, one may have painful joints from being in the cold ocean too long. The second type, "spiritual sickness" *(baca vakatevoro),* is caused either by witchcraft or by some violation of cultural norms, punished directly by the ancestors. While Western medicine is reserved for treating "true" sicknesses, both "true" and "spiritual" sicknesses are brought to Fijian healers. The same symptom pattern often can express either etiology.

There are a variety of traditional Fijian healers. We will concentrate on the *dauvagunu* or the spiritual healers, in distinction to the herbalists and massage specialists. Spiritual healers treat the broadest range of problems as well as the most severe. Sicknesses with a spiritual etiology are their special province, while the majority of cases present physical symptoms. Requests for help vary widely: a boy with a swollen neck, a childless woman who wishes to become pregnant, a family seeking protection against others' evil intentions, and an entire village wanting to make amends for violating a sacred custom.

Healers remain fully contributing community members. When they were compared with a sample of nonhealers matched on a series of demographic variables, healers were rated as more "respected," closer to the "ideal Fijian," and "harder working." Healers are villagers first and foremost.

Healers may request the healing influence of *mana,* but others may subvert the *yaqona* to request *mana* to work against someone. Fijians call this latter practice witchcraft. The healing ceremony deals with resolving uncertainty and making comprehensible the unknown. Most important, it is the primary arena in which the forces of good and evil — healing and witchcraft — struggle against each other. Because these forces are ever present, the healers must be educated in the *gaunisala dodonu* ("straight path"), so they will use *mana* exclusively for healing purposes. The journey along that path is what enables healers to direct *mana* toward healing. Though *mana* is accessible to many, not many become healers; one *dauvagunu* serves approximately three villages.[4] As one healer put it, "Few know how to begin walking on the path and even fewer know how to stay on it."

---

[4]Other healers are more common; there is one massage healer for every one of two villages, and frequently two herbalists may work in one village.

Traveling the straight path means living out attributes that characterize the ideal Fijian. The healer's character creates the possibility of healing work, and the development of character marks the continuation and deepening of that work. Information about healing techniques is available only to those with character. There is respect for technical aspects of healing, but character precedes and provides a context for healing technology.

The following attributes are often mentioned when prescribing the way a healer must live in order to follow the straight path:[5]

> *dauvakadina* (telling and living the truth): The amount of truth in each person determines the power of your healing. You must speak to your patients only what you have been told by your guardian ancestor. If you elaborate on that, and add your own opinions, or try to show how much you know, you are just lying.
>
> *dauloloma* (love for all): In this healing work you should love everybody, whether a relative or foreigner. They are all the same for you. You must help them all because of your love.
>
> *i tovo vinaka* (proper or correct behavior): The mana is getting weaker in Fiji because people are not now following ancient customs. We must observe these customs, . . . if our behavior is to be proper.
>
> *sega ni vukivuki* (humility): This work is your secret. Showing this work to everybody, even those who do not need your help, is boasting.
>
> *vakarokoroko* (respect): Everybody must be respected. Each person deserves our love and help. And the traditional ways of the land must be respected. We show our true nature by such respect.
>
> *sega ni lomaloma rua* (single mindedness): You must firmly and fully believe in your work and faithfully worship your guardian ancestor. Once you decide about something and judge what is right, you must stick by your word and seize the moment to act. No wavering or turning back.
>
> *veigaravi* (service): The power is to be used only for healing and serving others. You cannot use it to harm or kill others, or for your own personal gain, to get money or other things. That must be very clear. If you do, the power leaves you.

Though these attributes are often phrased in terms of the healing work itself, they prescribe the way a healer in particular, and Fijians in general, must live.[6] The characteristics of the ideal Fijian and those toward which the healer must aspire overlap. Becoming a healer means striving toward Fijian cultural ideals. Though the Fijian people are Christianized, important aspects of indigenous religion remain and support these ideals. Fijian healers are the guardians of this indigenous system.

[5]The quotes which describe the attributes come from several different spiritual healers.

[6]Although healers use phrases and describe values that are similar to those of Christian belief, there are many aspects of Fijian beliefs that are not identical with Western church doctrine. Where there is an overlap in the two systems, it is difficult to know the origin. But since identifiable elements of Christian beliefs are at present thickly blended with beliefs that do not seem of recent Western origin, and since traditional Fijian legends exemplify the attributes of straight path, it is likely that these attributes were also part of the indigenous system before the Christian influence.

On a variety of economic and social indicators, furthermore, healers are the same as nonhealers. Becoming a healer in Fiji does not bring economic rewards or increased social status. However, healers do differ from non-healers in their response and relationship to *mana*. Healers associate *mana* more frequently with healing than do nonhealers, respect it more, and consider it more powerful than do nonhealers. Healers also feel less surprised, afraid, and anxious when *mana* comes to them, since for them the experience of *mana* is more familiar. The healers' distinctiveness is focused in their motivations and beliefs which prepare them for their healing work, allowing them to work intensively with *mana* where others cannot.

A common metaphor of the straight path is a path cut by hand with a cane knife through heavy forest underbrush. In creating the path one must follow dead ends and shortcuts, torturously difficult passages and relatively easy ones, causing the healer's movement to fluctuate in rhythm and speed, sometimes circling back on itself. "Straightness" refers to a "correct" or "straight" attitude and motivation. As healers attempt to keep their motivation straight, they may be besieged by disequilibrium, involved as they are in transitioning. The straight path describes a process of the difficult and fluctuating evolution of a correct attitude or motivation; it is an inner journey expressed in behavior within community context. The straight path does not describe a process of orderly change characterized by equilibrium. It is not charted by clear directions, nor does it unfold in a linear progression, and its success is not defined by levels or stages of achievement. The straight path is not an externally measured career line.

Of those healers who embark on the journey, not all continue on the straight path. Some give up working with *yaqona,* as they find the path too demanding and see themselves as unwilling or too weak to continue. Others may continue practicing the healing ceremony, even though their commitment has become pretense. The ceremonies are empty performances and can be harmful. Clients receive false expectations, and practitioners are prone to attempt witchcraft.

Straying from the straight path is deviating from cultural ideals. But the process of straying is more a lack of striving for the ideals, than a failure to attain them, as the ideals are not seen as fully or permanently attainable. Traveling the straight path is living a life of special dedication to those ideals, more than in a step-by-step achievement of behaviors reflecting those ideals.

Healers in Fiji are not only respected but also feared. In deviating from the straight path, they become dangerous, as their power can then be used, at least temporarily, to harm others. Deviation represents not simply falling away from ideals but also gaining a dangerous, harmful power; deviation is therefore not without its rewards for certain people, who are thereby released to pursue their own interests at the expense of others. But such behavior is considered totally unbecoming for a Fijian, a violation of the order which is meant to govern Fijian life.

Sickness or misfortune is the common expression or manifestation of that deviation. In order to heal, the healer must stay on the straight path. Deviating from the path results not only in the loss of healing power but usually results in sickness as well. Sickness, though manifested in particular physical and psychological symptoms, can reflect social and spiritual imbalance, disturbances created by interpersonal jealousies or improper behavior. Sickness and health reflect the degree to which individuals and communities are living within the cultural ideals.

In the generic sense, the straight path is a means for negotiating the construction of experienced reality. Concepts of sickness and health imply patterns of meaning making with moral implications. In following the straight path, one constructs and reconstructs reality in a culturally valued manner, creating as well new and expanded constructions for the future. Morally correct living, and its consequence of health, is the ground from which such constructions become possible, as well as their reward. In contrast, failing to find or follow the straight path implies and leads to constructions of reality which are devalued by the culture. These "mistaken" constructions of reality are expressed in devalued (or "bad") behavior and eventually are manifested in sickness or misfortune for the person and his or her relatives.

But the straight path is not easy to follow, let alone find; it requires constant struggle and effort. The path itself is never straight, but filled with detours and dead ends; the travelers' intention must be straight, beset as it is by continual tests and challenges. The path describes a way of being *dodonu,* "straight" or "correct"; requires honest intentions and moral behavior. Though the path itself is not straight; the way one travels it should be:

Healers mark the beginning of their work with a first vision, one that calls them to healing. They place life-changing significance on the experience. Here is the first healing vision of Loti, a traditional spiritual healer or *dauvagunu:*

> I was sleeping or maybe just resting a bit. The ancestor of our village appeared to me as a woman. She told me to go to the cliff by the shore and jump on the ancient Fiji canoe that lay in the bay. I went to the cliff. The boat lay beneath, far below. I was afraid to jump . . . but jumped, landing on the deck. The canoe sailed out to sea. Suddenly a sea snake appeared, and around its neck, hanging by a gold chain, was the *mana*-box. The ancestor told me to take the box. She said it was for me. But I was very afraid, afraid the snake would bite. I approached carefully, using a long pole from the sail to try to lift the *mana*-box off the snake's neck. I hesitated more than once, and moved cautiously. I reached out with the pole . . . and failed. I was undecided about continuing on. A second time I reached out with the pole . . . and again failed to get the box. The ancestor said that I must return to the village. "The *mana* is not for you today," she said. The next day she appeared again. "You have one more chance. Leap

onto the canoe and take the *mana*-box." Again I went to the shore, leaped onto the
canoe and soon found myself facing the sea snake with the *mana*-box around its neck.
This time I did not hesitate. I slipped the *mana*-box off its neck and didn't even need
the pole. The ancestor told me that I was now to use that *mana* for healing, that I was to
begin the healing work. The next morning I awoke somewhat confused. How could I
begin to heal, I wondered, since I did not know how to perform the healing ceremony.
The ancestor spoke to me again: "Don't worry. You have the *mana* with you. Use the
mana for healing and the ways of healing will come to you." (R. Katz, 1981, p. 68.
Copyright © 1981 by the President and Fellows of Harvard College.)

The ancestor who wishes to provide *mana* for the healing work appears
during that first vision, offering the challenges of the straight path and the
potential for healing as those challenges are met. As Loti's indecision and
lack of courage threatens to turn his transitioning toward and away from the
mana into a paralysis of faith and action, he is inspired to become coura-
geously single-minded and to turn his transitioning toward healing actions.
With this new attitude comes sufficient character to make healing possible,
even though he knows no healing techniques. The techniques come to those
with the character to use them properly. The first vision calls for a commitment to use the power of *mana* only for healing.

These first healing visions, enhanced states of consciousness, vary in detail
and in intensity. For some, the vision occurs in a dream state, at times
moving into or out of a waking state; for others, the vision occurs while the
person is awake and, most often, alone. Frequently, the person sees the
ancestor, and usually they converse.

Altered states of consciousness in which the ancestors are felt, seen, or
heard are common among people of the outer Fiji islands, whether or not
they are healers. But fear dominates encounters between nonhealers and the
ancestors. These encounters are brief, and the opportunity for communication is not pursued. The prospective healer's acceptance of the ancestor's
communication and the commitment to work in alliance with that ancestor
distinguishes his or her experience from that of nonhealers.

The first vision presents to the healer a new way of being and behaving, of
viewing oneself as now capable of directing *mana* toward healing. The vision
signals permission to hold a healing ceremony. In affirming the healing value
of the ancestors, the healer shows courage in overcoming a fear that many
Fijians believe is "natural." This fear is supported by some urban ministers
who say that seeking communication with the ancestors can lead to working
with *tevoro* ("the devil") and the practice of witchcraft.

The first vision lays the foundation of the healing work — the connection
with the ancestor who will be the source of power and the commitment to use
that power for healing. It sets in motion a process we can call "envisioning"
(R. Katz, 1981). Envisioning helps healers to actualize the straight path
which unfolds along the lines suggested by the first vision, and to fill in the

details of healing techniques as they work. Envisioning is more than carrying out the intent of the first healing vision. It involves advice and instruction from a teacher, if there is one. It also involves subsequent visions, lessons learned from one's patients, and, most important, the actual practice of healing and learning to live with that practice in one's community. Becoming a healer is accomplished through envisioning, a recreation of that initial vision and subsequent visions, in daily life. The visions offer guidance for everyday behavior as that behavior in turn helps reshape the visions into actual guides to what is possible. The core transformational experience necessary to becoming a healer is thereby enacted and reaffirmed in daily life.

The first vision calls on the healer's emotional committment to healing rather than presenting information about healing technology. Healers must affirm their belief in *mana* often without knowing how precisely to conduct a healing ceremony; they agree to begin the healing work, trusting that specific healing techniques will come as the work is done. The call is felt as a painful challenge, a necessary responsibility, since Fijians are not meant to seek the healing power. One must try to refuse the ancestor's request, acceding only when the ancestor insists. As one intuits the pain and difficulty that characterize the healing work, a life filled with temptations, tests, and others' suffering one feels humble and unworthy of the responsibility of power. Many, especially those not yet adults, do not take up the healing work immediately after their first vision. Weeks, months, even years may pass. The vision may be reconsidered, its consequences reevaluated. Another strong emotional experience often precipitates the practice, perhaps an unexplained request for healing from a sick person.

Only one phase in the career of the Fijian healer is universal, the first healing vision. Visions most commonly occur in mature adulthood but can occur during adolescence or early adulthood. The first vision marks the entry onto the path, and the career of the healer consists of traveling on and developing in that path. The life of that healer is an unfolding of the first vision and an actualizing of the envisioning process. In traveling the path, the healer's power deepens as the ability to use and live with healing power matures.

Many prospective healers work first as assistants to established healers. Approximately one-third of prospective healers work as assistants to a healer who has just cured them and offer their help out of appreciation for the cure and respect for the healing power. About half of the healers, at the beginning of their careers, have a close relationship with an experienced healer, who helps the apprentice with difficult cases and provides general guidance. Through his or her behavior, the teacher demonstrates the straight path to the student. By traveling the path, the student learns how to walk it.

The straight path is characterized by "transitioning," the moving to and from situations and states. Being "betwixt and between" is the key experience rather than stasis. The key dynamic is the persons' ever-changing relationship to (spiritual) power. Though access to power generally increases with experience, that access constantly fluctuates. The continual points where the relationship to power is in flux are points of vulnerability for the healer, but they are opportunities for change, not merely times of danger. Traveling the straight path is a high-risk, high-gain activity.

The straight path challenges character, which unfolds amid confusing situations. The education of the healer deals with subtle movements back and forth along dimensions of character, at increasingly demanding levels. The movement itself releases increasingly potent healing power. But as one travels the path, living out the attributes of character becomes increasingly difficult. The healer is constantly tested through temptations to misuse power—tempted, for example, to charge money for a healing ceremony, to become sexually involved with one's patients, and otherwise to betray the attributes that define the path. Increased power is determined by meeting increasingly severe tests.

As the healer accumulates power, he or she begins treating broader problems, such as hostilities between villages. Because the magnitude of power makes it more volatile, and harder to control, the healer becomes more vulnerable. Also healers who are considered very powerful sometimes are suspected of witchcraft. Tests of the healer then become even more important.

Popular but sometimes superficial criteria for judging the healer's power along the path include: the number of clients seen, the importance of these clients, and the degree to which the healer's cures are considered "miraculous." The increasing severity of the tests faced and resolved by healers also determines his or her power. The accessibility of visions to the healer, their frequency, the number and power of the ancestors who visit, and the extent of direct communication between the healer and ancestor is said also to indicate the healer's power.

A criterion that is most important for judging healers' power is their total dedication to healing, expressed in the proper performance of the healing ceremony rather than in achieving specific cures. The healer's understanding, in contrast to knowledge, becomes most essential. Understanding is associated with the heart rather than exclusively with the mind, as is knowledge; it is a broadly emotional rather than a narrowly cognitive way of knowing.

Through the act of what we can call "moral exploration" the healer merges individual and sociocultural development (Katz, 1982c). The healer as "moral explorer" is sent as the community's emissary to unchartered realms of experience—areas of psychological, social, and spiritual ambiguity for the community, areas in which the meaning and structure of reality are confused or undeveloped. In returning, healers struggle to make meaning for the community as they interpret those realms. The journey is filled with risk — of being lost, of being wrong, of losing one's sense of place if not mind. The community's charge is simple: tell us honestly what you saw, and help us become clear about our reality with your interpretations, honestly made. The community's respect for healers is epitomized in its support of and reliance on these moral explorations.

Understanding the healer as a moral explorer suggests how the straight path functions in the creation, as well as maintenance, of cultural realities (Katz, 1982c). The core of the Fijian healer's education is finding and staying on the "straight path." It is this continual struggle which allows the healer to contact the most profound power in Fijian life and, more important, apply that power to healing. In this ever-demanding effort, the healer does indeed explore moral reality. Healers are faced with the task of defining reality in their constant interactions with the spirits and the realm of cultural mysteries. Defining reality, they impart meaning. Imparting meaning, they make judgments about morality. None of these activities is predetermined. Though the straight path has existed for many before them, all healers must find and travel the path for themselves. Encouraged and supported by the community, healers embark on a journey to new territories of experience. They formulate new questions of concern to the Fijian community about reality, meaning, and morality, and then the community looks to the healers for guidance in these areas. While seeking the enduring essence of their healing work — the transformation which allows them to release healing power to the community — healers are actively engaged in central issues of culture change. Though rituals of transformation recur, they are not necessarily static. In dynamic interaction with changing times, these rituals can provide guidance for the direction of change.

Crisis Points in Traveling the Straight Path

The following three examples collected by the senior author, the first based primarily on retrospective interviews and the next two on contemporary ethnographic data capture the movement and struggle to stay on the straight path and emphasize the accompanying processes of envisioning and moral exploration. The healer's increased power is accompanied by an increased vulnerability. The power is harder to control; the temptation to misuse *mana* is more overpowering; and staying on the straight path becomes more difficult. But these moments when the challenge of the straight path intensifies are the very moments when the healer also has the opportunity to facilitate significant individual and social change. The healer's development is always integrated with the development of the community. Though the examples which follow examine dramatic passages on the straight path, they illuminate the everyday dynamics of the path.

Visions of the New Fiji and Social Change

In the decades before World War II, there were several indigenous movements in Fiji calling for a return to traditional ways, a "return of Fiji to Fijians." One such movement, which traced its lineage to a charismatic leader named Jone, emphasized that Fijians should overturn the British colonial rule, shifting the government and especially economic affairs into their own hands. While not advocating violence, the movement did demand courage from its members as they had to proceed against a colonial regime that was firmly entrenched and liked by many Fijians. But the movement stressed that its path was correct, guided as it was by the *Vu* ("ancestors").

Saimoni, who came from a rural village on an outlying island, became a follower of Jone. Saimoni was very impressed with Jone:

> This man Jone was very special. When he spoke, we all listened. He had the Vu behind him. Then we knew the movement was right for Fiji.

At the urging of Jone, Saimoni set out to his home village to establish a community of "Fijians for Fijians." He began having a series of visions that guided his actions in this regard. At the start, his most difficult task was enlisting the support of other Fijians. Saimoni told a story about these efforts to gather supporters; it was a story told frequently during the establishment and running of the community and up until the present:

> When we reached the village it was just daybreak. The land was misty, with rain falling. As for myself, I left the village and went straight into the bush. In front was a big flat area of land with a very deep drain-pit. The drain-pit was filled with water about seven to eight fathoms deep. The bottom was also covered with gravel.
>
> I went straight ahead and jumped into the drain-pit, right to the bottom. When I landed at the bottom, I called the others to come down. They saw me, but withdrew.
>
> There was a path they could follow. I said: "If no one will follow me down here, then you should return . . . lest you shame me. Come! Who will come? Come Anare!" Anare was moved, so he jumped in. "Can't the rest of you see he hasn't broken his legs?" I said. "Come also Osea." Osea jumped down and came to us.
>
> "You others up there. Go away if you can't come down here," I said. We all had been tested in the jungle. Then another man jumped in, then another and another, until all had joined us down at the bottom of the water.
>
> We all went and stood around some stony places, and I told them the name: "This is the place where the word of God will fall upon you. Guard yourselves properly, stand fast and remember the Living God."
>
> We all stood there at the bottom of the water and looked straight up to heaven . . .

I said to them: "You had better watch out properly. Nobody to die, nobody to vomit, nobody to lose hope.

We all looked up . . . Then a thunderstorm cracked [above us]. When it cracked, it split in two, rushing toward one side with thunder and lightning. It was difficult to sit and face the sight.

The lightning came straight down onto my head. Because of this I was pressed down and my feet sank deep through the gravel. The others held one another so that they could stand still. The force of the lightning pulled me up again and hung me in the air for about five minutes. After that, it threw me back to the ground and told me to go and sit down and rest for ten minutes. I sat on the grass. My body was black. Then it gave its reply: "It has reached the fourth *gauna* (time or era)." Then it rose. The fourth *gauna* is at hand — now!

As Saimoni said, the fourth time *("gauna")* was about to arrive, and that was the time for Fijians. As he returned to his home village, this idea that the Fijian's time had come inspired his actions. He established a close-knit communal structure in which economic resources were shared, even more extensively than in villages at that time. He also removed expressions of British influence from the village, such as the British currency. Saimoni's movement captured the life of the village for more than a dozen years, and was well-known throughout the region.

The above story suggests the role that envisioning and moral exploration played in Saimoni's movements. Certainly, the story describes an incident in which people are challenged to explore unknown areas whose eventual meaning determines the course of their community structure. By jumping into the drain pit and struggling to stay underwater and face the terrible lightning, the men commit themselves to an uncharted direction but one which will establish the moral rules of the community where courage, hope, and group cohesion will be highly valued. In calling for indigenous self-rule, the entire movement, including Saimoni's community, was redefining reality. It was going against common understanding by stressing the negative aspects of British rule as well as stating that Fijians were capable, even ideally suited, for self-government.

The above story, and many others describing the formation and continuation of the community, was told many times. This combines Saimoni's own vision and a description of events. In retelling it, Saimoni and the community of listeners reaffirmed their commitment to the community; to keep community, such stories had to be relived as much as retold. The initial vision established the connection with the source of power Saimoni used for healing, calling for Saimoni's commitment, and calling upon him to confirm the commitment of others. The vision set in motion the envisioning process; Saimoni's behavior was thereby changed in response to his visions. As the story is told, it is offered as a description of life as well as an inspiration for living, a chronicle of events as well as a call to action.

The community was constantly beset by criticism from without and jealousies from within. Saimoni was accused of seeking personal power and rewards and, thus, of violating Fijian traditions of humility and service. Living out and living up to such stories was one method by which Saimoni and the community sought to keep on the straight path. Even today, as Saimoni — now old — tells the stories of his community, those who listen are deeply affected. One old woman, who was a member of the community, said: "Yes, his stories are true. That is how it happened. We had real power then." A young man, not yet born when Saimoni's community thrived, offered this comment: "Saimoni is a great storyteller. He makes us think about those days. We love to hear him tell stories." And an adult, whose uncles and aunts were involved in the movement, reflected:

> Saimoni and that community were special. They really got people to share with each other. They were the people who thought about Fijian independence long before we gained it from the British.

Through Saimoni's visions, the community felt empowered. Saimoni did not stop seeking the straight path after his initial vision. He worked to guide the movement in the past community and now, in retelling the stories, he works to make his present community "think about those days." Saimoni is indeed a moral explorer. Through his initial vision he was introduced to a new possible reality for his community — one of self-rule. Saimoni worked to bring this vision into communal consciousness and also to change attitudes and behaviors. The story-as-vision still stimulates the envisioning process in today's listeners, raising again the possibility — and for some the necessity — of moral exploration.

Indigenous Healing and the Imported Church

In Nagone, a rural village of approximately 100 persons located on an outlying island, there were four traditional Fijian healers and one Western-trained Fijian nurse. Tevita alone among the traditional healers was a spiritual healer *(dauvagunu),* as *mana* (the spiritual power) remained at the heart of his practice. People in Nagone turned primarily to the nurse and him to alleviate their problems and complaints. Although the nurse saw complaints that were considered due to "natural" or "true" causes, he saw complaints due to natural as well as "spiritual" causes, or so-called witchcraft.

Tevita was greatly respected both within his own village and the surrounding villages in the island chain. People spoke of his honesty and reliability rather than any great or dramatic healing power. They trusted him to do his best, without pretense or promising more than he can deliver. As one elder put it:

Tevita is one of us, just like the rest of us. He uses his healing powers carefully, to help the people, and doesn't brag about what he has done or take on cases which are not "his own" (beyond his ability).

In particular, people respected Tevita's understanding of traditional spiritual life. As the spiritual healer, he was called on to interpret dreams and custom, as well as to heal problems and complaints, all of which presumed an understanding of ancient spiritual knowledge.

Much of this respect was based on an even deeper respect for Tevita's teacher, Noa, who lived in the main urban area of Fiji. Likewise unpretentious and scrupulously honest, Noa was considered a model healer, an exemplary for following the straight path. He was widely respected as one who "knows the ancient ways and keeps true to them," who does not "publicize his practice," but "works quietly in his own way."

There had been many problems recently in Nagone. Three unexplained and unexpected deaths and one serious injury had intensified suspicions of wrong doing. Persons in the village came to Tevita requesting help; many requested interpretations of dreams that they believed portended further disasters. In requesting his interpretation, they were asking him not only to make meaning of the dreams but, in doing so, to prevent the dream content from coming to pass. As Tevita said, "There are many dreams; there are many problems."

Tevita remained the principle resource in Nagone for constructing meaning in life events from a spiritual perspective. Others in the village said that he was necessary for them to keep clear about the "right" and "wrong." As one of the older women put it:

These are troubled times. We are all confused about what to do, and suspicious of what others do. If it were not for Tevita, there would be a lot more sickness here.

Some in the village felt a different kind of help was needed and they invited Rev. Tale, an evangelic minister from the urban area, to come and preach. Rev. Tale was known throughout Fiji as a critic of indigenous Fijian religion. He felt it was unChristian. In a country which is nearly totally Christianized, his message was powerful, even though that conversion to Christianity has not displaced indigenous beliefs. Trying to be "better Christians," people in Nagone were receptive to his message, not explicitly recognizing that it would pit them against the indigenous healing that Tevita practiced.

Rev. Tale preached in Nagone village and condemned all things dealing with indigenous religion — the belief in Fijian Gods, the use of sacred objects, and the commitment to spiritual healing. He referred specifically to healing substances, such as ritual objects, herbal remedies and massage oil, which are said to contain *mana*, and are used for protection and healing. After his sermon, many in the village were convinced to "give up" their healing substances that were originally given to them by Tevita. The villagers handed them over to Rev. Tale, signifying their "new life" and their turning away from indigenous beliefs.

One morning, after Rev. Tale's departure, Tevita was sitting outside his house. We began a conversation, which quickly shifted to what was paramount in Tevita's mind. He stated his concern simply:

> I believe I must give up the healing work. Rev. Tale has said what I do with the healing is against God, that it is un-Christian. Already, most of those who help me in that work have given up their herbal remedies and massage oil. I just don't know what to do . . . but I think I must stop. I've decided to stop. I can't go on if it's against God.

Tevita appreciated that others needed his services, and therefore he hesitated to stop the healing work. But until he was clear about the value of his work in light of Rev. Tale's attack, he felt he must stop. He sent a message to Noa, his teacher, describing the recent events surrounding Rev. Tale's visit and seeking help:

> I have ceased the practice until I can be sure I am doing what is right. Please tell me what you think is proper, what you think I should do.

Several weeks passed until the message came back from Noa. In the interim, Tevita no longer practiced healing. During that time, there was an unusual number of serious illnesses; in 3 of the 12 households, someone lay in bed, unable to carry on with their daily routines. Several persons said the same thing: "There is sickness in our land." They also spoke about the value of Tevita's work.

The return message from Noa was brief and firm:

> Tevita, you must continue your healing work. It is a work honestly done, and most important it is a work given to you by the ancient, supreme God, who we Fijians have always known and most respected, the God who rules above all the other Gods. Remember the vision that gave you the work, it was a vision from the supreme God. Keep remembering that vision. Keep remembering that no person, whether it be Rev. Tale or anyone else, someone from the church or any other place, can take that work away from you. What is given by the supreme God cannot be taken away by man. Only if you no longer travel the straight path, if you cease being honest, and use the work for bad purposes, will the work be taken away, and then you will lose it because of your *own* failings.

On receiving Noa's response, Tevita resumed his practice. As he put it:

> I see now that my work is in the right direction. Even though it is criticized by Rev. Tale, it is not un-Christian because it is given by God and made powerful by God's *mana*.

This particular crisis in Tevita's work was not the first to mark a fluctuation or interruption in his practice. This particular time, there is a clash of paradigms which guides the way reality is constructed and meaning generated. Tevita, and the village that he serves, struggle between the apparent contradiction in paradigms. In the process, the straight path becomes hidden, the people wander, movement along the path seems to cease. With Noa's understanding, there is a resolution. What was labeled as "bad" or devious, and felt as confused and conflicted, becomes "straight" again. Traveling resumes a straight direction, though future obstacles are recognized by all as inevitable. Tevita expressed this thought:

> The healing work is difficult. One is always confronted with challenges which make you question what you are doing.

The New Road and the Old Way

As part of the central government's program of rural development, a road was being built between Nagone and the neighboring village of Tamana. The aim was to facilitate communication and exchange between the two villages, as the road would replace a footpath which was in some places difficult to negotiate. Initial planning for the road took place largely in the central government. Local involvement increased as the planners began to look at actual site characteristics and as they stated the need for local volunteer labor to assist government workers. This local involvement reached a point of moral crisis when it became clear that the road, as planned, would pass through a sacred area *(i sava)* where the *Vu* were said to reside. Tradition dictated that persons were not supposed to enter such sacred areas but to take a wide berth when approaching them, thereby showing respect for the *Vu* and their power.

For most people in both villages, the road represented "progress" and an occasion to receive some of the government's material largesse, which thus far had been directed disproportionately to the urban area. To the elders in both villages, the road also represented a threat to a sacred space and traditional ways.

After some discussion, the elders spoke to the road crew, seeking a redirection of the road so that it did not penetrate the sacred area. The road crew tried to accommodate but said they could not change the projected roadway to bypass the sacred area completely; it would have to touch on what the elders considered the outlying boundaries of that sacred area. The elders then decided they would make a ceremonial offering to the *Vu,* asking their permission to have the road go near the outskirts of the sacred area and ask their forgiveness for any disrespect thus implied.

The ceremony to contact the *Vu* was held, with all elders in attendance. Those who were in charge sought a compromise. In their offering to the *Vu,* they spoke not only of their respect for tradition but also sought a loosening of tradition, exempting the road from the usual strictures of avoiding a sacred place.

But some elders felt that tradition was not respected in the ceremony. They felt that those who conducted the ceremony were bargaining with the *Vu* to allow the road to be built, letting their desire to have the road interfere with proper performance of the ceremony. They even commented on aspects of the ceremony that were improperly left out and the unusual nature of some of the wording.

At the end of the ceremony, it was pronounced that the road could continue, in its redirected manner, without violating the sacred space or showing disrespect for the *Vu*. Some of the elders, in private conversations afterwards, disagreed. They felt the ceremony had not settled the issue but in fact made the dilemma even more difficult. For now tradition—expressed in the ceremony—had been misused, which they believed made the question of the road even more threatening. They also spoke of the disrespect shown the sacred place by the initial hesitation in requesting that the road's direction be changed.

At the village level, people were confronting a threatened deviation from the straight path. The village experienced this crisis; it was the village's sacred space, the village's proposed road. Through the agency of the elders, the village reached its compromise. It avoided a radical deviation from the straight path, but in the view of some, it deviated nonetheless, because it did not fully respect tradition. Nor was the village single minded—as a hesitating and ambivalent attitude characterized some of the discussion about the sacred place and the road.

The compromise did not represent a permanent solution. The specific challenge of the new road to that particular sacred place was met, but not fully so. More important, the challenge was but one of a number of situations—most others not so dramatic—in which the village would wrestle with the nature of the straight path and how to travel it. This particular crisis was enmeshed in the apparent conflict between "tradition" and economic "progress." The elders and the village they represented were moral explorers, seeking to define anew what, until the advent of "progress," had been relatively set by tradition. The straight path projects issues of individual development onto the macro level of sociocultural development, as the two levels are from the Fijian perspective, inseparable.

The straight path suggests a process of psychological development. The processes of becoming a healer and educating the healer are for all practical purposes indistinguishable; the core and aim of both is the transformational experience. Transformation is the key to the healer's development, a painful challenge which constantly recurs. As it recurs at increasing levels of difficulty, it helps define the healer's unfolding career. Essentially, there is one recurring developmental task, transitioning. This transformation can be seen as a paradigm for the devlopment of healers. As Fijian healers in their traveling the straight path represent the culture's ideal of development, that transformation can be seen as a paradigm for concepts of community development as well.

Toward a Transformational Model of Development

The data on becoming a healer among Fijians suggests a transformational model of development, that is, transformational experiences are at the crux of this model. For the Fijians, these experiences, described as "traveling the straight path," include an enhanced state of consciousness that leads to a new experience of reality in which the boundaries of the self become more permeable to contact with a transpersonal or spiritual realm. During the enhanced state of consciousness, potential healers experience a sense of connectedness, joining a spiritual healing power, themselves, and their community. But firmly rooted as it is in the context of ordinary life, this enhanced state of consciousness is only part of the transformational experience. The envisioning process requires that the visions offer direction for everyday behaviors and that the behaviors in turn help reshape the visions into guides for new possible behaviors. Thus, the initial vision is recreated, and subsequent visions are enacted and reaffirmed in daily life. Through this envisioning process the healer rediscovers his or her direction, and the bonding to community is renewed. The straight path charts a developmental path, a trajectory toward cultural ideals which by its nature also includes a movement away from those ideals. Though it is often followed most intensely by healers, that path functions throughout Fijian culture. It offers an order for all people which is both normative and actual; it describes both the life toward which people aspire, and the fact that aspiring *toward,* with its continual reaching and falling back from these ideals, is the actual condition of people's lives.

The transformational model distinguishes itself in several ways: in its focus on a spiritual dimension that leads toward interaction with the community; in the transitioning movement along the straight path that is neither unidirectional nor the basis for permanent developmental gains; in the flexibility in the sequence of development; in the association of power and vulnerability; and in the inseparability of individual and sociocultural development. To make these distinguishing features clearer, we will contrast the model with Piagetian theories.

First, the contribution of the spiritual dimension to developmental processes is fundamental to the transformational model. In Piaget's work, cognitive aspects of development are central—spiritual aspects receive scant attention, and affective aspects are merely correlates of the structural, cognitive side. But Fijian spirituality is not spiritual in the sense of a distant or abstract dimension. The dualism inherent in much Western thinking between the spiritual and various other dimensions, such as the material or the human or the psychological dimension, is not present in Fijian society. There is, for example, no word for "extraordinary" in Fijian. Eliade's (1965) analysis of the sacred and the secular as intersecting spheres suggests, for example, a more dichotomous conception than exists in Fiji.

The straight path is learning to live in harmony with spiritual principles. The distinction between secular and spiritual tasks is minimized. The power to heal in the form of *mana* originally comes from this spiritual dimension. The *mana* "makes things happen" in all aspects of Fijian life; it is said to make healers powerful as well as, for example, politicians or athletes. Though representing a realm beyond the community in Fijian culture, the spiritual dimension is also close at hand. The closeness of the spiritual dimension does not lead to a disrespect or diminution of its power. Instead, the closeness generates a familiarity, even an intimacy with that dimension, thus preventing it from being considered as separate from ordinary life. Healers are most dramatic in their affirmation of the spiritual as part of ordinary life. Fijian healers do not find the experience of spiritual power *(mana)* frightening or surprising, nor does it make them "feel different." However, those who do not heal feel just the opposite.

Many current developmental theories isolate particular aspects of development; these are, for example, theories on cognitive development (Piaget, 1952; Piaget & Inhelder, 1969; Flavell, 1977), affective development (Izard, 1977, 1978; Zajonc, 1980; Hesse & Cicchetti, 1982), and moral development (Kohlberg, 1976). Some recent theories attempt to integrate two aspects of development such as models of social–cognitive development (Selman, 1978, 1980), socio–emotional development (Sroufe, 1979), emotional–cognitive development (Cowan, 1982; Kagan, 1978; Lewis & Brooks, 1978), or moral–affective development (Hoffman, 1978). Others have recently acknowledged the role of spirituality in development but have tended to discuss spirituality in terms of "faith" as a somewhat separate area of development, though related to other areas of development (Fowler, 1981). The transformational model includes, in an integrative manner, the social, cognitive, affective, and moral, all infused with the spiritual dimension.

Fijians consider optimal human functioning to be living in and with the spiritual dimension. This demands an integration of those human capabilities labeled in the West as "emotions" and "cognitions" with spiritual guidance. The Fijian Gods not only represent the most complete expression of the spiritual dimension but are also considered to exhibit the full range of what is termed emotion and cognition in the West: jealousy as well as love, and trickery as well as honesty.

The spiritual dimension constantly directs the individual toward interaction with the community. Healers merit special respect as participants in the healing ceremony, but they are not consequently sequestered from the community and given a special status. Fijian healers are expected to fulfill their everyday duties as members of communities; healing is an additional responsibility. The elder's description of the healer Tevita bears repeating: "Tevita is one of us, just like the rest of us." Healers differ from other community members in internal psychological qualities predisposing them to work at healing but not in measures of everyday status or functioning.

The Fijian healer is not merely turning toward a spiritual reality, neither is he or she focusing inward on the individual self. The Gods penetrate the healer's consciousness through a vision and send the healer to his or her immediate community to serve. For example, when the Christian minister tries to convince Tevita that his healing work is harming the community, Tevita is extremely disheartened and believes he should stop his healing. The fruits of his transformed consciousness — his healing — amounts to little if it does not benefit the community. Healers are not seeking to extricate themselves from a secular realm, to replace it with a spiritual dimension. They seek to remain within their community, meeting their daily responsibilities while exhibiting changed behavior through a transformed state of consciousness.

Second, from the perspective of the transformational model of development, movement along the straight path is characterized by the transitioning process. In contrast to Piagetian models, the movement in transitioning is neither unidirectional nor the basis for permanent developmental gains. Movement is neither only toward — but also inevitably away from — becoming progressively less confused nor only toward — but also inevitably away from — deeper or more powerful visions. Life history is enlivened by that recurring process of movement and transition. Healers who are active in moral exploration alternate between clarity and ambiguity of comprehension. Transitioning was exemplified by Tevita who moved from clarity to ambiguity to clarity in his understanding of God's wishes regarding the Christian church versus indigenous healing practices.

Similarly, transitioning characterizes the envisioning process as healers move between their visions, altering their daily context as a result of those visions and experiencing new visions which result from their own changed behavior and sociocultural environment. For example, Saimoni's behavior was changed as a result of his vision, as he worked to remove the influence exerted by the British in his village. Saimoni frequently reexperienced his vision. Through the retelling of the vision, the community was able to reaffirm its commitment to the vision, newly experienced with each retelling. A continual process of transitioning is itself the crux of development, rather than a linear (or spiral) progression over the life course that culminates in an end state or stage. Life history in the transformational model becomes the continuous dialectic of meeting and being overwhelmed by one recurring developmental challenge: transcending the self in order to channel healing resources to the community (Katz, 1982a).

In Piaget's theory, developmental processes are completely continuous (Piaget, 1970). The direction of increasing generalizations and differentiation always remains the same. In the transformational model, movement in both directions is constant and the norm. Transitioning occurs toward and away from meaning, balance, connectedness, and wholeness. There is an oscillation around these issues, and each movement is considered important — regardless of direction — because it deals with the basic developmental challenge of transitioning.

Third, this transformation model of development is not characterized by hierarchical stages. Transitioning does not guarantee "success" in the next transitional challenge or assume "success" in the previous one. Experience does not follow a universal and irreversible order. No more than half of the healers begin their work as apprentices. All healers have initial healing visions, but their visions differ in intensity, detail, and state of consciousness experienced. No universal ages or developmental stages can be specified that apply to the development of healers. The focus is on maintaining contact with *mana*. If the Fijian data were viewed from the perspectives of a linear, teleological conception of development, these life histories might be described as stalled or stuck in an endless dialectical movement, instead of enlivened by constant transitioning. Moving into and out of states of consciousness rather than achieving a stage and regulating healing power rather than possessing a certain degree of power are the developmental tasks.

A career pattern can be delineated for Fijian healers, but the boundaries between stages are open; the sequence of stages flexible, and there is no one articulated end point toward which the stages progress or culminate. Most important, such a career pattern does not provide an essential organizing principle to the healer's life history. Achieving a certain stage is not cause of celebration nor does maintaining a stage bring on status or other rewards — especially since remaining at a stage is a dynamic task, which can easily be undone. The career pattern is a collection of behaviors and events that represent and express the quality of the transformational experience. In sum, traveling the straight path means developing a correct or "straight" attitude and motivation, not passing through a sequence of stages or career behaviors.

Piaget views development as an evolutionary process that can nevertheless be divided into stages. Each stage is age appropriate, falling within a particular order, representing a uniform patterning of viewing the world, and fitting into a hierarchy (Piaget, 1970). Knowing a person's stage points to the expected behavioral level. In the straight path, healers can be said to move through phases in their work, but these are surface categorizations which do not organize the transitioning experiences. A healer's development is not best described by a hierarchical organization. Once a particular meaning, for example, has been achieved in a certain setting, it is not thereby permanent. Meaning is undone as meaninglessness inevitably appears, and old and new meanings are established.

A fourth characteristic of the transformation model is its association of power and vulnerability. As the healer meets increasingly difficult challenges along the straight path, the healer has access to greater power. However, power cannot be used to make the healer invulnerable. Healers should not focus on trying to increase their power. The key dynamic is the healers' ever-changing relationship to power. Though access to power generally increases with experience, that access remains fluctuating. In recognizing healers' power, one attends to their ability to regulate, not possess that power. The most powerful Fijian healers are the most vulnerable to abusing that power—and thus losing the power and the straight path totally. Merely because a healer has access to greater power does not guarantee a "successful" outcome. Each act of transitioning is a risk, a deep and abiding confrontation of the integrity and continuity of self. One is reminded of the healer Saimoni jumping into the drain pit with water 8 fathoms deep. The terror that accompanies the transitioning is no less because the healer experiences numerous acts of transitioning in a lifetime.

Healers are constantly forced to reassess their relationship to the healing power. They continually reestablish the quality and basis of that power in their lives. Healers move between their fear of the transforming experience and their desire to heal others, their search for increased healing power and the difficulty of working with it.

In their continual struggle to regulate their access to and control of the healing power, healers exemplify this fluidity in the developmental process. Knowledge of how to transit must in the existential sense be relearned with each opportunity for transition; at times it is unavailable, even to the experienced healer. Furthermore, the process of transitioning is accompanied by a basic sense of vulnerability, both more frightening and liberating than the feelings of perplexity, confusion, surprise and insight that often accompany developmental transitions in the Piagetian framework. Though the use of power for healing rather than harm may be the pattern, that pattern is constantly tested through temptations for misuse. The continual points where the relationship to power is in flux are points of vulnerability for the healers and their community, but these points also are opportunities for change, not merely times of danger.

Finally, this transformational model of development suggests that an individual's development is inseparable from his or her sociocultural context and development on a macrolevel. Individual and community development merge through their reciprocating influence on each other; healers experience transformation in order to serve the community as the community experiences transformation in order to serve the individual. As a result, both individual and community benefit beyond what was possible for each alone. This embeddedness of self-in-community which is mutually supportive and enhancing and which produces benefits that are exponentially greater than could result from either individual or community alone, has been described as a "synergistic community" (Katz, 1984; Katz & Seth, 1987). For example, Saimoni's individual process of envisioning and moral exploration entailed altering the structure of a Fijian community. Consequently, the community that began to change influenced his own development.

The concept of self-embedded-in-community contrasts with the dominant Western value of individualism, with its individualistic concept of self, separate and separating from others and community (Bourguignon, 1979; LeVine, 1982). The embedded concept of self is much closer to the value and functioning of the connected self described by Gilligan (1982) and others in their work on female development. Western developmental psychology has been moving toward a broader model, one that includes a link between individual and group development. The exclusive focus on individual development is expanding to include the development of social systems (Bronfenbrenner, 1977; Lerner & Spanier, 1978; Kilner, 1986). The interactional perspective (Maccoby & Martin, 1983), and the combination of family systems and developmental theories (Minuchin, 1985) reflect a major shift away from traditional models of socialization in their focus on bidirectional and multidirectional effects and development as well as variables such as reciprocity and mutuality, which highlight processes in relationship rather than in individuals (Kilner, 1986). In Fiji, self is defined by one's place in the network constituting the community; it is experienced contextually, dependent on how one fulfills one's social obligations (R. Katz, 1981). Independence is valued as a *community* resource, not a vehicle for personal achievement. Creativity emerges in connection with others. For example, the sacred dance songs *(mekes)* exist as they are performed by the community; their beauty resides in the intricate and delicate interrelationships between performers and performers and audience.

The Western assumption that the individual is inherently in conflict with her or his community, pitting the needs of one against the other, does not dominate Fijian thought and behavior. When Fijians visit another village, they are received as a representative of their own village. After expressing this representative function, they can emphasize their more idiosyncratic personal characteristics. Personal meaning making is encouraged but as a resource to be shared with the community, not as a means to accumulate personal prestige or distinguish oneself from the community. Certainly, in Fiji there is a movement toward separation as well as connectedness, a tension between individual and community aims, but Fijian values of self and community assume an extensive interrelationship and sharing which can alleviate some of the tension.

While connecting the healer to healing resources beyond the self, transformation commits the healer to serve the community. The concept of transformation involves the individual and the society simultaneously. The idea is not merely that when the individual is transformed then the society will be but that as the individual is transformed so is the society. The Fijian data describe an interactional model where the education of the healer is itself the transforming process for individual and society. The concept is not education *for* transformation but education *as* transformation (Katz, 1981, 1982c).

The merging of individual and social development offers a sharp contrast to the more individualistic emphasis in Piagetian models. Piaget views development as an innate and unchangeable process. The theory describes inner processes that naturally occur, assuming the individual interacts with the environment. One can argue that education based on Piagetian principles can speed up the cognitive development of individuals who may, in turn, positively affect the community, but the individual may develop without the community also developing. The transformational model views individual and community development as intrinsically and inextricably linked. If the individual is to develop, the community must also. In the transformational model, development is a shared enterprise, a joining of self and community with unexpected benefits to both. The community offers support as the individual faces difficulties during transitioning while the benefits released by that transitioning are distributed to the community.

The application of the transformational model of development to Western cultures may be limited due to the enormous differences between Western and Fijian cultures and their respective econiches. It may be, for example, that the transformational model is relevant primarily to those persons in the West more concerned with healing and spiritual functions, even though in Fiji it is a model with relevance for all persons, as the healing and spiritual functions are not separable from other ordinary life functions. But one could argue that it is important to bring the spiritual dimension back into general developmental concerns in the West; there is evidence of the destructive effects of splitting off this spiritual dimension (Jung, 1952, 1982). One could also argue that the concept of healers be expanded in the West. Perhaps we should include as healers all those involved in the *generic* process of healing, namely those engaged in transitioning toward meaning, balance, connectedness, and wholeness (R. Katz, 1982b); thus we could include certain teachers and other helpers, as well as members of the human service professions, such as psychologists and physicians (Katz and St. Denis, 1986). Again, there is evidence of the negative effects of limiting the healing function to medical and medically dominated professions (e.g., Light, 1980). An examination of the transformational model seems worthwhile since it deals with issues in development that have been either identified as problematic or overlooked in much Western theorizing (Rappaport, 1978). The straight path may indeed suggest developmental tasks and patterns of general relevance.

Acknowledgments

We thank the Government of Fiji, especially the Ministries of Health and Fijian Affairs and Rural Development, for their kind permission to the first author to undertake the research and their generous support of it. We also want to thank Saimoni Vatu, Ratu Civo, Sevuloni Bose, and Ifereimi Naivota for their generous help and essential guidance in making the research possible and the people in the Fijian villages and urban areas where the work was done. People in the home village were especially wonderful in making the stay in Fiji like being at home. Pseudonyms are used throughout the text to protect the privacy of individuals and villages. Ellen Langer and Sally Powers offered helpful and perceptive comments on an earlier version of this chapter.

References

Ashton, P. T. (1978). Cross-cultural Piagetian research: An experimental perspective. In *Stage theories of cognitive and moral development: Criticisms and applications* (Reprint No. 13). Cambridge, MA: Harvard Educational Review.

Bourguignon, E. (1979). *Psychological anthropology.* New York: Holt, Rinehart and Winston.

Bronfenbrenner, U. (1977). Toward an experimental ecology of human development. *American Psychologist, 32,* 513–531.

Cheever, O. (1987). The training of community psychiatrists: A test of the model of "Education as Transformation". Doctoral Dissertation, Harvard University.

Cowan, P. A. (1982). The relationship between emotional and cognitive development. In D. Cicchetti and P. Hesse (Eds.), *Emotional Development* (pp. 49–82). San Francisco: Jossey-Bass, Inc.

Decarie, T. G. (1978). Affect development and cognition in a Piagetian context. In M. Lewis & L. A. Rosenblum (Eds.), *The development of affect.* New York: Plenum Press.

Demos J., & Demos V. (1969). Adolescence in historical perspective. *Journal of Marriage and Family, 31*(4), 632–638.

Durkeim, E. (1968). *The elementary forms of religious life.* New York: Free Press.

Eliade, M. (1965). *Rites and symbols of initation.* New York: Harper and Row.

Elkind, D. (1978). Pigetian and psychometric conceptions of intelligence. In *Stage theories of cognitive and moral development: Criticisms and applications* (Reprint No. 13). Cambridge, MA: Harvard Educational Review.

Flavell, J. H. (1977). *Cognitive Development.* Englewood Cliffs, NJ: Prentice-Hall.

Fowler, J. (1981). *Stages of faith: Psychology of human development and the quest for meaning.* New York: Harper and Row.

Fuller, B. (1963). *Ideas and integrities.* New York: Macmillan, Collier Books.

Gilligan, C. (1982). *In a different voice.* Cambridge: Harvard University Press.

Hahn, H., & Katz, R. (1985). Education as transformation: A test of the model. Harvard University, Unpublished manuscript.

Hampton, E. (1985). Towards an Indian model of education: The sweat lodge and the American Indian Program. Qualifying Paper, Harvard Graduate School of Education.

Hesse, P., & Cicchetti, D. (1982). Perspectives in an integrated theory of emotional development. In D. Cicchetti & P. Hesse (Eds.), *Emotional development* (pp. 3–48). San Francisco, CA: Jossey-Bass.

Hoffman, M. L. (1978). Toward a theory of empathic arousal and development. In M. Lewis & L. A. Rosenblum (Eds.), *The development of affect* (pp. 227–256). New York: Plenum.

Izard, C. E. (1977). *Human emotions.* New York: Plenum.

Izard, C. E. (1978). On the ontogenesis of emotions and emotion: Cognitive-emotional relationships in infancy. In M. Lewis & L. A. Rosenblum (Eds.), *The development of affect* (pp. 389–413). New York: Plenum.

Jung, C. (1952). *Transformation.* Princeton, NJ: Princeton Univ. Press.

Jung, C. (1982). *Two essays on analytical psychology.* Princeton, NJ: Princeton Univ. Press.

Kagan, J. (1978). On emotion and its development: A working paper. In M. Lewis & L. A. Rosenblum (Eds.), *The Development of Affect.* New York: Plenum Press.

Katz, M. M. W. (1981). Gaining sense at age two in outer Fiji Islands: A cross-cultural study of cognitive development. Unpublished doctoral dissertation, Harvard University, Cambridge, MA.

Katz, R. (1981). Education as transformation: Becoming a healer among the !Kung and Fijians. *Harvard Educational Review, 51*(1), 57–78.

Katz, R. (1982a). Accepting "boiling energy": Transformation and healing. *Ethos, 10*(4), 344–368.

Katz, R. (1982b). *Boiling energy: Community healing among the Kalahari !Kung.* Cambridge, MA: Harvard Univ. Press.

Katz, R. (1982c). Commentary on "Education as transformation." *Harvard Educational Review, 52*(1), 63–66.

Katz, R. (1984). Empowerment and synergy: Expanding the community's healing resources. *Prevention in Human Services, 3,* pp. 201–226.

Katz, R. (1986). Healing and transformation: Perspectives on development, education, and community. In M. White & S. Pollak (Eds.), *The cultural transition: Human experience and social transformation in the Third World and Japan* (pp. 41–64). London: Routledge & Kegan Paul.

Katz, R. (1987). The role of vulnerability in field-work. In A. Schenk & H. Kalweit (Eds.), *The Healing of Knowledge.* Munich, F.R. Germany: Wilhelm Goldman Verlag (German language edition).

Katz, R., & Lamb, W. (1983). Utilization patterns of "traditional" and "Western" health services: Research findings. *Proceedings of the Annual Meeting of the National Council on International Health.* Washington, DC.

Katz, R., & Seth, N. (1987). Synergy and healing: A perspective on Western health care. *Prevention in human services. 5* (1), (in press).

Katz, R., & St. Dennis, V. (1986). The teacher as healer, *AWASIS,* 5(1).

Katz, R., Montoya, V., & Hess, R. (Eds.) (in press). *Community healing systems:* Lessons from indigenous people. New York: Haworth Press.

Kett, J. (1971). .Adolescence and youth in nineteenth-century America. In T. Rabb & R. Rotberg (Eds.), *The family in history* (pp. 95–110). New York: Harper.

Kilner, L. (1986). The role of family relationships in adolescent development. Qualifying Paper, Harvard Graduate School of Education.

Kohlberg, L. (1976). Moral stages and moralization: The cognitive-developmental approach. In T. Lickona (Ed.), *Moral development and behavior: Theory, research, and social issues* (pp. 31–53). New York: Holt.

Labouvie-Vief, G. (1982). Dynamic development and mature autonomy. *Human Development, 25,* 161–191.

LeVine, R. (1982). *Culture, Behavior and Personality* (2nd ed.). Chicago: Aldine.

Lewis, M., & Brooks, J. (1978). Self-knowledge and emotional development. In M. Lewis & L. A. Rosenblum (Eds.), *The development of affect.* New York: Plenum Press.

Lerner, R. M., & Spanier, G. B. (Eds.) (1978). *Child influences on marital and family interaction: A life-span perspective.* New York: Academic Press.

Light, D. (1980). *Becoming psychiatrists: The professional transformation of self.* New York: Norton.

Maccoby, E. E., & Martin, J. A. (1983). Socialization in the context of the family: Parent–child interaction. In P. H. Mussen (Ed.), *Handbook of child psychology,* Vol. 4, *Socialization, personality, and social development.* New York: Wiley.

Maslow, A. & Honigmann, J. (1970). Ruth Benedicts notes on synergy. *American Anthropologist, 72,* 320–333.

Menary, J. (1987). The amniocentesis and abortion experience: A study in psychological healing. Doctoral Dissertation: Harvard University.

Nayacakalou, R. (1975). *Tradition and change in the Fijian village.* Suva, Fiji: Univ. of the South Pacific Press.

Nayacakalou, R. (1978). *Leadership in Fiji.* London and New York: Oxford Univ. Press.

Nesselroade, J., & Baltes, P. B. (1974). Adolescent personality development and historical change: 1970–1972. *Monographs of the Society for Research in Child Development, 39*(1), 1–80.

Nũnez-Molina, M. (1987). "Desarrollo del Medium": The process of becoming a healer in Puerto Rican "Espiritismo." Doctoral Dissertation: Harvard University.

Phillips, D. C., & Kelly, M. E. (1978). Hierarchical theories of development in education and psychology. In *Stage theories of cognitive and moral development: Criticisms and applications* (Reprint No. 13). Cambridge, MA: Harvard Educational Review.

Piaget, J. (1952). *The origins of intelligence in children.* New York: International Universities Press.

Piaget, J. (1970). *Structuralism.* New York: Basic Books, Inc.

Piaget, J., & Inhelder, B. (1969). *The psychology of the child.* New York: Basic Books.

Rappaport, R. (1978). Adaptation and the structure of ritual. In N. Blurton-Jones & V. Reynolds (Eds.), *Human behavior and adaptation,* 18. New York: Halsted Press.

Ravuvu, A. (1985). *The Fijian way.* University of the South Pacific, Suva, Fiji.

Sahlins, M. (1962). *Moala: Culture and nature on a Fijian Island.* Ann Arbor, MI: Univ. of Michigan Press.

Selman, R. (1978). Education for cognitive development. In *Stage theories of cognitive and moral development: Criticisms and applications* (Reprint No. 13). Cambridge, MA: Harvard Educational Review.

Selman, R. (1980). *The growth of interpersonal understanding: Developmental and clinical analysis.* New York: Academic Press.

Seth, N. (1987). "Baira Ni Vato" (Women's Talk): A psychological context for exploring fertility options in traditional societies. Doctoral Dissertation: Harvard University.

Simonis, J. (1984). Synergy and the education of helpers: A new community psychology approach to counselor training. Doctoral Dissertation: Harvard University.

Spencer, D. (1941). *Disease, religion, and society in the Fiji Islands.* New York: Augustin.

Sroufe, L. A. (1979). Socioemotional development. In J. Osofsky (Ed.), *Handbook of Infant Development.* New York: Wiley.

Thompson, L. (1940). *Southern Lau, Fiji: An ethnography.* Honolulu, HI: Bishop Museum.

Zajonc, R. (1980). Feeling and thinking: Preferences need no inferences. *American Psychologist, 35,* 151–175.

10

Child Psychiatry in an International Context: With Remarks on the Current Status of Child Psychiatry in China

FELTON EARLS

Introduction

The influence of child psychiatry on the provision of mental health services to children has been restricted to a large extent to regional and national spheres. Little evidence exists that the practice of child psychiatry in one country could be transplanted to another. Though the same condition is faced in adult psychiatry, the problem seems much more severe in child psychiatry. Even when the United States and Great Britain are considered, countries similar in culture and language, differences in training, theoretical persuasions, diagnostic criteria, and treatment approaches are encountered. While a number of explanations could be offered to account for these differences, they must, in part, be attributed to the relatively sparse scientific base of knowledge in child psychiatry. Current research activities are encouraging, however, and there is promise that child psychiatry is rapidly progressing toward a more secure and respected foundation in medicine (Earls, 1982a; Guze, Earls, & Barrett, 1983).

The aim of this paper is to stimulate interest in development of an international perspective in child psychiatry. Such a perspective must take into account the fact that over 80% of the world's children live in developing countries. This figure is expected to increase to 90% by the end of this century. Yet, nearly all the world's child psychiatrists work and reside in the developed nations. Considerations dealt with here will focus less on the problem of how to foster cooperation between child psychiatrists in developed nations and more with the global problem of how to stimulate the growth of child psychiatry in places where it hardly exists and is most desperately needed. Efforts to develop universal principles in the practice of child psychiatry may, nevertheless, prove beneficial to mental health services in developed countries as they force psychiatrists to develop theories and strategies which can be used in the context of developing countries, all of which will have limited resources.

Child Mental Health in Relationship to Physical Health

Diversity in training programs and treatment philosophies among the developed countries only partly explain why child psychiatry has not been readily absorbed into the health services of the developing countries. In such countries the high incidence of physical disorders creates a primary concern for the survival of children. Health programs sponsored by international groups have been primarily concerned with the prevention of nutritional disorders and infectious diseases. When faced with a fast growing population and quickly changing social phenomena, restriction of health objectives to these problems is much too conservative. Indeed, many developing countries are already achieving notable successes in decreasing infant mortality and increasing life expectancy. These changing population characteristics create the need for adjustments in existing health services and in some cases the introduction of totally new services.

A dramatic illustration of the successful implementation of a primary care program aimed at reducing mortality rates in Haiti is described by Berggren, Eubank, and Berggren (1981). In this program a rigorous campaign of health education and preventive services employing local community residents decreased infant mortality in a village to a level one fifth the estimate for the country as a whole and at the same time decreased mortality in children over the age of one to a similar extent. During the study's 5 year duration, life expectancy in the village increased from 45 to 66 years as compared to a national figure which remained at 47 years. Results such as these prove that infant and childhood deaths can be prevented in a short space of time and that this has a powerful effect on increasing the physical well-being of a population.

Although improving physical health is a necessary step toward improvements in psychological health, achieving the former does not automatically lead to the latter. Increasing numbers of surviving children will result in more children with chronic diseases, including mental and social handicaps. Just how health services are to respond to these children is poorly conceived in most developing societies. Behavior problems, learning disabilities, developmental deviations, mental retardation, and both physical and emotional problems resulting from the maltreatment of children make up a large proportion of the disorders from which children suffer the world over. Epidemiologic studies in developed countries reveal that about one in seven children from the preschool period to adolescence acquire such problems at some point, and many retain problems for long periods (Earls, 1981; Rutter, Cox, Tupling, Berger, & Yule, 1975). There is no reason to believe that the rate for such problems is any different in developing countries; in fact, available data support there being no difference in the prevalence of psychiatric disorder (Graham, 1981). Even in China, a developing country that has achieved notable successes in maternal and child health practices and family planning, several school-based surveys demonstrate that the prevalence of attention-deficit disorders is in the range of 5 – 10%, a figure quite similar to that in the United States (Earls, 1982b).

An associated factor limiting the growth of child psychiatry in developing countries is related to the rate of demographic and industrial changes taking place in these societies. In fact, there still exist economic conditions in some countries that encourage child labor (World Bank, 1979). As many developing countries enter a demographic transition associated with industrialization, infant mortality rates begin to fall (Teitelbaum, 1975). Together with the existence of new knowledge on reproduction and the acquisition of the technology to control both male and female fertility, conditions prevail to greatly reduce the length of time required to complete the transition from agricultural subsistence economies, large families, and high-infant mortality to urban, industrial economies, smaller families, and lower rates of infant mortality. To illustrate, the estimated proportion of children in the total population for four developed and four developing countries is shown in Table I. These eight nations were chosen because they cover the range of variation observed among member countries of the United Nations. Between 1975 and 1980 each of the developing countries shown, except Nigeria, witnessed substantial reductions in the percentage of children in the general population, a factor reflecting declining fertility and, consequently, smaller family size. Despite significant declines, countries like Mexico, India, Brazil, and Indonesia still have a considerable way to go before they approximate the age profile of a developed country. The range of variation in birth rates, infant mortality rates, and life expectancies is given in Table II. Despite general decline in birth and infant mortality rates and increasing life expectancies, wide variation in these indicators are predicted to continue into the foreseeable future.

Table I

Actual Number and Percentage of Population <15 Years for Four Developed and Four Developing Countries, 1975 and 2000

	1975		2000	
	Number	%	Number	%
Mexico	27,501,000	50.1	55,905,000	42.3
Nigeria	33,857,000	45.0	62,488,000	46.3
India	256,162,000	42.1	369,183,000	34.9
China	274,954,000	33.4	290,283,000	25.3
Canada	6,201,000	27.2	7,774,000	24.6
U.S.A.	54,046,000	25.3	59,693,000	22.6
Germany	13,468,000	21.8	13,568,000	20.5
Sweden	1,719,000	21.0	1,947,000	20.7

Once smaller families and physically healthier children are obtained, parents can be expected to shift their aspirations from a value system that stresses the importance of the economic benefits of having children (which is typical of agricultural societies) to one which emphasizes their psyhological value (Nag, White, & Peet, 1978). In developing countries it is conceivable that demographic changes might precede by many years changes in the social and psychological perception of children simply because of the rapidity of change. This may account for lags in both the parental perception of children and the reorganization of health services. A recent American study con-

Table II

Demographic Characteristics of Four Developed and Four Developing Countries

	Birth rate/1000		% Natural increase in population	Infant mortality 1975/1000 live births	Life expectancy at birth	
	1975	2000			1970	1975
Mexico	42.0	35.2	3.6	52	62.4	64.7
Nigeria	49.3	44.8	3.0	163	38.5	41.0
India	39.9	26.3	1.9	130	47.2	49.5
China	26.9	18.3	1.7	35	59.0	61.6
U.S.A.	25.3	17.0	0.7–1.2	16	70.3	71.1
Canada	18.6	17.2	0.8	15	72.9	72.0
Germany	12.0	13.1	−0.3	20	70.3	71.3
Sweden	14.2	14.3	0.0	8	74.5	75.3

ducted in an urban housing project in the Midwest is of interest in this connection (Slaughter, 1983). Group meetings with black mothers of preschool children were used as a means of exploring and changing the way in which these women perceived their young children. It was assumed that many of these women had retained a traditional value orientation toward child rearing which was reflective of rural life in the South. This value orientation had been retained despite the fact that most were second generation migrants from the South to the North. The hypothesis that changing their values from a traditional to a modern psychological orientation would be produced by the group discussions was impressively demonstrated. In addition, the study showed that this change in value orientation also was correlated with improvements in the cognitive performance of the mothers' children.

Even when the importance of psychosocial development of children is realized the addition of health and education programs to improve the status of children is prohibitively expensive for many developing countries. While recognition of the need for day care services, primary school education, special schools or classes, child psychiatric clinics, and expanded pediatric facilities might exist, the resources to build, staff, and maintain such services may simply go beyond the fiscal capacities of an individual nation.

Components of a National or Regional Plan for a Child Mental Health Program

The demand for public education and a growing appreciation for the importance of early nurturance produced a psychological orientation toward children that brought about the introduction of child psychiatry in Western societies. Much of this phenomenon was dictated by the recognition that delinquent children seemed to be deprived of parental love and effective discipline (Levy, 1968). In this respect child psychiatry differs from other medical disciplines in that its origins were not determined by the study of specific diseases or disorders but rather by social problems. For several decades child psychiatry was developed outside medical centers as auxiliaries to juvenile courts and schools. Absorption into a community context promoted an awareness of historical and demographic conditions that over the past century gradually redefined the economic and psychologic value of children.

The question now is to decide how child psychiatry, narrowly, and child mental health services, broadly, are to align themselves with the health needs and aspirations of developing countries. Because it is now a more advanced science than it was 80 years ago when most Western societies were undergoing a demographic transition, the integration of child psychiatry into health and educational services of a developing country is much more important than it was a century ago at the beginning of the mental hygiene movement.

As child mental health services become established in developing countries, an understanding of the demographic and cultural context (considering diet, sanitation, and psychosocial stimulation) in which children are reared must develop concomitantly. This task will bring into focus the psychosocial parameters involved in child health and development and how such factors relate to the need for psychiatric services. Consideration of the basic requirements of children's mental health services for developing countries has been the topic of some special study (World Health Organization, 1977). The following conditions are essential ingredients of a well developed child mental health service: (1) health maintenance of infants and preschoolers and the prevention of developmental attrition; (2) population-specific knowledge about rates of psychiatric disorders and medical conditions that are likely to be chiefly caused by psychosocial factors (e.g., child abuse) and information about the capacity of mental health services to meet needs of the population; (3) an understanding of how families adapt to a variety of stresses including work patterns, migrations, and housing which did not necessarily exist for previous generations; (4) liaison with pediatricians and pediatric facilities to help manage the psychosocial components of chronic and life-threatening diseases in children; and (5) adequate staff and facilities, both outpatient and inpatient, for the diagnosis and treatment of psychiatric disorders in children. Less pertinent to the daily activities of child mental health workers, yet germane to their potential contribution to social change, is an understanding of the relationship of individual aspirations of adults who are or will become parents to issues related to population dynamics, such as sex education, fertility patterns, and family planning.

These five areas represent a basic list of requirements considered important in the organization of a child mental health service, but, given limited resources, the setting of priorities will be necessary. The first, health maintenance and prevention of developmental attrition, is relevant to primary care (or in public health terms, maternal and child health care). Over the past three decades a considerable base of knowledge has been gained on the importance of cognitive, emotional, and physical nurturance to children's development during the first few years of life. This enterprise has been so successful that developmental psychology has emerged as a distinct scientific discipline. In the medical sciences, pediatrics has responded by emphasizing the importance of behavior development and problems of behavior alongside its traditional concern with physical development and morbidity. Pediatrics has also succeeded in designing and deploying preventive health services for young children in developing countries (Morley, 1973). There is little to parallel these developments in child psychiatry, although there are some efforts among psychiatrists interested in infant development to develop preventive strategies (Shaffer & Dunn, 1979). However, much in this work is compartmentalized by psychoanalytic concepts and may prove to be of limited usefulness.

Estimates of the frequency of various types of psychiatric disorders and their social consequences in children are essential. Such data can be used to determine how resources are to be allocated. Aside from administrative uses, this kind of information gathering can be useful in understanding how behavior disorders in children relate to a social context which influences the rate and direction of social change, economic and psychologic demands on parents, and cultural expectations (Earls, 1982c). This kind of information can considerably broaden the scope of a health service and at the same time contribute to its effectiveness.

Finally, child psychiatry has a traditional clinical responsibility for pediatric liaison and the provision of diagnostic and treatment services for children with psychological disorders. These are placed at the end of the priority list, because given the evolution of child psychiatry in the United States and Western Europe over the past three quarters of a century, it is assumed that the prevention and early detection of psychiatric disorder in the vast majority of children is more effective than treatment, though by no means is this firmly supported by scientific evidence. Certainly, designing and implementing the best possible preventive programs will not eliminate all psychiatric problems in children. In fact, there is evidence suggesting that the rate of psychiatric conditions have increased rather than decreased over the past century (Rutter, 1980). How much of this is attributable to improved recognition and detection and how much to social and cultural change is not clear. It is conceivable that both these conditions will be responsible for similar changes in developing countries over the next few decades.

For rare and severe disorders, and for those which are poorly understood, tertiary psychiatric services will be needed, but the clinical work of child psychiatrists should not be exclusively devoted to the management of children with such disorders. It is essential that child psychiatrists spend time in pediatric clinics and hospitals. It is not at all clear, however, how much time a child psychiatrist in a developing country should spend in primary care or hospital-based care, for this will change with time and with social and economic development. Child mental health in many developed countries is evolving slowly, but unevenly, and seldom within the dictates of a rationally planned scheme. The potential for rational planning in developing countries based on the experience of developed ones should be exploited.

An Illustrative Case: Child Mental Health in China

The author's visit to China was prompted by the belief that the development of child mental health services in the years following the Cultural Revolution might represent an ideal model for developing countries. The impressive public health achievement of substantially reducing infant mortality rates combined with numerous reports of Western visitors that Chinese children from the earliest years appear surprisingly healthy, industrious, and bright suggested that the conditions and support for child psychiatry might be optimal. With assistance from the World Health Organization, a 3-month visit to the Shanghai Psychiatric Hospital was arranged in late 1981 with the primary purpose of observing and working with child psychiatrists. For half this period diagnostic and therapeutic interviews with patients and case discussions with the hospital's staff were conducted. For the remaining half, site visits were made to schools, pediatric hospitals, and psychiatric clinics in metropolitan Shanghai and to children's psychiatric facilities in Nanjing and Beijing.

A review of the five essential components of a child psychiatry program described in the previous section is useful to describe the current status of child mental health services in China.

1. Prevention and health maintenance: Two general factors have powerful preventive appeal. First, the frequency and severity of perinatal distress is reported to be quite low in Shanghai, a statement that becomes intelligible given the strikingly low infant mortality rate of 10/1000 live births in this urban area (Wray, 1975). This does not necessarily hold for the remainder of China, although standards of preventive health have improved generally. Second, women are typically granted about 55 days of pregnancy leave. According to a traditional Chinese belief, a month of confinement following the birth of a newborn is important in preventing neonatal infections, initiating breast feeding, and giving the mother a sufficient period of rest and recuperation (Pillsbury, 1978). This period may also serve to encourage the development of a secure parent-child bonding. Aside from these measures, other possibilities for prevention include the provision of high quality day care by many communes and the frequent substitute care provided by grandparents.

2. Establishing the prevalence and types of psychiatric disorder: Two types of epidemiologic surveys relevant to child psychiatric disorders have been carried out in China over the past two decades. Several mass surveys of total populations in different regions were carried out during the years of the Cultural Revolution. The results of these surveys suggest that the prevalence of major psychiatric disorder at all ages is low compared to estimates made in the West. The prevalence of disorders such as schizophrenia, hysteria, and

manic – depressive disorder in children are, as would be expected, exceedingly low.

On the contrary, school-based surveys, which have been more recently carried out in several parts of China, reveal rates of attentional problems and overactivity which are comparable to those in the United States (Earls, 1985). A two-stage survey in a large Shanghai elementary school reported the prevalence of attention-deficit disorder to be about 5% (Earls, 1982b). A survey in Beijing produced comparable findings. These data are particularly interesting because they were based in part on parent and teacher questionnaires originally designed in the West. To what extent methods such as these preserve an acceptable degree of reliability and validity as they are transcribed from one cultural setting to another is a concern that has not yet been rigorously addressed.

3. Family stress, coping, and adaptation: This is a neglected area of clinical methodology and of research. Chinese child psychiatrists are trained to diagnose and treat the most serious psychiatric disorders. Because these types of disorders commonly have a biological basis, there has developed less interest in the causal role of social factors. Both traditional cultural beliefs and political factors may have also contributed to a diminished interest in social factors. Yet, clinical work with attention-deficit disorder represents a new challenge to Chinese child psychiatrists. The phrase "minimal brain dysfunction" was being used to diagnose this condition and, with it, a connotation of biological causation. Implicit in the use of such terminology is an indication to use stimulant medications. Although use of these medications typically produced some improvement in behavior, both the diagnosis and the treatment represent conceptually crude approaches.

The author's clinical experience suggested that family factors, especially prolonged parent – child separations associated with multiple parent surrogates, was an important area for further investigation. Since most of the children believed to have an attention-deficit disorder were school aged, they were born during the years of the Cultural Revolution. Many experienced prolonged separations from their parents. It did not always appear that the substitute arrangements during the parents' absence (usually because of work assignments) were satisfactory. Equally important is the problem of estimating the quality of day care experiences received by some children since infancy. Indeed, because the society is highly dependent on the existence of out-of-home care for infants and young children, systematic inquiries in this area are greatly needed.

Significant changes in family structure and adaptation are also taking place with the shift to small families. Of 35 families evaluated in the course of the author's clinical work, none had more than two children, and many had only one child. The eonomic and political incentives to restrict family size appear to have been particularly successful in Shanghai. The ramifications of the adjustments needed in child rearing attitudes, parental perceptions of children's health and behavior, and the health and educational needs of children require careful consideration. There is evidence that Chinese psychiatrists, and perhaps other social scientists, will be giving this problem serious attention over the next decade. While they are currently interested in what is to be learned from studies of one-child families in the West, such information may not be relevant to their own circumstances. Furthermore, Chinese child psychiatrists recognize the need to develop a point of view and a base of knowledge which is sensitive to their traditional culture, prevailing political ideology, and current social changes. Yet, because developmental psychology, cultural anthropology, and sociology are still relatively underdeveloped in China, it will be very difficult to carry out the research needed to address these issues. For this reason international collaborations may be quite beneficial to rapid development of child mental health in China.

4. Relationship of child psychiatry to pediatrics: There is already much evidence that Chinese society at-large is making a major shift to support the educational and psychosocial needs of children. However, there was, rather surprisingly, not much evidence that either the practice of pediatrics or the quality of care in children's hospitals were being much influenced by this newly emerging psychological perspective. Child psychiatrists in Shanghai seemed to have little to contribute to pediatrics. Developmental screening was being carried out by pediatricians in the outpatient department of a large children's hospital, but interest in the psychosocial parameters of chronic disease in children was minimal.

5. Diagnosis and treatment of psychiatric disorders in children: From the foregoing discussion it should be evident that the nature of child psychiatric disorders appear similar to those seen in the West. Indeed, during 3 months of clinical work the author saw no evidence of a culturally specific behavioral syndrome. There was also no evidence that Chinese children have any greater tendency to somatize psychological distress than American children, although this tendency has been described as characterizing the expression of mental distress in adults (Kleinman, 1978).

A distinct biological orientation characterizes the work of Chinese child psychiatrists, and this represents the most obvious contrast with child psychiatrists in the West. Another important distinction is that most Chinese child psychiatrists work alone, without the assistance of psychologists and social workers. Of scientific importance is the fact that their approach is conducive to many recent developments in Western child psychiatry, for example, the use of structured diagnostic interviews and the development of elaborate schemes for classifying types of behavior disorders.

Given the distinct biological orientation of the field as it has developed so far, the roles of the social and psychological sciences and the place of psychological therapies in the scheme of clinical work are not clear. This represents the major challenge for the immediate future of child mental health. Because child psychiatrists will continue to have responsibility for treating major psychiatric disorders in children, this biological orientation is, of course, essential. The problem the Chinese confront seems to be one of developing a comprehensive psychosocial perspective in mental health programs for children in a way that compliments the biological perspective. Since this problem has not been thoroughly resolved in many Western training programs, the Chinese are in a position to develop training and research programs that represent an improved synthesis of these two bodies of knowledge. If they should accomplish this, their willingness to share their experience with other developing countries should be highly beneficial. One can be enthusiastic about this potential because they have developed mental health services rapidly in the years following the Cultural Revolution and are now involved in training a large number of child psychiatrists.

Ways of Fostering an International Perspective in Child Mental Health

Knowledge in child psychiatry acquired over the past two decades, from developmental and social sciences, neuroscience, and public health, must be continually disseminated in international symposia. The International Association of Child Psychology, Psychiatry and Allied Professions has an international meeting once every 4 years, and smaller conferences involving predominantly European and American child psychiatrists are beginning to occur regularly. But there remains a need for more vigorous transactions between child psychiatrists from developed and developing nations, and the large number of scientists and health personnel working in areas relevant to child psychiatry must systematically be included in this dialogue.

International centers, such as the Centre Internationale de l'Enfance in Paris, are needed to encourage the assimilation of child psychiatry in developing countries. Such centers can also collect information about migration patterns, cultural variations in child rearing, nutritional needs, innovative health programs, and other kinds of data needed to define the specific needs of countries and regions of the world. International health and development agencies should be involved systematically in this effort; agencies such as WHO, UNESCO, UNICEF, OXFAM, and the Red Cross all have roles to play. The recent completion of a major study of child mental health services in eight countries (Costa Rica, Egypt, France, Greece, Indonesia, Nigeria, Sri

Lanka, and Thailand) provides an important point of departure toward true internationalism in the field (Sartorius & Graham, 1984). It is hoped that three consequences will be derived from such endeavors: (1) child psychiatry will become rationally organized into national and local health services; (2) child mental health specialists will encourage a public health orientation to children's emotional development in addition to maintaining skill in treating individual children and their families; and (3) international research projects will be established to study fundamental questions pertaining to cultural and national differences in child psychiatric disorder.

Over the next decade it is expected that at least 25 cities in developing countries will exceed 10 million in population size, due primarily to continuing high fertility and declining (in some instances, rapidly declining) infant mortality rates. The role of primary health care directed specifically at infants and preschool children will have important effects on the quality of health and educational attainment. Day care programs are likely to assume great importance in societies undergoing such change. Child psychiatrists will be necessary to train and supervise primary health care providers to recognize and treat behavior disturbances and to create and sustain programs to support family welfare.

Research programs on population screening (Earls, 1982c), the role of brain development in child psychopathology (Shaffer, 1977), the design of day care curricula (Rutter, 1982), and the efficacy of various psychotherapeutic interventions (Kolvin, Garside, Nicol, MacMillan, Wolstenholme, & Leitch, 1981) are becoming much more highly sophisticated in child psychiatry. Through these kinds of activities, child psychiatry will be in a position to provide a new perspective on the understanding of population dynamics, family planning, health promotion, and prevention of behavior and educational handicaps. Until now, preventive child development services have hardly been evaluated for their social and economic benefits in most Western societies. Some countries with centrally planned economies have placed high priority on infant psychosocial development through routine health screening, liberal time off work following delivery, and day care. It is important to closely evaluate these programs for their costs and benefits since they represent natural experiments. Indeed, this should become the basis for an international research study. At the same time the prospects for progress in some other parts of the world, the sub-Saharan countries of Africa in particular, are less promising. The tasks of caring for children's physical, emotional, and social development in such areas are among the most serious and difficult challenges of human welfare. This is a task deserving international cooperation for the benefit it might have for all other countries, developed and developing.

Benefits to Developed Countries

It is worth pointing out some of the ways in which developed countries may benefit from these kinds of undertakings, since the discussion so far has focused on developing countries. In the first place developed countries are far from solving all of their problems regarding social and intellectual development of children. Though the mental health needs of children have been recognized and in some instances given top priority in programmatic development, complex social problems continue to challenge the successes already attained in economic and material terms. As reflected in current mortality and morbidity statistics from the United States, the leading causes of death in adolescents are suicide, homicide, and accidents (Holinger, 1981). Antisocial behavior disorders, learning problems, and attention-deficit disorders have not been prevented despite sizable efforts. Depressive disorders have now been recognized to exist in prepubertal children and may well represent the most common illness in adolescents. Minority groups and the poor generally continue to experience a higher proportion of health problems including psychiatric disorders, and their care and treatment is still inferior to standards achieved by the majority population. Hispanics in the United States represent a case of particular interest since this population is increasing at a very rapid rate. From a demographic perspective they approximate the profile expected of a developing country. The situation prevailing in the United States also applies to various immigrant groups in European countries (Prouska, 1981).

As developing countries attempt to control the rate of change and the full impact of a predominantly Westernized style of technological development, developed countries may benefit considerably from discussions and research projects aimed at understanding how cultural traditions and cultural change relate to child development and child psychopathology. This represents an important potential for international development and may be of particular benefit to developed countries in regard to the social adaptation of adolescence. The influence of technological changes on family life are extraordinarily complex and yet poorly understood. A study examining such changes in the Sudan shows a marked increase in behavior problems over a 15-year period, with boys being much more affected than girls (Rahim & Cederblad, 1984).

Conclusion

A formidable clinical and public health program has been proposed for child mental health. The results of determined and systematic efforts in international development cannot be predicted. Child psychiatry in Western societies is going through a major period of revision which is reflected in a number of ways: an improved scientific quality of its journals and professional meetings, and an expanded relationship of child psychiatry to pediatrics. At the same time these developments are taking place the profession is still being introduced to many developing countries as the example of child psychiatry in China illustrated. This state of affairs demands careful observation and open-minded participation from child mental health workers everywhere. Over the next decade child mental health services could easily become absorbed by pediatrics, general psychiatry, or primary health care services. As is the case in the United States, children's mental health services may continue to evolve into a separate discipline with distinct educational requirements. It is on the basis of discussions and planning on the kinds of issues outlined in this paper that mental health services for children will reach full potential, with broad social and cultural implications, aimed at maximizing human potential.

Acknowledgments

This work was supported, in part, by a World Health Organization Travelling Fellowship awarded to the author for study in the People's Republic of China, August–November, 1981.

References

Berggren, W. L., Eubank, D. C., & Berggren, G. E. (1981). Reduction of mortality in rural Haiti through a primary-health-care program. *New England Journal of Medicine, 304,* 1324–1330.

Earls, F. (1981). Epidemiological child psychiatry: An American perspective. In E. F. Purcell (Ed.), *Psychopathology of children and youth: A cross-cultural perspective* (pp. 3–27). New York: Josiah Macy, Jr. Foundation.

Earls, F. (1982a). The future of child psychiatry as a medical discipline. *American Journal of Psychiatry, 139,* 1158–1161.

Earls, F. (1982b, July). *Some observations on child psychiatry in China.* Paper presented at the 10th International Congress, International Association for Child and Adolescent Psychiatry and Allied Professions, Dublin, Ireland.

Earls, F. (1982c). Cultural and national differences in the epidemiology of behavior problems of preschool children. *Culture, Medicine and Psychiatry, 6,* 45–56.

Earls, F. (1985). The epidemiology of psychiatric disorders in children and adolescents. In J. O. Cavenar (Gen. Ed.), *Psychiatry,* Vol. 3 (pp. 1–30). Philadelphia, PA: Lippincott.

Graham, P. (1981). Epidemiological approaches to child mental health in developing countries. In E. F. Purcell (Ed.), *Psychopathology of children and youth: A cross-cultural perspective* (pp. 28–45). New York: Josiah Macy, Jr. Foundation.

Guze, S., Earls, F., & Barrett, J. (1983). *Childhood psychopathology and development.* New York: Raven.

Holinger, P. C. (1981). Self-destructiveness among the young: An epidemiological study of violent deaths. *International Journal of Social Psychiatry, 27,* 277–282.

Kleinman, A. (1978). Clinical relevance of anthroplogical and cross-cultural research: Concepts and strategies. *American Journal of Psychiatry, 135,* 427–431.

Kolvin, I., Garside, R. F., Nicol, A. R., MacMillan, A., Wolstenholme, F., & Leitch, I. M. (1981). *Help starts here: The maladjusted child in the ordinary school.* New York: Tavistock Publications.

Levy, D. (1968). Beginnings of the child guidance movement. *American Journal of Orthopsychiatry, 38,* 799–804.

Morley, D. (1973). *Pediatric priorities in the developing world.* London: Butterworths.

Nag, M., White, B. N. F., & Peet, C. (1978). An anthropological approach to the study of the economic value of children in Java and Nepal. *Current Anthropology, 19,* 293–306.

Pillsbury, B. L. K. (1978). "Doing the month": Confinement and convalescence of Chinese women after childbirth. *Social Science and Medicine, 12, (1B),* 11–22.

Prouska, F. (1981). Immigrant children: A minority at risk. In E. F. Purcell (Ed.), *Psychopathology of children and youth: A cross-cultural perspective,* (pp. 200–219). New York: Josiah Macy, Jr. Foundation.

Rahim, S. I. A., & Cederblad, M. (1984). Effects of rapid urbanization on child behaviour and health in a part of Khartoum, Sudan. *Journal of Child Psychology and Psychiatry, 25,* 629–641.

Rutter M. (1980). *Changing youth in a changing society.* Cambridge, MA: Harvard Univ. Press.

Rutter, M. (1982). Social-emotional consequences of day care for preschool children. In E. F. Zigler & E. W. Gordon (Eds.), *Day care: Scientific and social issues,* (pp. 3–32). Boston, MA: Auburn House.

Rutter, M., Cox, A., Tupling, C., Berger, M., & Yule, W. (1975). Attainment and adjustment in two geographical areas: I. The prevalence of psychiatric disorder. *British Journal of Psychiatry, 126,* 493–509.

Sartorius, N., & Graham, P. (1984). Child mental health: Experience of eight countries. *WHO Chronicle, 38,* 208–211.

Shaffer, D. (1977). Brain injury. In M. Rutter & L. Hersov (Eds.), *Child psychiatry: Modern approaches,* (pp. 185–215). Oxford: Blackwell.

Shaffer, D., & Dunn, J. (1979). *The first year of life.* New York: Wiley.

Slaughter, D. T. (1983). Early intervention and its effects on maternal and child development. *Monographs of the Society for Research in Child Development, 48,* (No. 4, Whole No. 202).

Teitelbaum, M. S. (1975). Relevance of demographic transition theory for developing countries. *Science, 188,* 420–425.

World Bank. (1979). World Atlas of the Child, New York.

World Health Organization. (1977). *Child mental health and psychosocial development.* (Report of a WHO Expert Committee, Tech. Rep. Series 613.)

Wray, J. D. (1975). Child care in the People's Republic of China: 1973. *Pediatrics, 55,* 539–561.

Index